I0866531

MICHIGAN'S
VENICE

MICHIGAN'S VENICE

The Transformation of the St. Clair Maritime Landscape, 1640–2000

DANIEL F. HARRISON

Wayne State University Press
Detroit

© 2024 by Wayne State University Press, Detroit, Michigan 48201. All rights reserved.
No part of this book may be reproduced without formal permission.

ISBN 9780814349472 (hardcover)
ISBN 9780814349489 (e-book)

Library of Congress Control Number: 2023941363

On cover: *Untitled* (1885, oil on canvas, 11″ × 15″) by Seth Arca Whipple (American, 1855–1901). Private collection; used by permission of owner.
Cover design by Will Brown.

Grateful acknowledgment is made to the Wayne State University Endowment Fund for the generous support of the publication of this volume.

Wayne State University Press rests on Waawiyaataanong, also referred to as Detroit, the ancestral and contemporary homeland of the Three Fires Confederacy. These sovereign lands were granted by the Ojibwe, Odawa, Potawatomi, and Wyandot Nations, in 1807, through the Treaty of Detroit. Wayne State University Press affirms Indigenous sovereignty and honors all tribes with a connection to Detroit. With our Native neighbors, the press works to advance educational equity and promote a better future for the earth and all people.

Wayne State University Press
Leonard N. Simons Building
4809 Woodward Avenue
Detroit, Michigan 48201-1309

Visit us online at wsupress.wayne.edu.

This work is dedicated first to my wife and partner Deanna, who is not a bit fooled by the term "field work." Her support and patience in indulging my late-blooming ambitions go well beyond the bounds of reason, into the realm where love meets exasperation.

To my parents, who instilled in me the love of learning, and stimulated my curiosity in ways so subtle that it was years before I realized that in taking my own path, I was following in their footsteps.

To the colleagues and mentors who have taught, inspired and motivated me, I will strive to be as generous with others as you have been with me. If it is true that we see farther by standing on the shoulders of others, then we must do what we can so that others will have our shoulders to stand on.

Contents

Figures

Maps

Acknowledgments

This project would not have been possible without the assistance and encouragement of many talented and generous people. The following is a woefully incomplete list of the individuals and organizations who offered their inspiration, wisdom, expertise, advice, resources, encouragement, and occasionally, sympathy.

As this book began as my doctoral dissertation, my thanks extend to the members of my dissertation committee, for their willingness to take a chance on a late bloomer's ability to bring this project to fruition. Within the amazing community of scholars that is Wayne State University, I found four kindred spirits who, while different in many ways, each shared a passion and an area of expertise crucial to my needs. Drs. Thomas Killion, Stephen Chrisomalis, Krysta Ryzewski and Karen Marrero became my "dream team," each with a complementary and essential perspective.

Special thanks to Mark Holley, Ken Vrana, John O'Shea, and Gail Vander Stoep, who brought me to the realization that maritime archaeology wasn't something that occurred halfway around the world, and that good work can still be a lot of fun (and usually is).

Three individuals who deserve credit are no longer among us. Legendary underwater videographer Tony Gramer and diver Rich Castillo were on that dive in 2013 on an uncharted wreck in Lake St. Clair, when I first realized that this was a special place whose stories needed to be told. The late historian and conservationist Henry Barkhausen, another legend of the Great Lakes, conveyed his enthusiastic support and encyclopedic knowledge in emails and telephone conversations from his hospice home until his death at age 103. His last email to me was a congratulation on winning the Association for Great Lakes Maritime History's Henry N. Barkhausen Award for outstanding original research. His legacy is enormous, but for me, it lies in the appreciation that the big picture comprises infinite detail.

My remaining but boundless thanks go to the scholars and shipmates, dive buddies, local historians, and librarians and their libraries: C. Patrick Labadie and the Alpena Public Library; Luke Clyburn and Noble Odyssey Foundation; Joel Stone and the Dossin Great Lakes Museum; Brian Dunnigan and the Clements Library, University of Michigan; Daryl Wright; Fred Dufty; Bob McGreevy; the Association for Great Lakes Maritime History; Clarke Historical Library, Central Michigan University; Burton Historical Collection at Detroit Public Library; Harsens Island & St. Clair Flats Historical Society; Thunder Bay National Marine Sanctuary; Walpole Island First Nations; the US Army Corps of Engineers. You each have brought a piece (and sometimes a large chunk) of the puzzle.

Portions of this work previously appeared in *Michigan Historical Review* 49, no. 2 (Fall 2023).

About the Cover

Seth Arca Whipple (American, 1855–1901), *Untitled* (1885), oil on canvas, 11″ × 15″. Private collection; used by permission of owner.

Although the work is untitled, the evidence is clear that Whipple, a New Baltimore native, depicted an imagined scene set in a familiar place and a bygone era. He chose a moment of crisis dreaded by sailors in the St. Clair Flats, even today.

The curve of the narrow channel through the surrounding reed beds points to the setting as the notorious "Elbow" at the entrance to the North Channel in Anchor Bay. The numerous details—vessels, navigational markers, clothing—are consistent with a date in the mid-1850s, when negotiating the Flats was often the riskiest part of a Great Lakes journey.

In the foreground, a Mackinac boat laden with fish has just rounded the red buoy that marks the safe channel. Just ahead, however, a topsail schooner appears to have strayed too close to the tall barrel-topped stakes that mark the shoals. It may already be aground and has set its sails in hopes of breaking free in the dying breeze that barely stirs both vessels' pennants. Its mainsheet, hanging limp, does not bode well. In the distance, the schooner on the right has cleared the bar at the mouth of the North Channel, and now makes its way slowly upstream to Algonac. On the left, a handful of buildings along the far shore mark the future location of the artist's birthplace.

The eminent Great Lakes maritime artist Robert McGreevy observes,

> As a painter, Whipple was criticized for paying too much attention to detail, but it is the minute details that make this little painting so fascinating. His familiarity with the area and his own sailing experience open a window into what working a boat on the Flats in the 1850s was really like. The Mackinac boat in the foreground is richly detailed. The rigging looks like it could really work the sails, it has the right weight and tension—all things a sailor would be aware of. Even the aids to navigation that many painters seem to ignore are rendered in detail, not just suggested. It's a pleasing painting that goes far beyond its small canvas. Whipple has left us with an important historical document of life on the Flats as it once was.

Introduction

The universe is made of stories, not of atoms.
—Muriel Rukeyser, *The Speed of Darkness*

This is the story of a place. There are people in it—many different peoples, over the past four centuries alone—and the things they did, and said, and made, and left behind are the result of their being in this place. While this is true of everywhere that humans have gone, there are places that are so different from their surroundings that one finds oneself thinking and acting a bit differently when there. The Great Lakes are home to such places. A series of enormous freshwater seas in the heart of a continent is itself a thing of wonder. Depending on their mood, the lakes have either posed a dangerous obstacle or offered a broad highway stretching deep into North America. To those who dwell and travel in such places, access to the daily necessities of life, as well as remote resources and long-distance trade, requires taking to the water. The resulting complex of relationships between people, the land and water, and the things they make and use on both, creates a pattern of behavior known as *maritime*.

Among the more than ten thousand miles of shoreline where often one cannot see the opposite shore, there are a mere handful of places—choke points—where land nearly touches land. What unites these special places is that each, both its land and waters, presents a distinct change from its surroundings. These narrow passages, carved by ice and water, offer access to both the connected lakes and the land on either side. They are all liminal zones—places of transition. There, one may expect to find peoples, past and present, taking advantage of what is, in every sense, a crossroads, where travel may be both facilitated and controlled. The Indigenous peoples gave them names: Bow-e-ting, Ongiara, Michilimackinac, Bkejwanong.[1] Today they are known as Sault Sainte-Marie, Niagara, Mackinac Straits, and the St. Clair Flats, respectively. Each has a distinct, even dramatic, character: a treacherous rapids, a stupendous cataract, a fog-shrouded narrows, and an immense freshwater delta. In their presence, things must be done differently: dangers faced, obstacles overcome—and rewards gained.

As borderlands go, the delta of the St. Clair River is as much an idea as it is a physical fact. True, the modern political boundary between the United States and Canada, between Ontario and Michigan, bisects it. But that is an imaginary line that one can easily see across to the land on the other side, unlike the lines bisecting the Great Lakes, many miles from the American or Canadian shores. And unlike political boundaries on land, there are no man-made physical barriers: no fences, walls, or even signs. The buoys that mark the central shipping channel are much like those found anywhere in the world. Yet this place is unique. Along with two other rivers—the Saint Mary's River linking Lakes Superior and Huron; and the Niagara, between Lakes Erie and Ontario—the Strait between Lakes Huron and Erie is a zone of geographic and hydrologic transitions (map 1). Two great land masses—the Lower Peninsula of Michigan and that of southwest Ontario—almost touch. Two enormous bodies of water are linked by a passage that is slender and well-defined along most of its eighty-mile length. Aside from a handful of islands, one is either on one side or the other of the Detroit River or the St. Clair River.

---

1 According to Henry Rowe Schoolcraft, *niagara* is derived from Mohawk *ongiara*, "neck" (Schoolcraft 1847, 453; also Bright 2004, 325). *Bow-e-ting* has many variant spellings; the *Ojibwe People's Dictionary* lists *baawitig* as "rapids." *Michilimackinac* likewise has many variants but is generally agreed to be derived from Ojibwe—perhaps *mishee mackinakong*, "the place of the big turtle's back" (Johnston 1976, 60). *Bkejwanong* is Anishinaabmowin for "where the waters divide" (Nin.Da.Waab.Jig 1987), describing the multiple channels of the delta. Lake St. Clair had many names; among those recorded is *otsi-keta*, variously interpreted as Huron/Wendat for "foot" (as in the foot of the St. Clair River) or Anishinaabmowin for "sweet" or "sugar" (for sweet fresh water or for the maple trees found there). Another name, *ganatchio* or *kandechio*, appears to be Miami for "kettle," describing its rounded shape. This is discussed further in chapter 5.

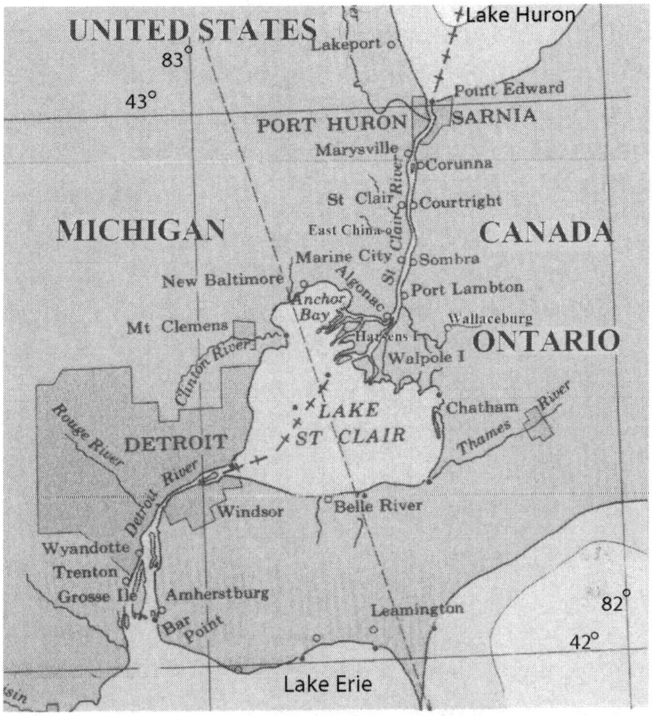

MAP 1. The Strait connecting Lake Huron (top) with Lake Erie (bottom). The St. Clair delta and Lake St. Clair are in the center. (NOAA)

The great exception is the delta where the St. Clair River fans out at the head of Lake St. Clair: roughly thirty square miles of multiple, winding channels creating dozens of islands large and small. It is a place of ambiguity. Land and water do not so much meet as interpenetrate, as river and lake merge subtly into reed bed and marsh. “Dry land” is often seasonal or cyclical as water levels rise and fall, and currents shift the location and depth of the channels. No wonder then, that such a complex space is the scene of constant transformation, both natural and cultural. While there have been successive dominant groups of inhabitants, each with its own capabilities and agenda, the trajectory of change has been anything but linear and chronological. To understand the interrelations between people and place, anthropologists use the concept of the *landscape* to describe an environment that is both ecologically grounded and socially constructed.

In the opening chapter, I lay out the key concepts of landscape, historical ecology, and maritime societies as they apply to the anthropological study of the environment. The resultant “maritime cultural landscape” is formed by four simultaneous and interrelated social processes: cognition of the environment; movement through it; dwelling within it; and communicating the knowledge of it to the larger social group through symbolic representation. The following chapter lays the ecological groundwork by describing the physical properties of the St. Clair region. Chapter 3 applies the process of landscape formation to the Indigenous societies immediately preceding European incursion and traces them to the present, while the following chapter outlines the two successive colonial occupations of the area, French and British. Chapter 5 presents contrasting forms of representation by the Indigenous, French, and British occupying societies, drawing principally on toponymic and cartographic evidence—place-names, maps, and their interrelations.

Chapter 6 focuses on transformations in maritime practice from Indigenous through modern times, while chapter 7 surveys the sweeping technological changes that characterized the nineteenth century, particularly as they were manifested in the St. Clair maritime landscape. The evolving material culture of maritime societies is further explored in chapter 8, as patterns in shipbuilding, a major regional industry throughout the nineteenth century, reflected the delicate balance between human ambitions and environmental constraints. Chapter 9 turns to the evolution of the built environment of maritime infrastructure, as expanding industrial capabilities permitted the physical modification of the landscape itself. This transformation had the effect of creating social space in what was once an impediment to navigation; chapter 10 traces the trajectory of "Michigan's Venice," as the channels that had confounded La Salle became the playground of nearby Detroit's social elite as well as its growing work force around the turn of the twentieth century.

By that time, hundreds of vessels had come to grief in the St. Clair region. While many decayed, were salvaged, or demolished as obstructions, there remain dozens of wreck sites in the area. The archaeological investigation of the submerged landscape, still in its early stages, is introduced in chapter 11. I present a necessarily cursory overview of this precious archaeological resource, with a program for further managing and interpreting it. The book concludes with a brief summation of the significance of the St. Clair maritime landscape to Great Lakes studies, and particularly to the cultural heritage of the Indigenous and descendant maritime communities that remain in this remarkable place.

The work exemplifies what I have termed "evidence-based storytelling" (Harrison 2017b), an acknowledgment of the human need on the one hand to make sense of what we find in the world, and the stubbornness of physical facts on the other. The emergent narrative is thus woven from many threads of evidence that both support and critique one another. Travelers' tales and old maps, long taken at face value, are placed in dialogue with potsherds and pine forests. Along the way are a colorful cast of characters, human and otherwise: individuals who will speak with their own voices, proud vessels that met their ends in ways both noble and ignominious, and always the flowing waters and shifting sands.

1

Maritime Landscapes and Their Study

There is little depth as you enter and leave Lake St. Clare, especially as you leave it. The discharge from Lake Orleans [Huron] divides at this place into several small channels, almost all barred by sandbanks. We were obliged to sound them all, and at last discovered a very fine one. Our bark was detained here several days by head winds, and this difficulty having been surmounted, we encountered a still greater one at the entrance of Lake Orleans, the north wind which had been blowing violently, and which drives the waters of the three great lakes into the strait, had so increased the ordinary current there. We could not stem it under sail, although we were then aided by a strong south wind; but as the shore was very fine, we landed twelve of our men who towed it along the beach for half a quarter of an hour, at the end of which we entered Lake Orleans on the 23rd of the month of August, and for a second time we chanted a Te Deum *in thanksgiving.*

—Father Louis Hennepin, *A Description of Louisiana*

With these few words, Father Louis Hennepin, chronicler of Sieur de La Salle's doomed expedition to the Great Lakes, recited a litany of the trials that awaited future mariners transiting the final leagues of the Strait connecting Lake Erie to Lake Huron. Strong currents, narrow obstructed channels, prevailing headwinds, and a churning rapids—all were arrayed against *Le Griffon*, the first European-style vessel to attempt the navigational gauntlet that led to the fur-rich lands to the north. In his selection and description of landscape features as obstacles, Hennepin reflected his cultural perspective on a place that, from an Indigenous viewpoint, was itself a repository of riches—all the necessities of a good life. So this "story of a place" is in reality many stories of many places—all of them occupying the same space, albeit at different times and seen through different eyes.

The Concept of the "Maritime Cultural Landscape"

When a place prominently features navigable water, *maritime cultural landscape* has become the preferred scholarly label. An early proponent of the concept, Danish archaeologist Christer Westerdahl enumerated such maritime activities as "human utilization (economy) of maritime space by boat: settlement, fishing, hunting, shipping and its attendant subcultures, such as pilotage, lighthouse and seamark maintenance." The physical features of such a maritime landscape include "the whole network of sailing routes, old as well as new, with ports and harbours along the coast, and its related constructions and remains of human activity, underwater as well as terrestrial" (Westerdahl 1992, 5, 6). Useful as this early formulation may be, the phrase now merits a bit of unpacking—a word-by-word tracing of its interdisciplinary roots and usages.

In studying the human dimensions of a place, anthropologists use the term *landscape* to denote the environment as it is experienced and understood by its occupants, especially in the course of routine or repetitive activities. The emergence of landscape as a central organizing framework comes rather recently to anthropology (Tilley and Cameron-Daum 2017, 1), although its concepts and themes have long been accessible and applicable across the social sciences, notably physical and social geography (Sauer 1956; Bradford 1957; Glacken 1967; Meinig 1979; Ingold 1993; Strang 2008).

From such diverse backgrounds come diverse perspectives. The foundational historical archaeologist James Deetz used *cultural landscape* to denote "that part of the terrain which is modified according to a set of cultural plans" (Deetz 1990, 2). By contrast, landscape has also been memorably described by ecologists as "the product of the collision between Nature and Culture" (Balée and Erickson 2006, 2; capitalization mine). I am inclined to regard most landscapes as lying somewhere between a plan and a collision, concurring with

Carole Crumley and William Marquardt (1990, 79), who define landscape as "the spatial manifestation of the dynamic relations between humans and their environments." This is close to the elegant expression of geographer P. W. Bryan nearly six decades previous, who saw an emerging consensus that "human activity, which takes place to satisfy human desires, adapts and modifies Nature, and is itself adapted and modified by Nature" (Bryan 1933, v). Without using the terms, Bryan foreshadowed two key concepts that figure prominently in present-day landscape studies: first, that of *agency* as the capacity of an entity, human or otherwise, to affect another (Dolwick 2008, 18); and second, the role of the *dialectic*—the dynamic resolution of disparate forces and agents through the emergence of new, synthesized entities and relations.

As a result, the landscape is "perpetually under construction" (Ingold 1993, 162). This is particularly true when one social group joins or replaces another. Through successive occupations and transformations, the landscape becomes the repository of memory, of identity, of the social order of occupying groups, whether dominant or remnant (Knapp and Ashmore 1999, 18). My archaeologically oriented characterization of landscape is as *context*—whether that of bygone lived experience or a current archaeological investigation. In either case, it supplies the physical setting within which individuals belonging to a society—whether of hunter-gatherers, colonial settlers, sailors, or archaeologists—create and perform their identity. Within the landscape, repeated past practice becomes inscribed and sedimented, awaiting discovery.

Critical to the formation of landscape is the role of *culture*—that is, patterned, purposeful behavior that has been developed, acquired, conserved, and transmitted within a given society. Group identities are defined in practice, as the behavioral attributes that define a group must be performed in the real world in order to be made visible to those within and outside the group. Identifying labels such as "Indigenous horticulturalists," "French traders," and "American settlers" are assigned based on evidence of those patterns and purposes. That evidence may be sought in cultural productions ranging from symbolic representations both textual (names, narratives) and graphical (maps, charts, plans, and diagrams) to instrumental material culture (tools, structures, and other features of the built environment). Anthropologists and archaeologists examine these cultural productions for evidence of the ideologies that characterize the group and distinguish it from others: worldviews, values, belief systems, social institutions.

Navigable water, and the practices that it permits and necessitates, is the sine qua non of the maritime cultural landscape. Maritime cultures may be characterized by the use of watercraft, but maritimity does not begin or end at the shoreline (Tuddenham 2010, 7–8). Littoral and coastal zones, as sites of landing places and wayfinding landmarks, expand the discussion of maritime contexts (Cooney 2003; Ford and Crisman 2018). Maritime infrastructure, both on land and in the water, must include critical features of the built environment that affect movement: landings, harbors, wharves, piers, jetties, quays, seawalls, pilings, careening sites, canals and their locks, even dredging spoils and abandoned hulks (Gould 2000; Ford 2013). Aids to navigation include lighthouses and beacons, range markers, buoys, and devices from radar stations and cell towers to GPS satellites.

Beyond the primary focus on watercraft and associated material culture, maritime patterns of settlement and subsistence are predicated on water bodies as direct sources of, or means of accessing, the necessities of life from ancient times to the present. Within the Great Lakes, Indigenous shoreline fishing camps, fish impoundments and weirs, middens of mollusk shells, and beds of wild rice (*Zizania aquatica*, or *manoomin*) appear in the archaeological and ethnohistoric record (Fitting 1965; Tanner 1987, 13–23; Langouët and Daire 2009; Barton 2016). Where the French settled in the strait between Lake Huron and Lake Erie, aerial photography confirms the persistence of colonial patterns of land use and ownership, notably "ribbon farms"—so termed from their narrow shape, sometimes extending a mile or more inland but invariably fronting on a navigable waterway (Butzer 1992, 357). In the present day, shipyards, marinas, salvors, ship chandleries, and warehouses are familiar features of the waterfront community.

Reassembled, the phrase "maritime cultural landscape" refers to an expansive yet finite locale where the repeated activities of a social group are determined by their relationship with navigable water. That locale comprises the water itself and adjacent natural landforms together with features of the built environment. It becomes a *place* through repetitive behaviors that fall into four categories of processes I have identified. These processes appear, in various manifestations, in most anthropological writings on landscape, maritime or otherwise. Three are essential to everyday life; the fourth is social, making possible the creation, maintenance, reproduction, transmission, and evolution of behavior-as-culture—in effect, the survival of the other three processes.

Creation of the Landscape: Four Essential Processes

In the literature of landscape anthropology, three human activities have been observed as working in combination to render a portion of the environment a socially constituted landscape. The first is cognition or *knowing* a place; the second is *dwelling* within it; the third, *moving* in and through it. To these I add a fourth, not absent, merely unacknowledged. That is the process of *representation*, whereby that familiar place that has been cognized, dwelt in, and moved through is rendered in symbolic form and thus made accessible to the rest of the group—made *social*. It is a process intimately related to, yet an order of magnitude higher than, the individual's process of cognition. This is so because it creates *collective* knowledge within a group using a shared convention of symbols and modes of communication. Like some cosmic "dark matter," representation is essential, omnipresent, and yet largely invisible in the anthological literature of landscapes. As evidence of the other three processes, it may be found hiding in plain sight, serving as the aggregation of a group's environmental knowledge and interactions over time (Balée and Erickson 2006, 9).

Far from being linear or sequential, the four processes operate constantly, simultaneously, and recursively, as each shared act of knowing, dwelling, moving, or representation further cements the nature and extent of the landscape. Collectively, goal-directed behavior—the seeking and getting of the means of existence within the landscape—is brought into conformity with social aims and norms.

Knowing: The Cognitive Process

I know the limits of my actual knowledge of the earth at any given time, but not the limits of all possible geography.
—Immanuel Kant, *Critique of Pure Reason*

Introducing my four-part model for landscape formation best begins with the individual's sensory *perception*. Inputs from the senses (sight, sound, smell, touch, taste) are linked through the higher process of *cognition* (literally, thinking) to existing patterns of knowledge and made useful, initially to that individual. Not all perceptions are treated equally, however—by the perceivers themselves or by those who later study them. Features of the landscape commonly understood to impact human behavior (that is, possess agency) are privileged and, for purposes of analysis, can be divided into two categories: *affordances* and *constraints.* Affordances—things that are necessary or useful—may also be labeled "assets," "capabilities," or "resources" found within the environment (Gibson 1979, 127). Complementing this notion of affordances is that of constraints: features in the environment that limit or prevent certain activities, particularly the exploitation of an affordance. These may encompass physical difficulty or impassability, risk, danger, or even social disapprobation (as a locale that is sacred or taboo). The interplay of perceived affordances and constraints literally shapes the cognitive landscape.

The variability from one social group to the next as to what is considered an affordance or constraint, even within the same physical space, has long been noted as a revealing indicator of diverse values and aims (Spoehr 1956, 94). The result is often a multiplicity of landscapes that overlap in space and time. For members of a group, the outcome of this process of knowing is a mental inventory of things that, through seeking or avoidance, affect their ability to remain and succeed in that place—that is, to *dwell*, the second formational process.

Dwelling: The Ecological Process

Gaining understanding of a place cannot come exclusively from "being there," but also requires constructing a perspective analogous to those for whom the place had significance.

—James E. Snead, "Trails of Tradition"

Dwelling, as the complement of *moving*, takes place in locales of maritime occupations (fishing camps, shipyards, lighthouses), in settlements of groups engaged in maritime livelihoods (waterfront communities supporting waterborne transport), and in transition zones between terrestrial and waterborne transport (harbors, landings, wharves, portages). In all these places, collective and repeated acts of dwelling inscribe patterns of activity associated with getting a living by seafaring. Factors influencing a group's choice of dwelling places include the location not only of affordances but of spaces where related occupational tasks are performed. For example, fishing may require long hours on open water, but drying the catch and mending nets are better done on the littoral, perhaps on a sheltered cove. Logs felled in the deep forest may be floated many miles to streamside sawmills where they are more easily processed and used to create shelter, ships, and other useful objects. Anthropologist Tim Ingold has coined the term *taskscape* to denote this integration of *things* to be done and the *places* where they are best done (Ingold 1993, 158). These maritime taskscapes thus require two additional affordances as means of access to the natural resources themselves: navigable routes and the wherewithal for building watercraft (Westerdahl 1998). A full accounting of a maritime cultural landscape requires an inventory of all the ancillary occupations and their taskscapes that support seafaring. Dwelling and moving—each makes the other possible.

Moving: The Technological Process

One of the underlying themes of our story has been mobility—the ceaseless movement of peoples.
—Barry Cunliffe, *Europe between the Oceans*

Landscapes may first be created through knowing and dwelling, but they are sustained through movement. Purposeful and repeated journeys are perpetuated through generations of following in collective acts of *inscription* (Tilley 1994, 31). In terrestrial contexts, repetitive movement along inscribed lines aids a society in consistently accessing affordances and avoiding constraints or risks. In leaving physical evidence in the form of pathways, inscription also aids scholars in reconstructing past landscapes. The matter becomes problematic when considering maritime movement, as water routes do not so readily lend themselves to inscription. Evidence of systematic wayfinding often becomes inferential.

A robust anthropological toolkit is called upon. Archaeology focuses on both shoreline infrastructure (settlements, landings, landmarks) and submerged material culture (notably shipwrecks) deposited en route. Ethnography looks at movement associated with seasonal activities, which in the Great Lakes will include fur trapping, spawning fish, migrating waterfowl, and ripening wild rice. Linguistics reveals past navigational practices through place-names like "Anchor Bay," so called for ships anchored awaiting a favoring wind, or "Teuchsagrondie," the Huron/Wendat name for the distinctive bend in the Detroit River, meaning "place where the channel turns." Together with historical archives of all kinds—charts, diaries, pictures, reports—the indirect inscription of movement may be traced within and across multiple occupying groups, each addressing the same classic questions of how, where, and why movement occurs.

Signature cultural features of a group dwelling and moving in their distinct maritime landscape will include first *their means of transport* (*how* they go). By its nature, movement by water is an act requiring technology in its classic sense of *techne*: craft or skill, in both the creation and operation of watercraft and their associated instrumentalities. Closely related is the question of their choice of routes or *transport zones* (*where* they go; Westerdahl 1998). Skills in wayfinding, seamanship, and risk avoidance figure among the many factors affecting which routes are chosen and inscribed through practice.

Finally, there is the question of their purposes and destinations (*why* they go *there*). This is invariably a reflection of the shared aims of the group, be they subsistence, trade, exploration, or conquest. The very need for movement, however, is driven by a key form of agency of the environment: the uneven spatial distribution of its natural resources. This unevenness and the mobilization of labor required to overcome it have been identified as the fundamental dynamic driving the formation of social networks (Cunliffe 2008, 26). Over successive occupations in the Great Lakes, the natural distribution of resources relative to their loci of supply, versus that of use or demand, has led to innumerable acts of movement producing elaborate trade routes many hundreds of miles in length.

Representing: The Cultural Process

Through the impact of memories . . . mankind attaches a meaning to its surroundings. The cultural landscape is being created. And it is being inherited to the following generations, who fill it with its own meaning and values. The layers of landscapes from different eras grow on one another.
—Kristin Ilves, "Place Names about Life by the Sea"

Implicit in all this environmental and technical knowledge is its symbolized *representation* and social transmission within and across groups and generations. Omnipresent yet seldom foregrounded, this fourth process underlies landscape formation's essential nature as a cultural phenomenon. Perhaps this oversight is simply a matter of taking the obvious for granted, yet without it, every landscape would remain, in a sense, a wilderness to all but those with direct experience. Sharing in a communicable form is the process that enables the social reproduction of all that knowing, dwelling, and moving that a group continually creates, adopts, and adapts. It is through familiar and persistent modes that the other three processes are represented and made to signify, chiefly language (oral and written narratives) or graphic symbols (notably maps and charts), completing the cycle of landscape formation. Without a system of representation to its own members, the landscape cannot be said to be truly cultural, in the essential sense of its knowledge being transmitted within and among social groups over time and space.

By the same token, in *studying* past maritime cultural landscapes, scholars find most helpful those representations describing features that an earlier population prioritized in accessing affordances, managing risk, and operating within constraints. Seen in this light, past representations are themselves artifacts, sharing primary significance with the thing represented. Collectively, symbolic representations provide a lens through which societies saw their own landscape as well as one through which we now view those societies. Representations have long served as primary data sources, data that are historically and culturally situated and must be contextualized by adopting a perspective analogous to that of their creators (Snead 2009, 44).

My objective is to raise *representation* up from its secondary status as mere evidence of the other three landscape formation processes. Instead, it assumes its role as a crucial process in its own right—shedding light on the "dark matter" that binds together a given landscape with its social constituency. We interrogate, albeit indirectly through their creations, the makers of texts, maps, paintings, names—all forms of symbolized representation—as agents operating in a historical and cultural context. Seeking evidence of such agency, I examine cases where a narrative account or a map representing the Great Lakes region (some intentionally vague or inaccurate) conveyed information that affected social and political decisions made far from the places represented. This is particularly impactful where natural resources, trading partners, political allies and enemies, and trade routes were concerned. A map of North America purporting to show a route to the Orient where earlier maps had shown only *terra incognita*—such a representation, regardless of its accuracy, would be a powerful motivating agent, mobilizing resources of manpower and treasure by the nascent European colonial empires. Half a millennium later, it serves to suggest to us what was on their minds.

Text is seductive. Its capacity to confirm our biases creates the illusion of deep knowledge. The overreliance on documentary sources privileges the literate (and dominant) societies of both the past and present—at the expense of Indigenous and other dominated voices. The alternative consists in placing multiple and culturally diverse representations in tension with one another, with the other three landscape formation processes, and with other forms of evidence. Recovering context, especially that of literate societies in historic times, requires not only skeptically inspecting what its members said, wrote, and drew but then critiquing that by interrogating the physical evidence: what they built, destroyed, traded, worshipped, broke, lost, buried, or discarded. Evidence-based storytelling consists in allowing textuality and materiality, history and archaeology, to critique each other to their mutual benefit.

Studying the St. Clair Region: How and Why

For both the archaeologist and the native dweller, the landscape tells us—or rather is—a story.
—Tim Ingold, "The Temporality of the Landscape"

Together with its strategic position, the distinct and bounded nature of the St. Clair hydrologic region—river, delta, and lake—permits a robust approach to every aspect of landscape formation. Each of the four processes is represented by multiple forms of evidence; moreover, each is repeated with variations within each of a succession of cultural occupations. Environmental affordances for the settlement and subsistence patterns of all occupying groups were accessible in the varied biomes along the corridor: stands of birch at its upper end, massive pine and hardwood forests, fertile alluvial plains, and a veritable estuarine pantry of fish and fowl in the marshy delta. Thus, the entire St. Clair system comprises a definable landscape-as-taskscape, furnishing the means of subsistence within a manageable space as well as commodities for exchange along regional maritime and terrestrial networks. Constraints, however, are mostly concentrated in one particular locale—the delta, or St. Clair Flats. Its confined sea room, shoals, wind, and currents render movement by water problematic. It is here that the greatest degree of transformation may be observed.

The dramatic nature of the successive landscape formations and transformations renders the four processes of knowing, dwelling, moving, and representation highly visible, even at the remove of many years. From hunter-gatherer and horticulturalist lifeways through to industrialization, by way of fur trappers and lumber barons, each society saw with divergent perspectives, was driven by differing ideologies and economies, and employed adaptive technologies.

In social and historical terms, there are at least five overlapping Great Lakes maritime landscapes: Indigenous, colonial French, colonial British, postcolonial American and Canadian, and modern. Adaptations, borrowings, survivals, and other blurrings of cultural lines inevitably occurred as these societies came into contact and persisted as remnant populations.

The approach taken here is to tease these landscapes apart chronologically, first along functional lines. Cross-cultural thematic comparisons of the four processes of cognition (knowing), settlement (dwelling), transport (moving), and cultural transmission (representation) will shed light on the similarities and differences of each of the societies that brought their own sensibilities, values, and aims to the Great Lakes and St. Clair region and in turn interacted with the ecological and social milieu in which they found themselves.

Multiple forms of mediation between nature and culture will be examined as evidence: *language*, whether written or oral; *material culture* (watercraft and their contents, maritime infrastructure) used in movement within and beyond the immediate environs; and associated *nautical practices* (seafaring, wayfinding, charting) required to operate there. Finally, all this must be contextualized against the social, economic, and political milieu of larger worlds: Indigenous alliances and enmities, rival colonial empires, nation-states, and global networks.

As the product of the interaction of a specific environment and society, each landscape is a unique phenomenon, discouraging the application of doctrinaire laws or ruling theories. Instead, explicating the complex relations between a landscape and its human occupants calls for a flexible and pragmatic approach to diverse yet interrelated data. Within the past three decades, a multidisciplinary research program known as *historical ecology* has emerged as a robust and inclusive methodological framework for the management of complex chains of mutual causation and contingency in human-environment relations (Crumley 1994, 2). As its name implies, this hybridized approach accesses both the humanities and the physical sciences, which find common ground in dialogue with anthropology, particularly its fields of linguistics, archaeology, and ethnography. Its proponents point to an absence of dogma and its resulting amenability to multiple theorizations (Crumley 2021; Biersack 1999; Balée 2006, 76). actor-network theory (Tuddenham 2010, 2012; Dolwick 2008; 2009), practice theory (Bourdieu 1977), and entanglement (Hodder 2012) are among the accessible means of relating social behavior to landscape formation.

Novel interactions, particularly disruptions of the status quo, provide the triggering mechanism for transformation of the cultural landscape, social practice, and material culture through innovative and adaptive changes over time. The processes of landscape formation empower other-than-human agents—water and wind, sand and rock, wood and iron. In the St. Clair landscape, the paradigmatic relations among an overloaded schooner, a contrary wind, and an uncharted sandbar formed a trajectory that was repeated (with predictable results) for decades, only to be radically altered within a few years by the development of nautical material culture in the form of accurate charts, the steam dredge, and the tugboat.

The life cycles of landscapes are measured variously, with fundamental transformations perceptible only when viewed across centuries or even millennia. By contrast, signal events forming inflection points in their trajectory may occur seemingly overnight. In between these extremes, decades of relative stability provide middle-range periods. These three temporal frames of reference all prove complementary in the analysis of social groups and their landscapes.

The multiscale segmentation of time was pioneered in the mid-twentieth century by a group of French thinkers known as the *Annales* school, from their signature journal, *Annales d'Histoire Économique et Sociale*. The versatility and pragmatism of multiple yet simultaneous time frames have proven popular with historical ecologists, who praise their absence of dogma and their eclecticism, problem-based approach, and broad embrace of the social sciences (Peebles 1991, 111; Knapp 1992, 3). Maritime archaeologist Johan Rönnby neatly synopsizes the preeminent *Annaliste* Fernand Braudel's three scales of history. Braudel, he writes, "rationalizes the temporal complexities of history into three levels: *les événements*, which is the short political and military history of events; *les conjonctures*, the interrelated medium duration cycles (*moyen durée*) of groups, institutions, economy and social structures; and last, *les longues durées*, which is the history of the almost unchanging structures in mentality, technologies and landscape" (Rönnby 2007, 67). As a characteristics of a cohesive society, especially over the middle-range *conjonctures*, *Annaliste* Lucien Febvre posited *mentalité*, comprising "ideologies, collective systems of belief, world views, which both reflect and can transform human life" (Bintliff 1991, 10). This notion of a shared mentality is particularly useful in understanding the encounters and interactions between groups representing dissimilar cultures, as occurred in colonial and frontier contexts like the Great Lakes.

The long-term view (*longue durée*) of the upper Great Lakes region is flexible, at its extreme spanning thousands of years since the lakes' creation by the most recent glacial retreat. Closer to hand are nearly four centuries of contested historical occupation, still a formidable task if one attempts either to view it in its totality or merely to recite the innumerable events that make up its details. In practice, the middle path—organizing the initial discussion by periods—provides the best initial context for underscoring both their typical and transformative features, while deferring the "big picture" view until its components are in place (Little and Shackel 1989, 496).

As the term *conjoncture* implies, periods of relative stability are produced by the ascendancy of the constellation of elements that form a group's mentality (*mentalité*) and endure only so long as that ascendancy persists. In Great

Lakes maritime landscapes, the historical succession of dominant groups serves as the middle-range framework. The result is a series of five periods: first, Indigenous occupation immediately prior to European contact circa 1640; second, the French colonial period (mid-seventeenth century to 1760); third, the British colonial period (1760–1815); fourth, a frontier period ending with the American Civil War; and last, the modern period beginning in 1865 that sees the political and economic emergence of the American and Canadian nation-states.

Significant *événements*, often the intersection of multiple causative factors (economic, political, technological, military), break the behavioral patterns established within a period and as such are critical to understanding and explaining change (Knapp 1992, 6). Sufficiently disruptive events not only alter the trajectory of a period but may trigger the transition from one period to another with the attendant transformation of the ways in which the landscape is understood, represented, dwelt in, and moved through.[1]

Formation of the Landscape: Seven Primary Elements

Historical processes are exquisitely sensitive to their initial conditions.
—Tristram R. Kidder, "The Rat That Ate Louisiana"

The plethora of factors affecting the processes of landscape formation appear dismayingly complex, but a nautical analogy proves helpful. Maritime archaeologist Jonathan Adams has identified a network of seven interdependent factors affecting shipbuilding: environment, materials, ideology, technology, tradition, economics, and purpose (Adams 2001, 301). Scaled up to the scope of the landscape itself, these same elements categorize the agents participating in the processes forming not only ships and boats but the world they and their creators inhabit.

1 Hereinafter, rather than maintaining the French terminology of the *Annales* school, I will generally use the English equivalents "long term" for *longue durée*, "period" for *conjoncture*, "event" for *événement*, and "mentality" for *mentalité*.

Using Adams's scheme, the agency of Nature constitutes two elements: first, as *environment*, the physical context (water bodies, landforms, weather) within which maritime movement and dwelling are both afforded and constrained. Second, the immediate locale either contains or furnishes a route to raw *materials*: such affordances as food and naturally occurring commodities (furs, timber, minerals) are unevenly distributed in the natural environment. The remaining five elements are Cultural, beginning with the *ideology* of the society, whose goals and values are expressed in the *purpose* of the social group's moving and dwelling. Labor is mobilized according to the *economics* of the society, thereby modifying and redistributing resources using culturally transmitted methods (*technology* + *tradition*).

Some elements, notably *environment* and *materials*, may be expected to change slowly over the long term, while the continuity of others (*ideology*, *purpose*, *economics*) is liable to be disrupted between periods, particularly with a transition in dominant societies. The tensioned relationship between the two remaining elements—conservative *tradition* and innovative *technology*—is the most volatile and dynamic in the network. By acting on the processes of dwelling and movement, they prove the most tangible in the transformation of the maritime landscape.

The evidence of past landscapes and their occupants may be divided into two broad classes of media: physical or artifactual and symbolic or representational. The physical evidence consists primarily of features of the built environment and the objects within it. Artifacts and sites may be found buried or submerged in archaeological contexts (lithic and ceramic artifacts, shipwrecks, abandoned vessels, disused infrastructure). Others are still serving in systemic contexts—that is, in active use (surviving wharves and landings, remnant settlement patterns, functioning lighthouses and aids to navigation).

These are complemented by myriad representations. Early acts of exploration, conquest, settlement, diplomacy, and commerce are attested in the form of official reports, travelers' accounts, diaries, correspondence, memoirs, charts, maps, and ship's logs (Crumley 1996, 559). Records of vessel construction, use, loss, and discard begin as a trickle but quickly become a torrent. By the nineteenth century, primary source material on every aspect of Great Lakes maritimity is not merely abundant; it is omnipresent, as the same Industrial Revolution that brought steamboats to the frontier also brought the telegraph and the printing press. This prototypical information explosion, driven by the bureaucratic practices of both the American and Canadian governments, created a treasure trove of primary source material. Registries of virtually every commercial vessel that has sailed the lakes are now easily accessible, thanks to a latter-day digital information explosion.

These textual and cartographic representations of the built environment and its associated material culture serve as proxies, signifiers for the vanished or transformed signified: ships and shipyards, fortifications, wharves, piers, lighthouses, and the waterside resorts from the St. Clair Flats' half-century heyday as "Michigan's Venice." But also present are invaluable accounts of maritime experience: seamanship from the days of paddle, sail, and steam; visions of vanished features of the landscape itself—treacherous sandbars, meandering channels, and seemingly limitless wildlife habitat. This reintegration of materiality and narrative, practice and place, creates a context for the recovery of maritime heritage and the transmission of identity within descendant communities, which form a significant rationale for, and value of, this work.

2

Bridge, Barrier, and Bottleneck

A Brief Natural History of the St. Clair Region

When we arrived we found the scenery here very pretty, the borders of the lake, for miles inland, being a savannah of long, bright green grass, with woods in the rear disposed in capes, islands, and devious avenues. I was delighted, and landed for a run, but to my surprise, I stepped into water ankle-deep, and forthwith returned. But a more serious evil was the bad quality of the water, as we were to be here for several days, and the weather sultry and close. It was tainted and discoloured by the dead bodies of a minute pink insect, and was only drinkable after straining and boiling. Our people spent most of the daylight in the insular channels, and Lieutenant Grant in sounding the lake. The natural result of all this was sickness; but while in the lake the only person seriously ill was my friend the lieutenant. He was attacked by the dangerous fever of the country, with great general excitement, delirium, &c, &c., but bleeding and other appropriate remedies brought him round, first by conversion of the continued fever into the remittent, and then into the common ague, which was driven off by quinine.

—John J. Bigsby, *The Shoe and Canoe; or, Pictures of Travel in the Canadas*

Dr. John J. Bigsby, physician and amateur geologist, led the British contingent of the International Boundary Commission's survey of the Great Lakes region in 1820. Like Hennepin before him, the good doctor quickly came to appreciate the rich ecology of their assigned locale, with its varied flora and fauna, pleasures and perils. In the intervening two centuries, our knowledge of and impact upon the Huron-Erie strait, including the focal delta at its center, have grown. A brief examination of its natural environment sets the stage for the explication of its varied relations with Indigenous, colonial, and modern inhabitants.

The scientific literature of the St. Clair system has its origins in the earliest European visitors, whose observations were admittedly motivated by considerations of colonization and exploitation but yield a wealth of detail about the landscape as well as a revealing look at the priorities of the observers. Among the first scientifically trained observers in the Strait were the American and British agents of the International Boundary Commission, Major Joseph Delafield and his friend and colleague Dr. Bigsby, both avid geologists. At the same time as the Commission was completing its survey of the St. Clair delta in 1820, a party led by Michigan's governor Lewis Cass made its way by canoe from Detroit to the headwaters of the Mississippi. In the party was an army engineer, David Bates Douglass, charged with documenting the natural history of their itinerary, a task not unlike that of the Lewis and Clark Expedition of 1804 to 1806. It was not until the turn of the twentieth century, however, that modern scientific publishing focused on the St. Clair system. A. J. Pieters's *The Plants of Lake St. Clair* (1894) and Leon J. Cole's *The Delta of the St. Clair River* (1903) addressed its botany and geology in twelve and twenty-five pages, respectively. Though brief by today's standards and written after much cultural transformation of the maritime landscape, they remain valuable resources and are cited to this day as ecological benchmarks.

Physical Geography

The St. Clair hydrologic system contains three major components: the St. Clair River; the St. Clair delta, or Flats; and Lake St. Clair. Together they comprise approximately 60 miles (100 km) of the 80-mile (130 km) strait connecting Lake Huron with Lake Erie (figure 1).[1] The upper portion of the river, at 30 miles

1 As most of the historical sources quoted give dimensions in English units (feet and miles), I will generally follow suit, adding metric units in parentheses. This is true both of distances and measurements of structures, notably ships.

FIGURE 1. "Gathering Wild Rice," painting by Seth Eastman (ca. 1853). (The American Aboriginal Portfolio, by Mary H. Eastman)

(48 km) in length, is generally about 1.5 miles (2.4 km) wide, running nearly straight north-south. Its depth ranges between 30 and 60 feet (9 to 18 m). The current is greatest at its head, a rapid averaging 4.5 mph (7.2 kph) as the waters of Lakes Superior, Michigan, and Huron pour into the Strait beneath today's Bluewater Bridge. There are tributaries along both sides, notably the Pine and Belle Rivers, both on the American side. The Canadian side is drained by several small creeks.

The delta occupies the lower 10 miles (16 km) of the river, featuring six major channels and numerous islands. The swift current has scoured the upper channels to a considerable depth, averaging between 30 and 40 feet (9 to 12 m), with the North Channel reaching a maximum of 90 feet (27 m) just below Algonac. All the channels are characterized, however, by a gradual shallowing, terminating in sedimentary bars across their mouths, reducing the depth to as little as 5 feet (1.5 m). Lake St. Clair is nearly 30 miles (48 km) long, and 24 miles (38 km) at its widest point. The mean depth is 18–20 feet (5–6 m). A natural channel, originally of some 22 feet (7 m) in depth, runs down its center to the lake's outlet into the Detroit River. In the past century this has been dredged to maintain a commercial shipping lane of approximately 30 feet (9 m) in depth. Weather events, seasonal fluctuations, and climatic cycles can cause all these measurements to vary by as much as 3 feet (1 m). The lake has two major tributaries: the Clinton River (once known as the Huron) on the American side and the Thames on the Canadian side. They access the communities of Mount Clemens, Michigan, and Chatham, Ontario, respectively.

Geology and Hydrology

At present, the Strait connecting Lake Huron and Lake Erie receives all the waters of Lakes Superior, Michigan, and Huron, but this was not always the case (Raphael and Jaworski 1982). During the Lake Stanley stage, 10,500 to 5000 BP, the retreating ice of the great Wisconsin glacier exposed a crustal depression northeast of present-day Georgian Bay, Ontario. Drainage followed the course of the present-day French River, passing northeast through Lake Nipissing, then east and south into the Ottawa River, finally emptying into the St. Lawrence River. This continued until the retreat of the Wisconsin glacier some 10,500 to 12,500 years ago. Relieved of the immense weight of two miles of ice, the earth's crust gradually rebounded, effectively tilting the land and its surface waters to the south to follow a course that persists to the present (Cole 1903, 19; Raphael and Jaworski 1982, 19; Bolsenga and Herdendorf 1993, 73). The glacial meltwater and sediment carried along this southerly route during the Lake Nipissing stage, 5,000 to 3,500 years ago, brought high water levels and deep sedimentation, resulting in the formation of a premodern St. Clair delta, some 5 feet (1.5 m) above the present level of Lake St. Clair. Crustal rebound has raised this formation well above today's shoreline.

Around 3500 BP, the Strait took on its present form, as newer, low-water channels carved through the older, higher delta and deposited the newer delta on its outer slopes downstream (Cole 1903, 8; Raphael and Jaworski 1982; Kaszicki 1985, 121). In its formative processes, the delta differs significantly from true riverine deltas opening into large bodies of open water (such as the Mississippi or the Nile). Its shape, however, exhibits the classic "bird's foot" pattern over an expanse of approximately 30 square miles (78 km^2), 45% of which

(13.5 mi^2 or 35 km^2) is emergent wetland habitat (Bolsenga and Herdendorf 1993, 367; Thomas et al. 2006, 739). As a strait emptying a chain of lakes rather than a true river, the St. Clair River lacks significant additional tributaries that would create a seasonal fluctuation of higher and lower flow rates and water levels (Raphael and Jaworski 1982, 13). Instead of spring floods and summer slack water, the river maintains a consistently high volume and flow rate, with a concomitant degree of force to transport sediment and shape its bed.

Despite the considerable force of the current in the river, these particles, being too heavy to be carried in suspension, are instead carried along the bottom as bed load (Cole 1903, 9; Raphael and Jaworski 1982). The lack of suspended particulates accounts for the unusual clarity of the river's waters (Cole 1903, 11). The currents in the channels lose force and speed as they divide and empty into the open waters of the Lake St. Clair, their sediment load being deposited in the form of bars across the channel mouths (Cole 1903, 13; Raphael and Jaworksi 1982, 12; Bolsenga and Herdendorf 1993, 86). This phenomenon was observed by the earliest of European explorers, and became a notable constraint upon, and determinant of, the maritime cultural landscape of the St. Clair delta, and indeed the navigation of the upper Great Lakes as a whole.

As a relatively small and shallow body of water, Lake St. Clair's wave action is not a significant factor impacting the natural shoreline, as windblown waves from any direction lack sufficient fetch and depth to grow to appreciable size. The wide and gently shelving margin causes larger waves to break well offshore, minimizing their erosive effects. Moreover, their energy has been further absorbed by the dense reed beds that were ubiquitous until recent years brought shoreline development (Raphael and Jaworski 1982, 20). This was noted by David Bates Douglass, the civil engineer attached to the Lewis Cass expedition of 1820: "Lake St. Clair may be considered a mere dilation of the river, being very shallow except in certain channels which pass through it. In many places at several miles from shore our paddles touched bottom and the rushes were growing thick" (Douglass 1969, 18; also Bigsby 1850, 299).

Also due to its shallowness, navigation on Lake St. Clair is disproportionately affected by any change in water level, as even a slight decrease can make the difference between clearing the bottom or running aground. Wind plays a significant role here, as Lake St. Clair is subject to a noteworthy phenomenon, one that mimics the lunar tidal action of the open sea. The shallow waters, despite offering wind-generated waves a maximum fetch of only 22 miles (35 km; Raphael and Jaworski 1982, 20), allow the generation of sudden local rises in water level, commonly termed *seiches* in the Great Lakes (Owen 2014, 987; Considine 2008, 4707). Pushed by a strong wind, the water entering a confined area such as a bay can temporarily "pile up," as it were (Ibrahim and McCorquodale 1985). Such is the case of Anchor Bay, at the mouth of the North Channel in the northwest corner of the lake. Southerly winds, Cole observed, "may raise the general level a foot or more" (Cole 1903, 18). As surveyors Delafield and Bixby learned in the early nineteenth century, wind direction and periodic water level fluctuations affecting the delta's navigability carried political implications in defining the boundary between the United States and Canada.

Climate

The archaeological record of the Strait indicates long-term occupation by Indigenous groups, most practicing a mixed horticultural/foraging economy (Cleland 1992; Goddard 1978). The locale's climate is generally temperate, consistent with its latitude near the forty-second parallel and its proximity to large bodies of water with their moderating influence. At the outset of the historical period, French visitors made favorable comparisons to the climate and soil of their native land. One must consider the motivations of the informants, however. Cadillac, shortly after his arrival, wrote in 1702 that "the climate is as temperate there as in Touraine, and the Winter (according to what the Savages say) lasts only six weeks at most" (Cadillac 1904, 131). Beauharnois, in 1731, reported that "the Climate is fine, the Lands are very good and can produce anything that grows in France in the province of Guienne" (Beauharnois 1906, 141). In the case of Cadillac, it may be that he was intentionally painting a rosy picture of Detroit for the benefit of his overseeing officials, prospective sponsors, and potential colonists. Considering that the "Little Ice Age," lasted until approximately 1715 (Heckert 2016), Cadillac's optimistic reference to a mere six weeks of winter could be his own purposeful narrative, conditioned perhaps by his recent sojourn well to the north at Michilimackinac. The same may be true of his Native informants, painting a rosy picture of their own to encourage French fortification of the strategic Strait against their inveterate enemies to the east, the Iroquois Confederacy.

More convincing is the consistent description through the seventeenth and eighteenth centuries by multiple European authors of the vegetation in the Strait, particularly along the St. Clair River (Hennepin 1966, 92; Galinée 1917, 196; Duluth 1902; Lahontan 1905). There, extensive and well-established anthropogenic orchards and vineyards reliably indicate long-term temperate conditions, possibly moderated even farther along the shoreline by a littoral microclimate that would enhance its attractiveness to horticulturalists, whether Indigenous or French.

A mid-twentieth-century study using the Geiger-Köppen climate classification system places the Strait on the border between the "humid continental, hot summer" (classification Dfa) and a narrow band of "humid subtropical, no dry season" (Dfb) zones (Himmler and De Long 1963). For comparison, the climate of western France is classified as the more temperate "marine west coast" (Cfb; Veregin 2010, 30–31), despite lying several degrees to the north of the Strait. That the Detroit climate of that time should compare favorably in its vegetation zones with the highly productive French landscape may speak to both the moderating effects of the surrounding Great Lakes and perhaps the greater impact of the Little Ice Age in Europe than in central North America. In either case, the contrast in the Strait's local zonation provided a mild area favoring settlement and horticulture, while offering ready access via rivers to inland biomes supporting the flora and fauna that supplied the fur and timber industries.

Flora

The Huron-Erie strait and the surrounding lands of southeast Michigan and southwest Ontario lie entirely within the Carolinian biotic province, characterized by Fitting and Cleland (1969, 289) by "essentially southern plant and animal species and both soils and climate [that] are amenable to agriculture." The relatively constant water levels in the St. Clair delta and Lake St. Clair, and the dynamic processes that have created its landforms, have led to the distinct zonation of both the aquatic and terrestrial plants found there (Raphael and Jaworski 1982, 7).

The distribution of aquatic plants is dependent primarily on water depth and bottom composition (Pieters 1894, 9; Raphael and Jaworski 1982, 20). Likewise, the terrestrial plant life shows zonation related to the geological strata and elevation of the landforms. The higher premodern delta now hosts oak-ash hardwood forests, while dogwoods, willows, ferns, and grasses dominate the transition zone above the sedge marshes (Bolsenga and Herdendorf 1993, 390–91). On the American side of the delta, the Michigan Natural Features Inventory identifies at least six natural communities in the St. Clair delta and along the St. Clair River: Submergent Marsh; Emergent Marsh; Great Lakes Marsh; Lakeplain Wet Prairie; Lakeplain Wet-mesic Prairie; and Mesic Southern Forest (Kost et al. 2007). Historically, the Strait circa 1600 has been classified as a deciduous-coniferous biome, mixing maple, beech, birch, hemlock, and spruce (Tanner 1987, 14). Beyond creating a locale ideal for settlement, this diverse forestation of the upper St. Clair River carried implications for timber production, both as a resource for local boat- and shipbuilding as well as a commodity to be shipped throughout the Great Lakes.

A survey of a section of wet prairie on Harsens Island in 1960 documented the presence of ninety-two plant species, all but six of which were perennials (Hayes 1964). As an indicator of healthy diversity, this survey compares favorably to approximately one hundred species observed on adjacent Walpole and Squirrel Islands a half-century previous (Dodge 1914). In both studies, the authors noted the regular use of intentional burning to suppress invasive annual and woody-stemmed species. This preferential creation and maintenance of floral (and thereby faunal) biodiversity using fire is a diagnostic indicator of long-term anthropogenic landscape transformation (Sauer 1956, 55; Erickson 2010). In terms of affordances, the multiple St. Clair biomes have historically hosted a dense and diverse floral population within a highly accessible and manageable taskscape.

Fauna

The result of such varied and sheltered habitat is an abundance of wildlife. Migratory waterfowl are seasonal visitors; game fish and their prey flourish in the estuarine and open waters; mammals inhabit every niche, including the aquatic, where economically significant species—beaver, muskrat, otter, and mink—made their homes (Kost et al. 2007, 65–68). Present-day studies still document a complex food web with avian, mammalian, piscine, and reptilian apex predators (Bolsenga and Herdendorf 1993, 392). The abundance of game species in the Strait caught the attention of the earliest French visitors. Hennepin in 1679 remarked on the deer, bear, turkeys, and swans (Hennepin 1903, 109), while Lahontan in 1688 noted the ease of hunting deer in the delta: "When we came to little islands, we scour'd 'em, in order to oblige these Beasts to cross over to the Continent, upon which they offering to swim over, were knock'd on the head by our Canow-men that were planted all round the Islands" (Lahontan 1905, 139).

The constricted and shallow waters of the Strait provided both habitat and access to stocks of fish, caught in shoreline weirs and net impoundments. A 1718 French government agent reported that Lake St. Clair was "well stocked with fish, especially whitefish, which, however, is not so good as that at Missilimackinac" (Chauvignerie 1855, 1058; also Tanner 1987, 23). Notables including Henry Rowe Schoolcraft (1821, 82) and Alexis de Tocqueville (1959, 143) chronicled the continuing abundance of game. Today the St. Clair Flats offer world-class recreational hunting and fishing side-by-side with the persistence of Indigenous subsistence practices, though not without some cultural friction (Martin 1971; Nin.Da.Waab.Jig 1987, 33). On the Michigan side, the St. Johns Marsh preserves some 3,000 acres of managed wetlands hosting nearly 160 plant species, attracting flocks of migratory waterfowl. Accounts from every succeeding dominant group make it clear that each found the St. Clair locale a rich source of ecological resources, whether considered as subsistence, commerce, or sport (Spoehr 1956, 94).

Economic Geography

As a maritime cultural landscape, the St. Clair River and its delta feature two key economic affordances: as a locale offering natural resources, and as a transport zone linking other landscapes. The former draws on the economic properties described earlier, whether resources from fish and wild rice to furs and timber are considered as subsistence needs or as commodities. The transport zone derives from the nature of the Strait as an interface of two land masses—the peninsulas of Michigan and southwest Ontario—and two Great Lakes. The settlements, transportation routes, and maritime industries that emerged and evolved there were contingent on these geographical realities. Throughout the historic period commencing in the seventeenth century, peoples occupying the Strait between Lake Huron and Lake Erie had access, either through local production or trade along extensive maritime and terrestrial transport corridors, to the means for the full range of affordances—literally, food, clothing, and shelter plus the material means for transport itself in the form of resources for building watercraft.

The operations of Adam's element of *economy* in the processes of landscape formation are generally concerned with at least one of these activities: subsistence in the local taskscape, extraction of commodities for shipment elsewhere, the manufacturing of watercraft, waterborne commerce through the local transport zone and beyond, or the creation and maintenance of the maritime infrastructure in support of transportation and commerce. These economic activities were generally conducted along the transport corridors at points of supply, processing, and consumption (sawmills and shipyards near timber stands); support (drydocks, repair and salvage operations); or transshipment (wharves at roads and railheads). The result was a zoned taskscape linked by a common dependence on waterborne transportation of goods, information, and people: a networked economic maritime landscape.

Political Geography

Being socially constructed, landscapes are inevitably political. Even before the arrival of Europeans in the historic period, the strategic landscape of the Strait had been claimed and contested by a succession of societies and their political institutions. The Huron/Wendat, Haudenosaunee/Iroquois, Anishinaabeg / Three Fires, France, Britain, United States, Canada—all have occupied or laid claim to the lands and waters of the Strait (Tanner 1987; Cleland 1992; White 1991). For each of these maritime societies, the Strait was a membrane permeable by both land and water. Only in the past two centuries have the channels of the Strait served double duty as political boundaries: the demarcations between the United States and Canada and between Ontario and the Walpole Island First Nations.

Contestation over these boundaries and the territory they traverse centered not only on access to long-distance maritime trade and transportation networks but on local affordances and settlement sites as well. Unequal distribution of resources on the two sides of the Strait meant that any artificial constraints placed on movement carried both political and economic consequences. This became evident, for example, in the case of pine forestation, which was more extensive on the Michigan side of the Strait than in Ontario (Moore 1915, 154). The ramifications for Canadian shipbuilding triggered an international incident as late as 1870, when a load of timber was seized after being unloaded on the wrong side of a disputed section of the American/Canadian border. A brief and bloodless episode of mutual saber-rattling was the seriocomic result, dubbed "a Speck of War" by the *Detroit Free Press* of October 12. The working out of these economic and political contestations is an integral component of the processes of dwelling and movement in an evolving landscape.

Considered from any perspective or time period, the Strait in general, and the St. Clair delta in particular, offers a complex, dynamic, and strategic environment. Throughout the historical period commencing in the early seventeenth century, the ecology of the St. Clair system has consistently been perceived and exploited as one of great diversity and natural abundance. The natural hydrology, by contrast, has shifted from being perceived and utilized by Indigenous inhabitants as an unalloyed affordance, both in terms of transportation and habitat. To arriving Europeans, the convoluted channels were a problematic source of difficulty and risk, even danger.

While none of the ecology of the present-day Strait can be regarded as pristine, some areas, such as Walpole Island, appear to have preserved much of their long-term biodiversity. Urbanized areas have altered the shoreline, mostly by seawalls and other hardened surfaces, so that the interface between land and water is not so permeable and variable as in its more natural state. The extensive forestation that formed a principal affordance until the end of the nineteenth century has been replaced by urban and agricultural areas. Nevertheless, the focused development of artificial navigational channels through the central zone of the Flats has allowed much of the natural hydrology at its periphery to remain comparatively unaltered.

3

Indigenous Landscapes and Identities in the St. Clair Region

It is true that many men of all countries have listened to your words. I look toward the rising sun and toward the setting sun, I look on all sides, and I see that everywhere you have made the ancient customs disappear. In truth, the changes you have made in the world are many. I contemplate them and am amazed. Most nations have rejected the blessings of their Ancestors. And that, my brother, is what you are asking of me, that is what you are reserving for me! After having traveled far, on all sides, you come to me on this small island where I live. Could you not leave me in peace to enjoy the blessings of my Ancestor? Soon, I will not even remember them. No, that cannot be; I remain faithful to my Ancestor. Here at least the fire he left me will burn for me and for my children. So my brother, do not worry about me; take no more interest in my fate, and let me live in peace, on my little island, in my humble dwelling.

—Chief Petrokeshig

These words were spoken on July 31, 1844, by the Ojibwe chief Petrokeshig to Father Pierre Chazelle at Bkejwanong, or Walpole Island (Delâge, Tanner, and Chazelle 1994, 313). In a debate lasting hours, he and the great Shawnee chief Oshawana politely but firmly rejected the Jesuit missionary's arguments for establishing a Christian congregation in their midst. This act, both an assertion of identity and a rejection of cultural imperialism, crystallizes Indigenous resistance to the transformation of their lifeways and homeland. Petrokeshig and Oshawana, who had fought alongside Tecumseh, stood astride the transition between European colonialism and the emergence of the American and Canadian nation-states. Their land remains poised between past and present, between tradition and modernity.

Background and Early Habitation in the St. Clair Delta

Among the remarkable aspects of the St. Clair locale is its preservation of an Indigenous occupation that is essentially continuous from the precontact period. Moreover, this presence persists in spite of, rather than because of, government intervention. The Walpole Island First Nations were not relocated from elsewhere; rather, they remain on unceded ancestral land. The early processes of knowing, dwelling, moving, and representation, whereby the Indigenous peoples of the Archaic and Woodland periods created their own landscapes, lie outside the time period of this study. The result, however, forms the cultural substrate upon which descendant communities, and those of European and American arrivals, continued to transform the landscape. The suppression, persistence, transformation, and appropriation of Indigenous modes of landscape formation may be observed in their interaction with successive arrivals. These will be revisited as subsequent landscape transformations are addressed in the following chapters.

The present overview proceeds from the foregoing discussion of the corridor between Lake Huron and Lake Erie. In this transitional environment, the life that flourishes, both flora and fauna, is adapted to its range of conditions. And so must it be with the human presence. What is remarkable is that despite over three centuries of incursion by non-Native cultures, an Indigenous presence not only survives but thrives. Surrounded by the political, economic, and cultural pressures of the developed world of the twenty-first century, a viable First Nations presence—and moreover, the landscape upon which its identity is founded—persists in this "place where the waters divide." This chapter introduces their story, about the ways people find the balance between what they need and what the environment affords them and, in doing so, create their unique dwelling-place in the world. As a *maritime* cultural landscape, Bkejwanong is characterized by an intimate connection between people and water—as a source of subsistence, a means of transportation, and a mark of identity.

It is a commonplace observation in maritime studies that water can serve both as a bridge and a barrier, depending on a given culture's technology, practices, and ideology—in short, on their ability and willingness to take to the water (Adams 2001; Cooney 2003; Ford 2011, 2017; Delgado et al. 2016). Archaeological evidence suggests that Indigenous peoples living between Lake Huron and Lake Erie had been settling on both sides of the Strait long before European contact, beginning no later than the late first millennium CE. A good indicator of cultural continuity during this period can be found in the archaeological record. Whether it indicates a flow of peoples, goods, or ideas is not clear, but characteristic "Wayne ware" ceramic vessels appear throughout the length of the Strait: near Port Huron (Hoxie 1980), at the Rivière au Vase and Fair Haven sites near Lake St. Clair's Anchor Bay; near Chatham, on the Ontario side; at Springwells, below Detroit; and in Gibraltar, at the mouth of the Detroit River (Fitting 1970, 150–60; Stothers 1999). Communication and cohesion were facilitated by the maritime corridor.

By the outset of the period of European contact, the picture becomes clearer and far more complex. The Strait area became highly dynamic as rival Indigenous groups contested control of a new economic reality: the fur trade. At issue were not only the beavers and their habitat but the water and land routes that the pelts and trade goods traveled to and from market. Definitely not a barrier, and more than merely a linear bridge, the Strait was a logistical and strategic nexus, a multidimensional crossroads of maritime, riverine, and overland routes that penetrated the North American continent from the Atlantic to the farthest navigable reaches of the Lake Superior drainage at the edge of the Great Plains, with portage routes into the Ohio and Mississippi basins.

War and Depopulation

The earliest French maps of the Great Lakes region date from the early 1640s, at a time when the Beaver Wars precipitated large-scale population displacement throughout the Great Lakes region. Although the French headquartered their transatlantic fur trade in present-day Quebec, the supply of beaver had already dwindled there (Witgen 2012, 46). Moreover, such European-introduced diseases as smallpox, measles, and pneumonia had ravaged those peoples with whom they had already come into contact (Warrick 2013, 72). Iroquois raiders from the Lake Ontario area, intent on gaining control of the resources and trade routes to their west, relentlessly attacked their Huron neighbors, effectively destroying them as a nation in their Georgian Bay homeland of Huronia or *Wendake*. Pressing on, the Iroquois waged war against the nations occupying southwest Ontario and the Lower Peninsula of Michigan (Wolf 1982, 170). These included the Mascouten, Fox, Sauk, and Potawatomi, who fled across Lake Michigan to Green Bay, where the Iroquois offensive, now overextended, lost momentum.

The intervening space, only recently a killing ground, became a depopulated landscape (Tanner 1987, 30–31). What remain are labels locating its peoples on maps drawn by missionaries and explorers. These, together with linguistic, ethnohistorical, and archaeological evidence, allow us to visualize how groups distributed themselves preceding the arrival of the French. Clues to group identity take the form of subsistence and settlement patterns, group names, and other linguistic evidence. Sources of such information during this period come from cartographic and first-person accounts, with archaeology contributing both scope and detail (Nassaney 2015).

A recurring theme in this process of linking peoples, places, and practices is that of *fire*. An anonymous map entitled *Novvelle France*, attributed to one Jean Bourdon and made no later than 1642, shows the locations of Great Lakes tribes prior to the dispersals of the late 1640s and the 1650s (Steckley 1990, 17). A large area west of Lake Erie is labeled as the territory of the *Gens de Feu* ("people of the fire"), while one of several smaller labels identifies a subgroup, the *aictaeronon*. Citing Bourdon's imperfect knowledge of Huron, ethnolinguist John Steckley interprets this as a corruption of *atsistaeronon*—again, "people of the fire," the Huron name for the Mascouten nation. The other labels give the Huron names for the Potawatomi, Fox, and Sauk nations (Steckley 1990, 21). This clustering of several groups around the general term "people of the fire" echoes the summation of ethnohistorian Charles Cleland that the "Fire Nation" was not a single group. Rather, it comprised groups of small, independent Algonquian-speaking agriculturalists occupying the southern third of what is now the Lower Peninsula of Michigan and included the Potawatomi and Mascouten (Cleland 1992, 87).

What united them in the eyes of the arriving French was their use of fire. Early accounts from Huronia suggest that after clearing the land, the inhabitants regularly burned only the weeds; moreover, by planting the ecologically complementary "three sisters"—corn, beans, and squash—nutrients were not as readily depleted from the soil (Doolittle 1992, 393). The name "Mascouten," which was initially construed as "fire people," may be more accurately translated as "people of the small prairies"—a reference to the man-made clearings that were created and maintained by controlled burning and soil regeneration (Goddard 1978; Fitting 1970, 197).

The first French eyewitness account of the ravaged homelands left behind by the fleeing Hurons and Fire Nations comes from René Brehan de Galinée and François Dollier de Casson, a pair of Sulpician missionaries who in 1669 journeyed from Montreal to an Odawa settlement at Sault Ste. Marie by way of the Strait of Detroit. Galinée's observations indicate an awareness that they were traversing an unpeopled landscape but not that it was also a man-made one. Of their winter camp on the north shore of Lake Erie, the priest wrote, "*Although it has no cultivation* it does not fail to produce grapes in great quantities as large and as sweet as the finest of France" and "The woods are open, interspersed with beautiful meadows" (Galinée 1917, 196–97; emphasis added). Yet on his accompanying map, he noted that only a few miles inland from that same place, "here was once the Neutral nation," acknowledging the destruction of that group's homeland.

Paddling up the Strait, the priests encountered a large war party of Iroquois camped at Springwells, an ancient habitation site featuring several large mounds, located just below the future location of Detroit, at the present site of historic Fort Wayne. There, a painted idol marked a ritual site along the Iroquois maritime war path, as sacrifices of food and pelts to "this god of stone" were said to ensure their raiding parties safe passage across the lakes (Galinée 1917, 204; Smith 1939, 5–6). Upstream, the missionaries encountered the so-called *Lac des Eaux de Mer* or "Salt Water Lake" (later Lake St. Clair), as it had been termed since the time of Champlain in 1616 (Dunnigan 2001, 9). This possibly derived from Indigenous informants referring to a salt spring among its tributaries; to this day, "Salt Creek" enters Anchor Bay near New Baltimore.

The missionaries, however, did not display the interest in seawater that would be expected of an explorer in search of a route to the Orient. By contrast, in 1634, the ambitious Jean Nicolet had traveled with an ornate Chinese robe in anticipation of meeting with the Great Khan (Wien 2003). Galinée's party observed neither salty water nor inhabitants (Galinée 1917, 204).

The perception of a depopulated landscape was inadvertently corroborated by Père Louis Hennepin, La Salle's Jesuit companion on his ill-fated *Griffon* expedition of 1679 from Niagara to Green Bay. Along the Strait, Hennepin "left a promised-land description wherein there is no mention of the presence of any inhabitants, red or white" (Lajeunesse 1960, xxxv): "The Banks of the Strait are vast Meadows," the cleric enthused, "and the Prospect is terminated with some Hills covered with vineyards, Trees bearing good Fruit, Groves, and Forests, so well dispos'd that *one would think Nature alone could not have made, without the Help of Art*, so charming a Prospect" (Hennepin 1903, 109; emphasis added). As with Galinée's winter camp on Lake Erie a decade previous, such paradisiacal bounty was viewed as a gift of divine Providence, or a beneficent Nature. The former inhabitants, of course, had only recently fled their carefully created and tended horticultural landscape, and they would have to wait two more decades before regaining their ancestral homelands, this time in collaboration with Cadillac.

Repopulation of the Strait

When the Mascouten, Sauk, Fox, and Potawatomi fled the southern Lower Peninsula in the 1640s, they took refuge at La Baye (present-day Green Bay, Wisconsin), finding a significantly shorter growing season. As their new home lay within the Carolinian-Canadian transition biotic province (Fitting and Cleland 1969), they evidently subsisted by supplementing their crops with hunting and fur trapping along with the trade goods and supplies that the latter brought. The principal French trading center was at the Straits of Mackinac, accessible to the peoples of northern Lake Huron, with a secondary outpost at La Baye. When in 1701 Antoine de Lamothe Cadillac, commandant at Michilimackinac, declared his intention to move his headquarters south to the Huron-Erie strait, it precipitated a displacement of his Indigenous trading partners. In effect, it was a homecoming for the refugees at La Baye but a dislocation for others who had been at home in the north all along. This difference can be perceived in the settlement patterns of these Native groups in the resulting landscape surrounding the French nucleus at Fort Pontchartrain on the Detroit River.

The standard Eurocentric narrative of the "founding" of Detroit places the credit squarely with Cadillac, who "invited" the Native trading partners from his tenure as commandant at Michilimackinac to join him at his new settlement (Dunbar and May 1995). These included Huron and Odawa residing in the St. Ignace area as well as recent refugees from Green Bay: Fox, Sauk, and Potawatomi. It would also have extended to long-term Anishinaabeg residents to the northeast, including the Mississauga/Ojibwe on the mainland north of Lake Huron and Odawa on Manitoulin Island.

To the refugees returning from Green Bay, the founding narrative's perspective would have been quite different. In effect, they were using the French against their inveterate Iroquois enemies to regain their vacated homelands (Witgen 2012, 294; also White 1991, 14). The settlement pattern these groups formed relative to Cadillac's Fort Pontchartrain gives credence to this notion. The Potawatomi villages were close both to the fort, and to sacred landscape of ancestral burial mounds in the Springwells area. Likewise, the Huron settlement was now much closer to the Huronia/Wendake homeland that lay just across the Strait. A shift of viewpoint reframes their relationship with the French, whom they were utilizing to reclaim and defend their homeland and thereby their traditional settlement pattern and life ways. For the long-term horticulturalists, this included a return to their anthropogenic landscape with its longer growing season and thus more plentiful crops for consumption and trade (Tanner 1987, 21).

Significantly, the hunter-trader Odawa established their villages across the Detroit River, where Sandwich and Windsor, Ontario, now stand. Not being native to this region and having relocated many miles south from their Manitoulin Island homeland, they may have found it politic to keep their distance as newcomers and not to compete for the same economic niche as the Potawatomi and Huron. The Odawa acted prudently, considering the reception the Saginaw-area horticulturalist Fox and Mesquakie refugees received when they attempted in 1711 to relocate to the Detroit locale and claim a share of the trade there. The "Fox Wars," fought by the Potawatomi and Huron with

French aid, drove the Fox and Mesquakie interlopers back to Wisconsin, where they settled and remain (Tanner 1987, 39).

Similarly, the Mississauga/Ojibwe, having traveled from territory even farther to the north, settled farthest from Fort Pontchartrain. Galinée's map of 1670 shows the "Mississaugué" originally dwelling along the north Lake Huron shore, while that of Boishébert in 1731 shows a village of "Les Misissagi" now relocated to the St. Clair delta, on the eastern shore of "Île de Nénehe," present-day Harsens Island (map 2). Like the Odawa, these northern Anishinaabeg were native to the Canadian biotic province, where their subsistence followed the "Chippewa Pattern" characterized by trapping and hunting for exchange with the neighboring Odawa to the south, including agricultural products (Fitting and Cleland 1969, 293). It appears that these hunter-fisher-gatherers from the north, the Mississauga—whose name means "river with many outlets"—chose the delta of the St. Clair River as a locale that suited their traditional patterns of settlement and subsistence: a place that felt like home. There they found their customary seasonal resources in abundance: fish, game, and wildfowl. They also found the birch and spruce trees needed to make their distinctive canoes.

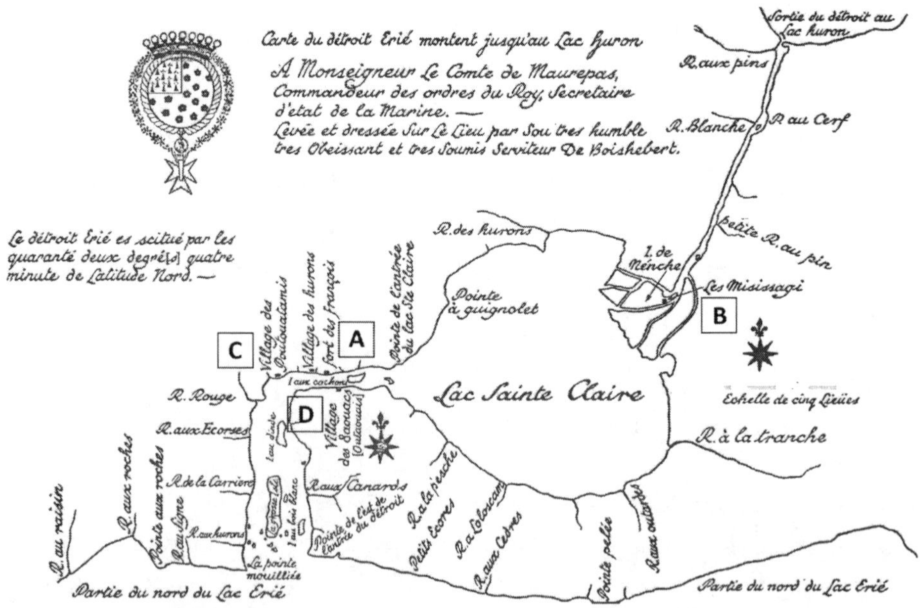

MAP 2. Map of Detroit, copy after Boishébert, 1731. (A) Fort Pontchartrain; (B) "Les Misissagi" on "Île de Nénehe" (Harsens Island); (C) Potawatomi and Huron (Wyandot); (D) Odawa (Archives Canada).

With these supremely adapted watercraft, they were a true maritime culture, capable not only of accessing Fort Pontchartrain but of conducting long-distance trade across open waters, penetrating inland rivers for food and furs, and harvesting wild rice (Monk 1999, 73; figure 1). The river and its delta offered an expansive and varied landscape through which they moved seasonally, from fishing camps during spring spawning (Storrow 1872, 155; McKenney 1959, 151), to estuarine reed beds, to wooded hunting grounds and sugar maple groves in winter (Hudgins 1935). The Mississauga could barter for corn and vegetables with their old neighbors from the north, the Odawa ("traders" in Anishinaabmowin) much as they had done on Manitoulin Island (Nin. Da.Waab.Jig 1987, 7–8; Rogers 1978). Pelts and hides were exchanged for trade goods from the French at Fort Pontchartrain (Jenks 1912, 47). Throughout the French colonial period, the Mississauga—gradually joined by their Anishinaabeg relations, the Ojibwe and Saulteurs from the north—were an acknowledged presence in the St. Clair delta, appearing in censuses taken in 1718 and 1736 (Chauvignerie 1855, 1058; Tanner 1987, 61) and routinely offering hospitality to travelers, as in the case of Pierre de Charlevoix during a stormy passage in 1721 from Detroit to Michilimackinac (Charlevoix 1966, 40–41).

With the arrival of the British regime in 1760, promptly followed by Pontiac's uprising in 1763, the Indigenous Anishinaabeg population of the St. Clair delta, now collectively termed "Chippewa" (variant of "Ojibwe"), became increasingly peripheral to the British colonial economy and its maritime trade. Unlike the French adoption of Indigenous watercraft in the upper Great Lakes, British-style navigation emphasized traditional shipping in large-hulled wooden vessels. An armed schooner, the *Gladwin*, was stationed at a fortified base along the St. Clair River at the present site of the town of St. Clair. Thereupon the St. Clair Flats became a mere obstacle to shipping between Detroit and Michilimackinac, its Indigenous population increasingly marginalized.

Emergence of the Walpole Island Community

These simultaneous processes of Indigenous aggregation of related Anishinaabeg groups and their marginalization by the Euro-Americans were accelerated by the War of 1812. Following the Treaty of Ghent (1814) and the work of the International Boundary Commission (1817–20), the St. Clair Flats were divided between the United States and Canada along the course of the South Channel, bisecting the Chippewa homeland between Michigan and Ontario. On the Ontario side, Odawa were forced by the Crown to cede their villages in the strategic Detroit area, both on the mainland and on islands including Bois Blanc (Anonymous 1869).

Across the river, Michigan's governor Lewis Cass questioned in 1827 whether "a few naked wandering barbarians should stay the march of civilization and improvement, and hold in a state of perpetual unproductiveness, immense regions formed by Providence to support millions of human beings?" (Cass 1827, 392). Ironically, one of Cass's companions on his 1827 voyage, Thomas L. McKenney, began to realize that the remarkable fecundity and orderliness observed by Europeans along the St. Clair River from first contact might not be purely providential: "Near our walk on the bank [of the St. Clair River]," he wrote in his journal, "are growing the wild gooseberry, and the garden currants. From the regularity of the bushes, it would seem that they had been planted. But we see no remains of the habitation of man near. Still, Indians might have once lived near this spot, and their lodgings being so frail have left none of their remains. Time and the elements soon destroy an Indian tenement" (McKenney 1959, 154–55).[1] Lewis Cass, for his part, was determined to finish the job of eradication.

Pressured by both the Canadian and United States governments, Native groups displaced by land cessions were forced to decide between removal or refuge. On the American side, land cessions were the prelude to removal to the West throughout the 1830s. Among the Potawatomi, resistance often took the form of joining their Anishinaabeg relations on Walpole Island (Tanner 1987, 126; Nin.Da.Waab.Jig 1987, 36–37). Simultaneously, the Canadian government pursued a similar policy of land cessions. Despite their efforts to remove aboriginal

1 McKenney, an official of the Indian Department accompanying Governor Lewis to the negotiations of the Treaty of Fond du Lac, described commencing his trip through the Flats in 1826: "The night was dark and stormy; but we got underway." This foreshadows Bulwer-Lytton's notorious opening line from his 1830 novel *Paul Clifford* by four years. Credit for coining the epic phrase "It was a dark and stormy night," however, goes to Washington Irving, whose sketch "The Doleful Disaster of Anthony the Trumpeter" appeared in 1809.

communities in southwest Ontario to Manitoulin Island, however, Walpole Island has remained unceded to the Crown.

With a diverse Indigenous population composed of multiple tribal affiliations and subsistence and settlement patterns, plus numerous non-Indigenous squatters, Walpole Island only gradually began to take on the attributes of a homeland to all Three Fires of the Anishinaabeg. Fortunately, the diverse affordances of the landscape matched the varied needs of the inhabitants and their lifeways: arable land, woods, marshland, and waters to support a semisedentary pattern of horticultural subsistence, with a substantial amount of traditional hunting and fishing. By 1852, Neal Ferris notes, "most of the Walpole Island community was still characterized as being away from the reserve a good six months of the year"; a decade later, a quarter of Walpole Island households were still not engaged in agriculture at all, and a third engaged only marginally (Ferris 2009, 71, 74).

Ideologically and politically as well, the emergent Walpole Island community forged its identity in its relations with the institutions of the dominant culture. In 1844, a pair of Jesuit priests, unannounced, erected a mission on the sacred Highbanks ground, cutting down a sacred oak grove in the process. Challenged to a debate by Oshawana, an ancient Shawnee and comrade-in-arms of Tecumseh, and the Chippewa chief Petrokeshig, the clerics were unable to convince their would-be converts of the superiority of their religion. Before long, the mission mysteriously burned, and the priests gave up their efforts. An Ojibwe commented that though the chapel might be rebuilt from brick and stone, it would burn again. Today the Tecumseh memorial stands on the site (Delâge, Tanner, and Chazelle 1994, 297).

Politically as well, solidarity emerged. In 1869, a coalition of the Three Fires petitioned the governor-general, Sir John Young, as the "Chippeway, Pottawatomy, and Ottawa Indians of Walpole Island," asserting their claims to their ancestral homelands along the Detroit River and western Lake Erie (Anonymous 1869). Although unsuccessful in regaining their ceded territory, the action demonstrated that the Three Fires nations could act collectively while maintaining tribal identity. A remarkable map from 1915 depicts the resources of Walpole Island, shedding light on both its vegetation zonation and its settlement pattern. The lower-lying modern delta is largely marshland, while the higher premodern delta shows extensive timber stands, dominated by elm, oak, basswood (linden), and ash. The centrally located Potawatomi settlement shows an area of "good farm land," immediately to its south, with a larger area labeled "well suited for agriculture" (presumably not yet under cultivation), just beyond. A similar situation obtains in the north of the island, where the Chippewa settlement has "land under cultivation" adjacent and "good farm land" nearby.

With sustained effort, the Walpole Island First Nations have engaged with, yet remained distinct from, the American and Canadian cultures, whether it be politics, commercial agriculture, industry, or tourism. The community-based research arm of the Walpole Island Band Council, known as Nin.Da.Waab.Jig ("those who seek to find"), has made its mission the preservation and understanding of their multifaceted heritage: environmental stewardship, oral and archival history, language, foodways, music and dance, arts and crafts (Beckford et al. 2010; Wetzel 2006; Hoefnagels 2002). As a result, today's Walpole Islanders are performing and communicating their identity in a twenty-first-century Indigenous landscape—a term that once might have been regarded as an oxymoron—that has truly become a "landscape of knowledge . . . a repository of memory . . . holistically incorporating every aspect of culture and its material expression" (Strang 2008, 52–53).

Archaeological and ethnohistorical evidence makes it clear that Indigenous peoples have pursued a maritime culture, and created a maritime landscape, for over a millennium in the strait connecting Lake Huron and Lake Erie. Their intimate relation with water and waterborne transportation was a common element of groups who subsisted as horticulturalists, hunter-fisher-gatherers, and traders, whether living in semisedentary settlements or in seasonal camps. These peoples shaped their landscape with fire and water, creating spaces for crops, game, fish, and wild rice. Even before their physical presence on the scene, Europeans had disrupted this balance, so that their perceptions were distorted by the appearance of abundance without human agency. As the Strait was repopulated, the delta of the St. Clair River became a landscape reminiscent of the homelands that the Mississauga and Ojibwe had left behind in the north.

These peoples of "the place where waters divide" found themselves in a place where emergent nations divided as well. Ironically, its very liminality created a cultural and political niche as well as an ecological one. Walpole

Island was only a short paddle away from two new nation-states, both simultaneously pursuing policies of removal or forced assimilation. These outside pressures and challenges operated, however, as shaping, not determining, forces. The marginalization beginning under colonialism, rather than resulting in the extinction of Indigenous culture, failed to dispossess (Pasternak 2017, 55–56). Today, both from a narrative and material perspective, the Indigenous experience of colonialism is being reclaimed (Atalay 2006; Keehnen, Hofman, and Antczak 2019).[2] The Three Fires—each with its own identity and traditions but sharing needs, values, and goals—have forged a community within the marginalized lands along the international border. The result, a persistent Indigenous maritime landscape, now forms a locus of identity for the greater Anishinaabeg community of the Great Lakes.

The two incidents involving the desecration of Indigenous sacred landscapes in the Strait serve as bookends to this process. Both cases, although separated by nearly two centuries, involve missionaries as representatives of an invading culture assailing the materiality of sacred artifacts and features. The desecration and destruction of the stone idol at Springwells by Galinée's party in 1669 was an attack on an Indigenous entity believed capable of granting safe passage—even to the hostile Iroquois. It set the pattern for years of suppression of Indigenous identity and agency. The felling of the sacred oak grove at Highbanks by the Jesuits in 1844 too was a direct affront to the spiritual world of the Anishinaabeg in their homeland. The Indigenous agency expressed in burning the missionaries' chapel in response was an act of resistance and reclaiming of the landscape, culminating in 2015 with the memorialization of Tecumseh on that sacred spot.

With the Indigenous maritime cultural landscape of Bkejwanong thus outlined, the stage is now set for the discussion of subsequent landscapes within the St. Clair locale—their formation and transformation and their interaction with these Indigenous neighbors.

---

2 In my own experience, the demonetization of our perception of wampum, and its restored role in the present as a powerful instrument in a highly sophisticated process of negotiation and record-keeping, is a striking and encouraging instance of the shift in the perception of Indigenous material culture away from the colonial and toward the Indigenous perspective (Harrison 2017a).

4

Colonial *Conjonctures*

Cognition and Dwelling during the French and British Eras

It is a delight to see that River bordered by an infinite number of apple-trees, a number of plum-trees of several kinds, chestnuts, walnuts and French nut-trees; and to come upon the vine there, which forms one of the finest ornaments, the grapes of which are tolerably large and good. At intervals there are very large prairies, dry and damp, full of grass which is more than three feet high; they are interrupted only by fruit trees, or by natural trees of very great height of many kinds. In the prairies, in Lake St. Claire, and the river, in which there are several islands, a great variety of game is met with. If this settlement is continued it will be a means of preventing the English from coming and seizing upon it in order to take from us the trade with the tribes of the further districts; of curbing the Iroquois; and of holding our allies to their duty, and it will be easier to frenchify them, and to proclaim the Gospel to them.

—Cadillac, "Account of Detroit"

In penning his 1702 dispatch to Governor-General Marquis de Vaudreuil, his superior in Montreal, Cadillac expressed in great length and detail his rationale for removing the upper Great Lakes hub of the French colonial enterprise to the Strait, or *detroit*. The landscape was seen through French eyes, cognized, and represented in relatable French terms to a critical French decision-maker. Significantly, the hospitable coastal landscape was deemed sufficiently France-like. Not so the inhabitants, however. For Cadillac, the demographic approach to the local colonial enterprise was to "frenchify" (*francization*) the Natives through cultural assimilation (Morrissey 2013, 57–58). By contrast, the British colonial *conjoncture* would see and treat both the landscape and its peoples very differently, with attendant shifts in dwelling and movement patterns leading to the marginalization of both Indigenous and French remnant populations.

The Colonial Landscape of the Strait as a Frontier

When the first Europeans entered the upper Great Lakes region, they encountered a landscape that had been intimately experienced by generations of Indigenous inhabitants, albeit of differing, shifting, and most recently, warring groups. Those inhabitants had long since solved problems of dwelling and movement by adapting their behavioral repertoire, developing technologies, and modifying the environment. All these practices had been transmitted and curated through symbolic representations: place-names, narratives, songs, and graphical depictions from birch scrolls to petroglyphs. The options for the French arrivals, particularly in terms of dwelling and movement, can be summarized as follows: adopt, adapt, or invent. Indigenous lifeways could be emulated, often unmodified. Alternatively, their own old-world practices and technologies could be applied, with varying degrees of adaptation, in their new environment.

While the hybridization of Indigenous and colonial maritime practice and material culture is abundantly evidenced, there is little if any indication of significant innovation in practices or technologies during the colonial eras. Not that the Europeans were risk-averse; rather, the colonial mentality, both French and British, favored the imposition of the cultural norms of the mother country on the landscape and its inhabitants (Cadillac 1904, 137; Gilman 1836, 61). It would take more than a century for the entrepreneurial character of the newly independent American polity to trigger a veritable cascade of transformational inventions and innovations.

A group's decision to enter and occupy a remote environment is largely predicated on their socially grounded perception of its critical qualities: affordances versus constraints, acceptable risks versus prohibitive dangers. Whether a group's mission is economic, political, military, religious, or scientific, determining those qualities must be a high priority, and the knowledge gained in the field must be represented and shared with the larger group. In the Great Lakes region of the French colonial period, these representations survive primarily as texts and maps. In particular, the landscape of the St. Clair locale was sufficiently picturesque, problematic, or eventful that it seldom failed to earn a passage in firsthand accounts of even the most transient encounters. Close readings of dozens of primary sources reveal patterns in the nature and value of things perceived.[1] Primary texts and maps offer insights into the social construction of landscapes that articulate well with anthropological evidence: archaeological, linguistic, and ethnohistorical.

An unavoidable challenge in studying primary documents during the early historical period was to interpret expressions of the relationship between Nature (as environment) and Culture (as the domesticated landscape). Even today, the terms *frontier*, *civilization*, and *wilderness* remain fraught with the ideological baggage of decades of Eurocentric scholarship. Much of the secondary literature on frontiers over the past century has been a long-term reaction to Frederick Jackson Turner's 1893 formulation of the American frontier as "the meeting point of savagery and civilization." Until comparatively recently, scholarly discussions of the frontier (half-seriously branded as "the 'F' word") remained shunned in the social sciences (Klein 1996, 185). In seeking to recuperate the term and its usefulness, historian Stephen Aron (2005, 176) proposed to retain the term *meeting point*, stressing "the fluid character of frontier zones" with an attendant blending and blurring of cultural distinctions: "Lying on the margins or in the interstices of cultural networks," concur Rodseth and Parker (2005, 9), "frontiers are the quintessential matrices of change." This dynamism and mutability are inherent in their nature, they add: "Like the word

1 All French texts used are available in good translations. I seldom needed to consult the original language. In the interest of accessibility, I have avoided presenting lengthy passages in the original; occasionally, however a French term best conveys the flavor of the source. In the case of maps, I have translated the labels and annotations cited.

'culture,' 'frontier' names a 'thing' that is really a set of processes, a busy field of intersecting forces" (Rodseth and Parker 2005, 16). It is certainly the case that along the Strait, one observes what Richard White (1982, 387) terms "the rough and tumble of social interaction" where inherited behaviors encounter altered circumstances. When those behaviors are repeatedly and deeply inscribed in the landscape, as they are in the St. Clair locale, physical evidence of a frontier is liable to persist over time and cultural replacement.

While long ubiquitous in the secondary literature, however, the notion of frontier or wilderness is all but absent from first-person narratives, particularly early encounters. The binary opposition of "savagery and civilization" is not found in the French narratives of the Strait. Whether the missionaries and explorers of the seventeenth century somehow anticipated the Enlightenment and Rousseau's "state of nature" by a full century or matter-of-factly accepted *les sauvages*, literally "people of the forest," the dichotomy that looms so large in retrospect seems not to have occurred to them at all. Further, upon the British takeover of the Great Lakes region, the dominant perspective understandably became one of an inherited French maritime landscape, not a purely Indigenous one.

Cognition of the Landscape during the French Colonial Era

On the eve of French contact, the St. Clair landscape was the product of subsistence practices by many generations of Indigenous inhabitants. The use of fire to create clearings for horticulture, the selective practice of forestry to produce economic fruit and timber species and provide game habitat, aquaculture aimed at harvests of wild rice and fish—all these caused early French commentators to marvel at the "natural" abundance of the landscape. A few days before entering the Strait, Galinée had praised the abundant fruits along the Lake Erie shore, noting that "the vine grows here only in sand, on the banks of lakes and rivers, but although it has no cultivation it does not fail to produce grapes in great quantities as large and as sweet as the finest of France. We even made wine of them, with which M. Dollier said holy mass all winter, and it was as good as a *vin de Grave*" (Galinée 1917, 196). This comparison of the New World with the Old, favorably or otherwise, is a recurrent feature of colonial accounts. It served to situate the new experience in the known universe of both the author and his audience, who frequently had some form of oversight as an agent of a social institution, whether religious, political, military, or economic. Such comparisons, especially when signifying affordances, were mutually accessible within a functional context: How does the colonial landscape compare with the home country—to a patron, an investor, a prospective colonist?

Hennepin, La Salle's chronicler, enthusiastically inventoried the edible affordances throughout the Strait, pausing like Dollier along the St. Clair River to "make some little wine." Clearly the landscape was fit for dwelling, but movement was another matter. Traveling by ship, rather than by canoe as had Galinée and Dollier, he noted both a strategic maritime affordance ("there is timber fit for building") and its signature constraint, the delta. In his account, quoted earlier, he showed an awareness of all four aspects that made this landscape problematic to mariners: its shallow outlets ("there is little depth as you enter and leave Lake St. Clare"); the current, or "discharge"; the multiple channels, "almost all blocked by sandbanks"; and the prevailing "head winds [by which] our bark was detained here several days" (Hennepin 1966, 92–93). This brief but telling passage outlines the cognitive picture that frames waterborne movement through this landscape for the duration of the next two centuries. Much of what followed, whether found in French, British, American, or Canadian accounts is, to some degree, postscript.

With the loss of the *Griffon* and the subsequent shift to small watercraft, French colonial accounts of the St. Clair locale tended to focus on inventorying affordances. The reports of Duluth (1686), Lahontan (1688), and Cadillac (1704), all directed to officials and patrons who oversaw and controlled their activities, were replete with glowing descriptions of pleasant climate and natural bounty—often, as noted earlier, in comparison to France. This familiarity proved useful when the French turned from cognizing the landscape in passing to actually settling within it.

Dwelling in the French Maritime Cultural Landscape

In transferring the hub of the upper Great Lakes fur trade from Michilimackinac to Detroit in 1701, both Cadillac and his Indigenous trading partners were either creating or reclaiming a landscape that was cognized as home-like. Like his Potawatomi and Huron horticulturalist neighbors, the French commandant quickly set about reproducing a familiar landscape and its crops, "the land having shown its quality, and taught me that the French tillage must be followed" (Cadillac 1904, 137). Militarily, the royal orders to Cadillac, like Duluth and Lahontan before him, were aimed at preventing British inroads into French-controlled territory (Cleland 1992, 79; Dunbar and May 1995, 40–41; Tanner 1987, 39).

Economically and ecologically, the fur trade was best promoted by leaving the habitat of the beaver and other fur-bearing mammals, as well as the Indigenous trappers who brought their pelts to market, largely intact (Woodford 1994, 5). The thin veneer of French settlement along the waters of the Strait, rather than a sign of their inability to domesticate the interior, indicates that French priorities were best served by securing access along waterborne transport routes while leaving the productive interior relatively undisturbed. Although the French colonial era ended politically with the specific event of the French and Indian War's conclusion around 1760, the French maritime cultural landscape, like its Indigenous predecessor, survived for generations, sustained by its descendant community.

The classic French settlement pattern of narrow shoreline ribbon farms, with their limited agricultural production aimed at subsistence and local markets, reflects this. As a member of the 1820 Cass expedition, David Bates Douglass described the still-extant French-era farms: "At St. Clair settlement," he wrote, "are many well cultivated farms of long standing with an abundance of fruit and ground cleared and tilled to the distance of half a mile from shore" (Douglass 1969, 19; also Vigne 1833, 138). Deep but narrow, each parcel featured a sloping frontage that could accommodate a shallow-draft watercraft: "The early settlers went to mill and did their trading at Detroit," recalls St. Clair County historian William Mitchell. "They took their produce in canoes, following close to the shore along Lake St. Clair to Detroit, and exchanged a bushel of wheat for a yard of calico" (Mitchell 1884, 413). This adaptation demonstrates the complementarity that evolved between landscape, settlement pattern, and transport.

In fact, the very nature of the French colonial economy was not dependent upon (and arguably inimical to) the modification of a landscape that supported both the hunters and the hunted. Such was not the case with their successors, the British colonial empire. Historian Arthur Woodford has succinctly expressed this dichotomy: "The gathering of fur and the taking of land represented two conflicting visions of the North American continent; the fur trader kept the country and its native people much as he found them, but the settler remade the country and drove out the Indians. The French garrisoned the area west of the Alleghenies while the British colonists established a land company to settle it" (Woodford 1994, 5). The colonial French regarded both the unmodified interior and the maritime network of open lakes and inland rivers as affordances. This mentality remains inscribed in surviving shoreline patterns of descendant French communities along the Strait between Lake Huron and Lake Erie, including property lines in Algonac, Detroit, and Monroe, Michigan.

Given their disparate values and lifeways—their mentalities—British commentators disparaged what they perceived as French indolence. The trader Jonathan Carver, an early British visitor to the newly conquered Great Lakes, complained in 1766 that the defeated and displaced French, "on giving up the possession of [their lands], took care to leave the places they had occupied in the same uncultivated state they had found them" (Carver 1781, iv). The newly minted Americans were no less critical. Attorney and politician Solomon Sibley's 1798 impressions of Detroit were generally favorable, "but unfortunately for the country the settlers are almost to a man French and exceedingly ignorant and lazy." Nevertheless, he admitted, "Fruit of every kind is plenty. Provisions are scarce and dear owing wholly to the idleness of the farmers and not, as some have alleged, to the barrenness of the soil" (Sibley 1917, 40).

A generation later in 1817, an American officer named Samuel Storrow adopted much the same tone toward their remaining descendants along the St. Clair River, incidentally confirming the persistence—and utility—of the ribbon farm: "The country bordering the two waters [Lake St. Clair and the St. Clair River] I found level and fertile. It is scantily peopled by French Canadians, who reside on the margin, and make no improvements to the interior. The small surplus of their produce is purchased by vessels coasting between the lakes. In the rear of the settlements is a growth of timber, and an abundant supply of natural grass" (Storrow 1872, 154). Not to be outdone, the American journalist and politician Calvin Colton wrote in 1830 in praise of the natural beauties of the St. Clair River: "and then to see the French huts . . . to look upon the habitations of that indolent race, so mean and sordid, as they are, resting upon the river's brink, and demonstrating by their every feature a dull and lazy existence, akin to that of the savage" (Colton 1833, 61).

Journalist Chandler Gilman, aboard the schooner *White Pigeon* in 1835, aimed some of his most pointed barbs at the French and their ways: "An hour's sailing," he wrote upon departing Detroit, "brought us to the entrance of Lake St. Clair. The shores are still flat and uninteresting; and where the land is under cultivation, 'tis commonly the French; and their poor sickly cornfields, and crowded unproductive orchards, speak of the wretchedness of their mode of farming" (Gilman 1836, 60–61). He continued his diatribe, pointedly critiquing French arboriculture and, by extension, French identity:

> [The Frenchman's] orchard is a curiosity; the trees stand so closely together, that scarce a ray of sun can penetrate their centre; and consequently, though the outer row, particularly on their outer side, are loaded with fruit, those in the centre have scarcely an apple apiece, and those of the most indifferent kind. Yet Monsieur goes on after the French custom, year after year the same, always perfectly convinced that his orchard is the best, his trees the finest, his fields the most productive, his ways the wisest, because his orchard is a French orchard, his trees French trees, his fields French fields, and his ways are French ways. Ah, la belle France! Thou art most happy in the affection of thy children. (Gilman 1836, 80)

Yet he could not deny that the fresh eggs, bread, milk, and butter his party, becalmed in the river, bought from *les habitants* (ethnic French) were most welcome (Gilman 1836, 74–75).

The French practice of providing, like their Mississauga antecedents, hospitality and sustenance to hapless travelers was already a matter of long standing (Duluth 1902, 129; Lahontan 1905, 139; Cadillac 1904, 131–32; Porteous 1939, 90). Its persistence is further confirmed by the journal of missionary Elisha Loomis in 1830: "November 2. We lay at anchor last evening in St. Clair River, there not being enough wind to enable the vessel to stem the current. I went on shore to the house of a Frenchman and procured some apples, for which his lady generously declined receiving payment. She also sent us some milk in the morning" (Loomis 1953, 38). Had Gilman been a man of God, or perhaps less condescending, he too might have dined gratis.

Evidently, the maritime cultural landscape of the French colonial period, and that of the French-descendant community in the early decades of British and American ascendancy, reflects a society content to "reside on the margin," as Storrow disparagingly yet accurately observed, between land and water or even "wilderness" and "civilization." Farming the interior would have come at the expense of habitat, of both their trading partners and furbearers, and complicated the transport of their own produce to market. The maritime cultural landscape of the Great Lakes during the French colonial period was not so much about controlling territory as it was about controlling connectivity—between trading partners, furs, and the market.

The early French military presence in the Strait, as a form of dwelling, reflects this view. Sent to establish a fort in 1686, Duluth garrisoned a position near the head of the St. Clair River, near the eventual site of Port Huron: "If we continue to maintain this Establishment," he wrote to the Comte de Pontchartrain, "it will be a means of preventing the English from coming to take possession of it, to deprive us of the Trade with the Nations up above; of holding the Iroquois in check; and of maintaining our allies in their duty" (Duluth 1902, 129). By 1688, however, Baron Lahontan, sent to command the fort, found it manned by unregulated fur traders called *coureurs de bois*. Evidently adopting a laissez-faire policy that favored robust economic relations over military deterrence, he deemed his new post unnecessary and burned it: "The Garrison," he recorded, "surrendered their Post very chearfully to my Detachment; and then pursued their Commerce with our Savages, for every one had leave to go where he pleas'd" (Lahontan 1905 140). So stood French military matters in the region until Cadillac's move from Michilimackinac to Fort Pontchartrain in 1701.

Under the succeeding British colonial period, the Natives lost economic importance and were socially marginalized. With the extirpation of the beaver stock, the interior landscape, while remaining an affordance, shifted from fur production to commodity extraction, commencing with timber. In time, agriculture came to dominate the cleared landscape. The Great Lakes transport network remained an affordance—except the St. Clair Flats. There, British maritime practice and tradition, formed over generations of seafaring throughout its global empire, increasingly regarded its navigation as a constraint, strategically limiting the carrying capacity of the entire colonial maritime enterprise, military and commercial.

Cognition of the St. Clair Delta during the British Colonial Era

Three decades of exclusive British colonial control spanned the end of the French and Indian War in 1763 and the relinquishing of the Michigan Territory to the United States in 1796. This period evidenced a changed attitude toward the landscape that reflects a shift in values and objectives to those of the now-dominant British. Where the French excelled in the appreciation of the edible (and potable) affordances of the Strait, the British took careful note of its forestation. The fur trade was no longer the economic engine of the region: the remaining stocks of beaver, already declining in Cadillac's time (Cadillac 1904, 144) had receded far to the north and west (White 1991, 477). Thus, while the transportation network required to move furs and trade goods ever-longer distances remained more crucial than ever, the commodity now most abundant, accessible, and valuable in the St. Clair locale was timber.

Upon the British takeover in 1760, Lieutenant Dederick Brehm submitted a report to Governor-General Jeffery Amherst, describing the newly acquired lands between Montreal and Lake Huron. Sailing upstream from the head of the St. Clair delta, he noted that

> four small creeks run into the [St. Clair River] at the west shore and 3 at the East which I have not named as the guides differed in the names. Except that they agreed with that river called De Pine, for the number of white Pyn trees that stand about it. The Inhabitants of Detroit had a Sawmill at said creek and got all their boards and Pyn Timber from it. The Pyn trees continue so far as we went up the west shore of Lake Huron, mixed with oak shrubs, higher up it begins to mix with Hemlock, maple, cedar, poplar, Beech & Swamp ash. (Brehm 1883, 25)

Significantly, the Pine River flowed through the southern extremity of the great coniferous forest, which then stretched north across the Lower Peninsula of Michigan (Moore 1915, 154).

This affordance, as Brehm observed, had been both perceived and exploited by the French, as the mill was already supplying the market of Detroit at the time of the British takeover. The modest scale of production, however, suggests that the local French timber industry was, like their agriculture, a subsistence economy rather than the production of a bulk commodity for distant markets. The British, once in firm military and economic control of the rivers leading into the interior following Pontiac's uprising, would see far more than "boards and Pyn timber" at their disposal. The building of larger settlements and a merchant fleet to ply between them would require large amounts of timber of all kinds.

Where the French fur trade had quickly adapted its maritime technology and practice along Indigenous and vernacular lines following the loss of the *Griffon* in 1679, the British were determined to pursue European-style navigation on the inland seas. Their chief constraint was the complex condition of the delta. As with landscape formation in general, *cognition*, the knowing of a place, was a precondition of effective *movement* and *dwelling* there. They promptly set about surveying its hydrology. Lieutenant Brehm wrote to Amherst of his party's initial reconnaissance in the late fall of 1760: "Lake St. Clair, the upper end of it, is drowned land or Islands of rush and canes in swamps," he reported. "By taking my bearings to them and by approaching found difficult to find a channel to a fixed object, was obliged to leave the intended line and only guess it which wants greatly to be corrected. In my return went the Easternmost channel [Chenal Écarté] in order to return by the shore but found itself losing itself in the Rushes and froze, which obliged me to return back a larger channel" (Brehm 1883, 25). The delta remained shrouded in mystery—and ice.

Accordingly, the following spring the British command sent one Lieutenant Charles Robinson back to the Flats: "Surveyed the various entrances to the St. Clair River," Robinson testified before a court of inquiry.

> Found the natural channel from Detroit through Lake St. Clair, finding two fathoms, and ten feet [22 ft.], much closer to the north shore [the North Channel] than we did on the South [Channel]. The wind blowed very hard so we could not hawl upon a wind [sail close-hauled] but was oblig'd to run into a deep Bay [Anchor Bay] where we stay'd all night instead of going to Lake Huron River [the St. Clair River] as we intended.

> The 30th at 11 A.M. we cross'd over a large Bay Steering E 1/2 N, finding in some places two Fathom [12 ft. or 3.7 m] water, but coming within two miles of the Rushes on the south side of the Northernmost Channell we came into four foot, then we cross'd over the entrance of the [North] Channell and in our way found ten foot, and two Fathom 1/2 [18 ft. or 5.5 m] Water. (Campbell 1762)

Without realizing it, Robinson had negotiated the Elbow, a sharply curving natural channel through the shallows of Anchor Bay that was to figure prominently for the better part of the next century (maps 8 and 11).

A third survey party did not fare so well. Major Henry Gladwin, commanding at Detroit in 1763, "being desirous to know whether the lakes and rivers between that place and Michilimackinac were navigable for vessels of a greater burden than the small bateaux they made use of," again ordered Lieutenant Robinson to "go with a party consisting of six soldiers and two sailors in a large bateau with the necessary implements to sound the lakes" (Rutherford 1958, 219). Unfortunately, their departure coincided with the outbreak of Pontiac's Rebellion. The party was ambushed below Fort Gratiot, at the site of present-day Port Huron. Among the few survivors was a teenage John Rutherford, who was adopted by his captors and survived to fight in the Forty-Second Highland Regiment in the American Revolution. Such were the hazards of exploration.

Major Robert Rogers (of Rogers's Rangers fame) was quick to appreciate the lay of the land and its resources, while noting its Native population and their mode of travel. As he wrote in 1765,

> The country on both sides of the [St. Clair] river is level and good, the timber is white pine, oak, maple, &c of a good growth. The river where it enters Lake Sinclair [*sic*], is divided into several branches, by which are formed five or six islands of various dimensions. The Lake Sinclair is nearly circular, and is about eighteen miles across. On the east-side are large marshes of eight or ten miles extent from the water; and near the lower end, on the east-side, a river [the Thames] enters it of a considerable bigness, from which by a short carrying-place is an easy conveyance to Lake Ontario, used by the Indians who inhabit the banks of this river, who are a branch of the Souties [Saulteur/Ojibwe] or Attawawas [Odawa]. The land on the

> west-side of the lake is also tolerably good, the timber chiefly beach [*sic*] and maple. (Rogers 1765, 166–67)

In 1788, the British military engineer Gother Mann, while conducting a survey of the military facilities in the upper lakes, offered his recommendations on the navigation of the St. Clair River. Noting the bar across the South Channel, he added that "from the general prevalence of the Northerly and Westerly winds, and the strength of the Current upon this communication, it is often a difficult and tedious operation to get up[stream] from Detroit; and vessels are not infrequently a fortnight or more in accomplishing it." His ingenious but drastic solution lay in an acceleration of the ongoing shoreline settlement pattern of clearing for agriculture: "For the banks of the river being cleared, Vessels may then in contrary winds be tracked [towed by draft animals on shore] most of the way up the Rapid" (Mann 1888, 33). His suggestion was not adopted but foreshadowed the practice of radically modifying the landscape to human designs.

Instead, in a repeated pattern of catastrophic disruption that had commenced with the Iroquois Wars and continued with the French and Indian War, large-scale conflict drew British attention away from the frontier. The American Revolution, it has been argued, did not end in the Great Lakes region until 1815, with the conclusion of the War of 1812 (Taylor 2010). The tangible outcome was the survey of a new international border. The political partition of the landscape was a pivotal phenomenon that created impacts across every aspect and process of social life (Mauss 2011, 36). The resulting charts and documents, themselves a social representation, exerted powerful agency over dwelling and movement in a maritime landscape that was now territorially divided among multiple occupying groups.

Dwelling in the St. Clair Landscape during the British Colonial Era

Such new settlement as was initially implemented under the British was confined to the construction of the fortified trading post of Fort Sinclair, midway up the St. Clair River. Unlike the colonial French, who frequently mentioned visits to the Mississauga living in the Flats (Cadillac 1904, 680; Charlevoix 1966, 40; Chauvignerie 1855, 1058), the British seem to have had little to do with the Indigenous population of the delta during this time. The local fur production was now negligible, with trapping reduced to hides for leather.

Their relations with the French *habitants* were not much more extensive, being of two principal kinds. Besides offering hospitality and provisioning for becalmed upbound ships (Storrow 1872, 154), *fermiers* passing to and from Detroit regularly aided British ships aground in the Flats by "lightering"—that is, temporarily transferring its cargo into bateaux until the vessel could get clear (Porteous 1939, 89). Henry Wolsey Bayfield's chart of 1817 shows ribbon farms along the north shore of the North Channel where place-names like "Pointe aux Trembles" (aspen point) and "Pointe aux Chênes" (oak point) indicate the French presence at precisely the point where they could take advantage of such opportunities.

They appear to have been joined in the delta early in the nineteenth century by Scottish settlers farming the south side of the channel, known as Stromness or Laughton's (later Dickinson) Island. Charles Trowbridge, a member of the Lewis Cass expedition of 1820, described "scotch peasants" on "Lautons Island" who offered refuge to the battered paddlers following a storm on Lake St. Clair. Historian Milo Quaife opines that Trowbridge's benefactors were refugees from Lord Selkirk's failed "Baldoon" settlement nearby (Trowbridge 1942, 136n). Formed in 1804 along Chenal Écarté, the easternmost channel of the delta near present-day Wallaceburg, Ontario, the colony of impoverished Scots Highlanders had suffered since its inception from malaria and, more recently, from the ravages of the War of 1812. A remnant of its scattered survivors evidently relocated along the North Channel to exploit the economic opportunities developing at Anchor Bay, giving it the distinctively Scottish name of Stromness, after an Orkney village.

Midway up the St. Clair River, additional settlements developed at the mouth of the tributary Pine River, where Brehm had observed a French sawmill in 1761. Two more sawmills were built in 1763: one by "a French gentleman at Detroit," the other by Captain Patrick Sinclair, commander of fort that bore his name, at the site of the modern town of St. Clair, Michigan (Rutherford 1958, 222n; Jenks 1912, 93). By August 1766, Fort Sinclair had taken on a traditional British maritime role as the southern terminus of the schooner *Gladwin*'s route to Mackinac. The smaller boats that transferred cargo to and from the *Gladwin* came up from Detroit or even Lake Erie (Porteous 1939). Jonathan Carver, an agent of the fur trade, noted in his journal that a blockhouse guarded the wooden platform "at which the vessel is careen'd and lies during the winter season" (Carver 1976, 69).

This humble feature is the first recorded maritime infrastructure along the St. Clair River—a landing at the mouth of the Pine River, an indicator of a transshipment nexus in a maritime transport network (Ilves 2009). That nexus developed where the timber supply in the interior interfaced with the water route to Detroit, as trader John Porteous observed in his journal of 1767: "Above F[ort] S[inclair]," he wrote, "is a pinery from which D[etroit] & all the settlement is built, the timber being carried down on rafts. This swamp affords excellent pine & sufficient masts for any vessel" (Porteous 1767, 9). The Carver and Porteous accounts suggest a nascent shipbuilding industry on the upper St. Clair River very early in the British rule. There, locally sawn planks and spars could be used not only to repair and maintain the Niagara-built *Gladwin*, careened on its platform, but to build entire vessels.

Unlike the Pine River locale, the landscape of the delta to its south offered no special affordances to a colonial economic system driven by the movement of pelts, timber, or trade goods in increasing quantities. Rather, it posed a constraint to the mode of movement most familiar to the British empire: long-distance trade networks featuring navigation by ship. Even the movement of rafted timber posed problems when traversing the Flats. The shallow water was not a serious difficulty, but the confusing channels could be. Porteous described a 1765 encounter with a party of local French on their way to retrieve a raft that had been "wrongly conducted" down the Chenal Écarté, a sluggish, winding distributary terminating in an enormous marsh (Porteous 1939, 90).

As with the process of cognition, British dwelling within the St. Clair landscape remained superficial during their early colonial occupation. Contestations with the French, Indigenous groups, and finally their own rebellious colonists thwarted any ambitions toward the settlement of the interior. As did mosquito-infested swampland; the fiasco of Baldoon was a lesson in overreaching in *terra incognita*. When settlement resumed after the protracted disruptions of war, it was on a very different footing: along a borderland facing a former subject, only recently a military foe, and now increasingly an economic rival.

5

Representations of the St. Clair Maritime Landscape

In May of 1820, Michigan territorial governor Lewis Cass led his exploratory expedition to Lake Superior, accompanied by future luminaries Henry Rowe Schoolcraft, geologist Alexander Woolcott, ethnographer Charles Trowbridge, Army engineer David Bates Douglass, and a twenty-one-year-old James Duane Doty, future governor of the Wisconsin Territory. Taken together, their reports and memoirs comprise a kaleidoscopic snapshot of the American frontier along the Great Lakes. On the second day of their journey from Detroit, the party had encamped at Grosse Pointe, minus Cass. Doty's journal relates their passage into the St. Clair delta:

> Friday, May 26. Wind ahead. At 12 o'clock the Governor arrived, and the wind having ceased, we embarked, steering NNE. At ½ past 1 passed Milk River point [Gaukler Point]—6 miles. Landed at 4 o'clock below Huron point. The point is about 1½ miles long, immediately above which the [Clinton] river empties itself. Crossed the Lake—wind high and ahead. The waves broke over the canoes very fast and one man was kept continually bailing and we were all considerably excited by the danger. The most of us were unused to canoes, and the traverse was very unpleasant. Our course was about north. We arrived at Lauson's Island [Dickinson Island] at ½ past 9 in the evening, where we found the Governor, from whom we

> had parted on the Lake, and who had taken a different channel of the river, encamped. Both channels were east of the ship channel [North Channel]. We were shivering with cold when we landed. Distance from Detroit 60 miles. This Island is supposed to belong to the English.
>
> Saturday, May 27. Rose at 4, breakfasted and at half past 6 embarked. In a short time came into the Ship channel. Hursons [Harsens] Island lies opposite to our encampment. Passed several houses. The land appears fertile and the farms comfortable. The river is beautiful; The banks descend gently to the water's edge, covered with fine thrifty timber. (Doty 1895, 166)

On the present-day nautical chart of the St. Clair Flats (NOAA 14853), there is a natural channel slightly over a mile long (2 km) labeled "Doty Highway." It connects Chenal à Bout Ronde ("round-ended channel," locally pronounced "Snybora") with the Middle Channel by way of Big Fisher Highway. These numerous maritime "highways" offer shortcuts between the main channels. I have paddled the Doty Highway any number of times, usually after refreshing myself at Brown's Landing, a waterfront establishment at the intersection of the Middle Channel and Snooks Highway. Reading Doty's journal, I realized that this name commemorates a storm-tossed trip across the mouth of Anchor Bay over two centuries ago.

Corroborated by Schoolcraft, Douglass, and Trowbridge, Doty's account allows us to reconstruct the near-disaster in detail. Blown east of their intended course into the North Channel ("ship channel") and seeking sheltered water, the scattered paddlers made their way up separate routes. The canoe carrying Doty entered the Chenal à Bout Ronde while that of Cass was blown farther east to the Middle Channel, which separates Dickinson and Harsens Islands. As darkness fell, Doty and his companions found a short connecting passage, and the expedition luckily regrouped. Resuming the journey the following morning, Doty recorded the incident. The surviving cartographic detail serves to illustrate how a simple water feature, a name on a map, and an eyewitness account can likewise regroup to tell their story. Together, they illustrate the trajectory of a landscape in the moment that it was being cognized and appropriated, even by a young canoeist who went on to become governor of Wisconsin.

The Agency of Representations

The essentially cultural moment in an act of landscape formation—be it one of cognition, dwelling, or movement—is when it is shared. The inhabitants of each St. Clair maritime landscape were like any other society: they transmitted needful information in words, whether spoken or written, and in pictures. Such symbolized representations are the means by which individuals learned from their contemporaries and conveyed their knowledge to posterity. That these pragmatic representations have since become objects of scholarly analysis is liable to obscure their essential nature and original purpose. While naming and mapping are not absolute preconditions for purposeful movement through a maritime landscape, they greatly facilitate the successful repetition of achieving goals and minimizing failure. Place-names are arguably among the most highly charged and richly evocative of all linguistic symbols, and the process of place-naming is a universally primary means for appropriating physical environments (Basso 1988, 102–103). The choice of what to name and the name chosen become valuable indicators of the features of the landscape deemed worthy of such appropriation.

Those people who gave and used place-names did so primarily as a means of navigating and using the landscape. The resulting toponyms often reflect their origin and the relations between people and locations (Ilves 2006, 92–93). Moreover, one may learn about power relations between groups as well. The act of naming (and particularly renaming) is a socially embedded act, frequently exercised by a hegemonic group (Vuolteenaho and Berg 2009, 9). The results reveal that like human and material actors, place-names are liable to possess not only meaning but agency. Within the St. Clair landscape, the toponymic contest between "Bkejwanong" and "Walpole Island" presents a dramatic case and will be examined more closely.

The cartographic symbolization of the landscape, especially maps combining text labels, symbols, and pictorial features, is an information-dense medium of conveying ideology, as reflected in the selection and expression of map features. The foregoing instance of *Lac des Eaux de Mer* is a good example. Today, that briefly used name for Lake St. Clair is a mere footnote, a tenuous link to our geological knowledge of the vast salt deposits underlying southeast Michigan and its recent history of commercial salt mining.

To a seventeenth-century Frenchman viewing that map, however, that sort of information possessed agency—the power to influence behaviors ranging from curing venison to packing a silk robe for an audience with the Great Khan.

The appreciation of representation as a vital process in landscape formation lies in the acknowledgment that place-names and maps are not merely reflective symbols of landscape features but potent agents of cultural transformation. While not every name or map can be expected to be impactful, a case may be made for the potential agency of both modes of representation: linguistic (toponymy) and graphic (cartography).

Toponymy in the St. Clair Maritime Landscape

Naming is power—the creative power to call something into being, to render the invisible visible, to impart a certain character to things.
—Yi-Fu Tuan "Language and the Making of Place"

Place-names will be considered first, not only because they generally predate the maps that bear them as labels, but because they readily lend themselves to classificatory systems that can reveal patterns of seeing and knowing (Waterman 1922; Thornton 1997; Van Gijseghem and Whalen 2017). Many places have borne several names, often marking a transition from one dominant culture to another, each name revealing something about its giver. I have created for illustrative purposes a rudimentary and very incomplete typology, using a sample of names from the St. Clair maritime landscape. Some categories offer numerous instances, some only a few, occasionally none.

The classification scheme is structured by the three landscape formation processes that form the objectives of representation, beginning with *knowing*. The first group contains names of cognized features that are impactful to the mariner's mission, whether affordances, constraints, or natural landmarks used in wayfinding. The second group deals with navigation, the process of purposeful *movement* by water along an intended route and utilizing artificial or modified aids to navigation and infrastructure (Westerdahl 1992). Finally, there are names that are indicative of *dwelling* by a social entity, be it a dominant occupying group (Indigenous, French, British, American, Canadian) or a functional sector within a society (military, fishing, recreation). The categories are fluid and nonexclusive, especially as they reflect both the nature of the signified and the positionality of the name-givers.

Typology of Maritime Place-Names in the St. Clair Landscape

- Names *cognizing* a landscape feature or attribute
  - affordance: Salt Creek, Pine River
  - constraint: the Elbow, Blind Channel
  - danger, obstruction: St. Clair Middle Ground (reef)
  - physical appearance: Ganatchio, Bkejwanong, Chenal à Bout Ronde
  - flora or fauna: Pointe aux Chênes, Stag Island, Swan Creek, Goose Bay
- Names indicating maritime *movement*
  - passages, transport corridors: the Elbow, New Ship Channel, Grocery Cut
  - landings, wharves: Ward's Landing, Palmer's Landing, Roberts Landing
  - harbors, havens: Anchor Bay, New Port, Fair Haven
  - navigational landmarks: Plum Bush Island, Old South Channel Light
  - shipyards and associated infrastructure: Marine City, Sarnia "boneyard"
  - portages: [none present in the St. Clair locale]
- Names indicating *dwelling* by a social group
  - Indigenous: Otsi-keta, Chematogan Channel
  - French: Chenal Écarté, Sans Souci, Belle River
  - British or Canadian: Baldoon, Stromness Island, Walpole Island
  - American: Yankee Point, Algonac, Anchorville
  - military: Fort St. Joseph, Fort Sinclair, Fort Gratiot
  - recreational: The Old Club, Canada Club, Tashmoo Park

In the discussion that follows, a few cases have been selected to illustrate the process by which places received their toponyms. The resultant linguistic representation (the signifier), as much as the thing signified, can be seen as possessing agency—power—in the formation of social relations between peoples and their landscapes.

From the few surviving Indigenous names in the St. Clair landscape, it appears that those of places needful to be known for either their affordances or their physical appearance were the most likely to persist through successive occupations. Even when the original names have been lost, it is likely that in many cases their meanings survive in French translations. "Rivière de la Belle Chasse" (River of Good Hunting), surviving as Belle River, is almost certainly a French rendering of a Native reference to a universal affordance, food; likewise, Salt Creek and Pine River exemplify the naming of landscape features to indicate access to a subsistence need and a commodity, respectively. As for names based on physical properties, the rounded shape of Lake St. Clair informs an early French name, "Lac Chaudière" (Kettle Lake), derived from the Miami *Ganatchio* (Jenks 1912, 24), both of which appeared on early French maps.

Within the second category, that of maritime movement, two classes stand out in relation to each other. Landings were numerous from the outset of navigation in the St. Clair but with an evolving nature and function. During the French colonial era, the waterfront of every ribbon farm was a landing, where flat-bottomed bateaux accessed the minimally improved riverbank. Hence Doty's appreciative remark on the North Channel, whose "banks descend gently to the water's edge." With the British came sailing vessels that, when becalmed in the current, dropped anchor where they stood as the crew sought provisions ashore, either using the ship's boat or that of the local farmer. It was not until the arrival of steam that the "landing" became a specific type of infrastructural feature and a conventional label. Lack of fuel, not of wind, sent the steamboat men ashore for the wood that was still plentiful along the St. Clair River above the Flats. The loading of bulk commodities, beginning with firewood and lumber, required an investment in the built environment. At least four entrepreneurs gave their names to the "wooding stations" below Port Huron, two of which became nuclei of urbanization: Ward's Landing (later incorporated into Marine City) and Palmer's Landing (now part of the village of St. Clair).

Of the harbors listed, Anchor Bay derives its name and significance from the nautical practice of sailing vessels anchoring there, awaiting favorable wind conditions. "New Port" (later Newport) formed at the mouth of the Belle River. Together with Ward's Landing, it coalesced into the early center of shipbuilding known as "Marine City": an ambitious name adopted in 1865 by a community that evidently wore its new maritime identity with pride and a certain assertiveness.

To European and American eyes, the nearly featureless terrain of the Flats as seen from the water gave rise to few named natural navigational landmarks. A conspicuous example of this type of feature is the Sleeping Bear formation on Lake Michigan. That they were both few and inconspicuous may be inferred from the frequent accounts of early travelers losing their way. A revealing example of such naming occurred in 1856 while Captain George Meade of the Topographic Engineers was surveying the Middle Channel. He observed a bush on a tiny, otherwise featureless island marking the outer end of the Middle Channel. It duly appeared on the resulting chart—as "Bush." When the survey was updated in 1872, the lonely bush, now known to be of the plum variety, was still there, doing its job marking the channel mouth in the absence of any artificial navigational aid. The name "Plum Bush Island" remained in use for at least another two dozen years, appearing on R. J. Mackey's 1896 "Guide Map of the St. Clair Flats" (map 15). Alas, the bush is no more, and its picturesque name no longer appears on the current navigational chart.

Names indicating Indigenous dwelling, while plentiful in the historical and cartographic record through the French period, become few thereafter. One exception introduced in chapter 3, Bkejwanong, "where the waters divide," is more a revival than a survival. To better understand this conspicuous absence, I must tell a story about a stick-in-the-mud—several, in fact. The official name of Walpole Island actually displaces indigeneity in two senses: symbolically and politically. According to the *Encyclopedia Canadiana*, Walpole Island is named for one Lieutenant Arthur Walpole, a surveyor in the Royal Engineers (d. 1842) who prepared the plan for Fort Erie in 1818–19.[1] Alan Rayburn's *Place Names of Ontario* accepts this without comment (Rayburn 1997, 361). In her account of a journey through the Great Lakes in 1840, however, writer Eliza Steele remarked on "a body of Chippeway Indians who reside upon *Warpole* Island" (Steele 1841, 96; emphasis added).

While this is the earliest printed instance found to this toponym being applied to the island, a reference to "warpoles" had occurred in the log of the British sloop *Welcome* for June 5, 1780 (*Welcome* 1779–82). They were implanted

1 *Encyclopedia Canadiana*, 1975 ed., s.v. "Walpole Island."

along the shoreline above Russell Island, where the main course of the St. Clair River first divides into the North and South Channels. The term "Warpole *Channel*," applied to the South Channel, began to appear on maps beginning with Thomas Smith's in 1809, where "St. Mary Island" was the label given to present-day Walpole Island. The concatenation of *Warpole* with *Island* recurred in the guide map accompanying an 1819 travelogue (Darby 1819) and, most influentially, in the 1821 report of the British delegation to the International Boundary Commission (Bigsby 1850). This naming appeared in American and British atlases in 1835, 1839, and 1844. "St. Mary's Island" persisted in other sources until at least 1848. In 1867, however, it was labeled "Walpole Island" on William F. Raynolds's "Chart of Lake St. Clair" (US Bureau of Topographic Engineers), begging the questions, by whom and to what purpose?

By 1841, "Warpole Island" had evidently become sedimented into the local toponymy through informal usage, where Eliza Steele acquired it in her travels. At that same time, both the American and Canadian governments were dispossessing Indigenous populations in the area, largely through removals west to Kansas and north to Manitoulin Island, respectively. As related in chapter 3, Walpole Island became a liminal yet contested landscape to which Potawatomi refugees from the American side were fleeing and from which non-Indigenous squatters were being evicted (Nin.Da.Waab.Jig 1987). As St. Mary's Island and Warpole Channel tipped toward merging as "Warpole Island," it appears that the beleaguered Canadian government, in naming the island after a recently deceased surveyor, was writing "hegemonic history" (Vuolteenaho and Berg 2009, 11). The late Lieutenant Walpole, who likely never set foot on the island, had the advantage of a name that could be neatly grafted over the emergent Indigenous identity, creating a toponymic palimpsest where the earlier name was obscured but not quite obliterated.

In reproducing the hegemonic history of the *Encyclopedia Canadiana*, Rayburn inadvertently commits a sin of omission: true, the island is officially named after the dead surveyor. No lies are told, but neither is the whole truth. The Indigenous name *Bekejwanong* counters this with "subaltern history" (Berg and Kearns 2009, 27–28) as presented by the Other, recuperating both the Anishinaabmowin language's formal structure as well as descriptive content. Navigationally, "Where the waters divide" is both a useful physical label and a common Indigenous naming convention. The point is this: both names,

"Walpole Island" and "Bkejwanong," have *agency*—they are the instruments of dominance and resistance, respectively. They empower persons, whether Anglo-Canadian or First Nations, in the creation, performance, and transmission of their identity. In the latter case, that identity is also maritime, referencing dwelling and movement by water.

Nearly lost in the fog of this war of words is the *materiality* and the *maritimity* of the poles themselves. A recent study of the Indigenous use of poles for wayfinding offers the intriguing suggestion that the "war poles" observed in 1780 by *Welcome* were in fact painted "lopsticks," commonly used as directional markers along fur trade routes (Podruchny, Gleach, and Roulette 2014, 42). The inference to be drawn is that in taking them to be "war poles" marking Indigenous boundaries, the British misinterpreted navigational aids placed for the benefit of the French fur traders, intended to direct their canoes to the Mississauga and Ojibwe who had relocated south to the St. Clair delta. With the displacement of the French and the decline of the fur trade, the original economic intent would have been lost upon the British who, reflecting their own imperialist ideology, inferred a military symbolism.

Meanwhile, at the same time on the other side of the river, the opposite process was occurring yet with the same result—cultural dispossession. Whereas "Walpole Island" represents a straightforward assertion of hegemony, the Michigan community of "Algonac" was meant to sound like an Indigenous name yet was a death-knell for the vanished Native presence. Coined by Henry Rowe Schoolcraft circa 1843, it is a concatenation of "Algon[quin]" and the Anishinaabmowin suffix "-ac," meaning "place of"—hence "place of the Algonquin" (Romig 1973, 17). Termed *anticonquest*, this practice of appropriating the culture of a subjugated people involves glorifying the Other at the same time that the Other is denied real power. As the colonizer's attempt to recapture the disappearing Other out of a nostalgia for the lost exotic, anticonquest is a part of conquest that is in no way antithetical but only masquerading as different by operating backward (Herman 2009, 103). Here again, both the act of signifying and the *signifier*—that is, the name given—possess agency in asserting dominance. The *act of representing* not only marks but effects the process of landscape transformation as a shift in power relations.

In the transformation of the St. Clair landscape through two colonial eras, the Indigenous presence was first seen as an economic agent (trading partner) or a military agent (as ally or enemy). In the postcolonial period of expansion and exploitation, the policies of Indigenous marginalization or outright removal were thus marked by new representations, whether by overwriting, suppressing, appropriating, or fabricating the past.

Cartography of the St. Clair Maritime Landscape

Nearly all the place-names listed above have appeared as textual labels on maps, diagrams, and charts. The two-dimensional matrices upon which those labels were applied combine language with the graphic representation of the physical world, its features and its inhabitants. Like place-names, the maps produced during a given period not only reflect but reinforce and, in cases, act as agents in the construction of social relations. A key indicator of the ideology of the society creating a map is the choices it makes as to what to represent on its finite area and in what manner.

As with the toponymy of the Great Lakes, Indigenous symbolizations lead, through the French and British colonial periods, to the postcolonial era. In cartographic terms, this can be dated from the work of the International Boundary Commission in 1820. Each of these periods, however, preserves something of the past, whether descriptive or ideological. It is here that the metaphor of the palimpsest—erasure and overwriting—is most apt, as the obliteration of the past is seldom total. Evidence of previous representations persists—however faint, flawed, or transformed—in their replacements.

Arguing for the social construction of space, the *Annaliste* Henri Lefebvre poses a thought experiment. How many maps, he wonders, might be needed to exhaustively represent a given space, to code all its meanings and contents? The answer, he decides, is an infinite number, bolstering his case for the inextricable intertwining of social spaces of all kinds (Lefebvre 1991, 85–86). But this argument, tossed off as a reductio ad absurdum, can be played backward to even better effect. If an extensive yet imperfect knowledge of a socially selected array of features, represented by labels and symbols, must be inscribed in a single sheet of paper—what then? This is the conundrum that has faced every successor to the first mapmaker to scratch lines in the dirt with a stick. Priorities must be set, decisions made, and in their making, ideology is instantiated, reproduced, transmitted—and revealed. In using maps anthropologically, the task is to decode what others have coded, looking for patterns in the choices made—patterns that reflect underlying values and assumptions that distinguish one society, dwelling within and moving through its own unique landscape, from another. In doing so, the social features become visible: the objects chosen to be symbolized and the scale at which a society considers a given piece of its physical world to be meaningfully bounded. As in the case of place-names, the map is not merely the representation of the disposition of features-as-agents within the landscape; rather, the map itself acquires agency.

Whether as conservative documents or agents of change, maps are never neutral (Harley 1992, 247). As a form of discourse and exercises of power, maps are legitimate subjects of social criticism. By controlling official mapmaking, hegemonic institutions dictate ideology in the time and place represented. The resultant hegemonic discourse persuasively conveyed through maps, geographer John Pickles explains, is "a particularly good example of a 'text' which has been presumed to require a straightforward literal reading, but which actually poses great problems of interpretation and requires a rigorous hermeneutic analysis" (Pickles 1992, 223). Dozens of maps of the Great Lakes region were made during the critical period between European contact and the modern era. Techniques of deconstruction and hermeneutic analysis of power relations offer a means of demonstrating how these maps served as instruments of hegemony in their original social and political contexts (Harley 1992). At the same time, when interrogated as a diachronic assemblage, the maps offer an insight into long-term physical and cultural transformations in the maritime landscape.

As normative agents, maps and their makers create and control movement through maritime transport zones by selectively providing and withholding knowledge of resources, risks, and opportunities. In emphasizing maritimity, features have been selected that indicate not only the ideology of each ascendant group but its nautical technology and nautical practices as well. An Indigenous map will serve to introduce the maritime landscape first encountered by the colonial French.

Indigenous Mapmaking in the Great Lakes

Early French visitors to the Great Lakes observed the Indigenous practice of making birchbark scroll maps that, curated and interpreted by elders, were "used to make long voyages without straying" (Lewis 1998, 79–80). The perishable nature of the medium has prevented the survival of any known specimens from the encounter period. However, an insight into what they would have looked like and how they encoded knowledge of the landscape may be inferred by preserved migration scrolls of the Ojibwe. An outstanding curated example will serve here: that of Red Sky, an Ojibwe elder of the Lake of the Woods community in Manitoba. As interpreted by its owner, the scroll depicts the westward diaspora of the Ojibwe people from their original homeland on the Atlantic Seaboard (figure 2). Its significance here lies in its documenting a specific pattern of maritime movement.

The ancestors of the Ojibwe, then part of a general Anishinaabeg diaspora, first left the St. Lawrence River near the present site of Montreal, ascending northward along the Ottawa River. From there, they portaged into the Lake Nipissing drainage, descended the French River to Georgian Bay, and proceeded

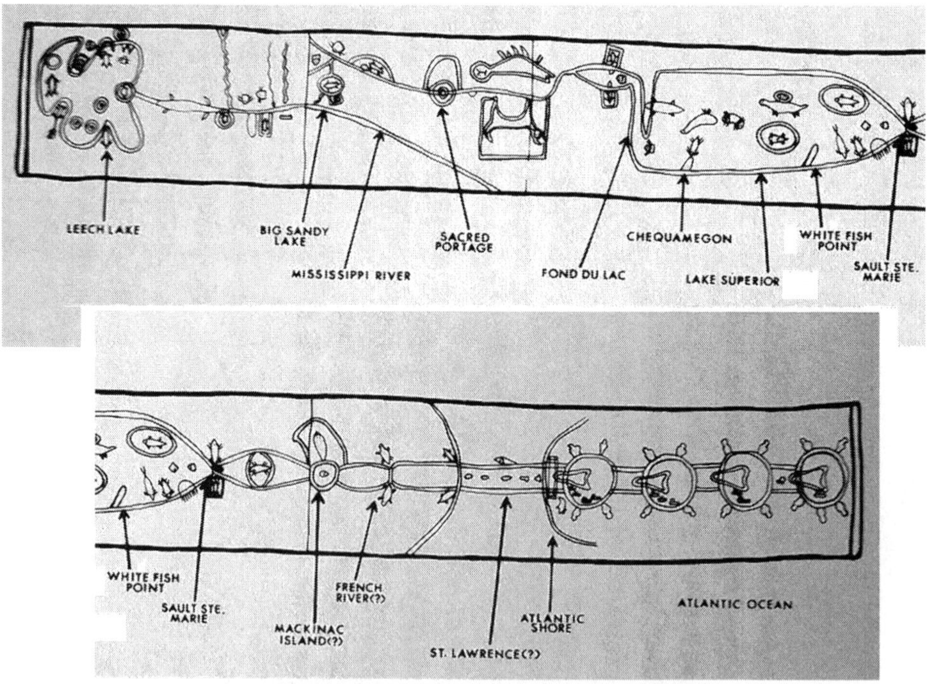

FIGURE 2. Red Sky's migration chart (Ojibwe). The lower section is thought to depict the Anishinaabeg diaspora from its origins on the Atlantic Seaboard westward to Lake Superior by way of the St. Lawrence, Ottawa, and French Rivers. (Dewdney 1975)

to Sault Ste. Marie. After an extended stay, the Anishinaabeg migration continued westward, radiating throughout the upper Great Lakes and into the lands bordering the Great Plains (Dewdney 1975). This route may have been chosen in order to avoid the territory of their inveterate enemies the Iroquois, which lay ahead had they continued on the southerly route through Lakes Ontario and Erie (Tanner 1987, 30).

Besides its documentation of the Anishinaabeg diaspora, another significance of this scroll lies in its ability to contextualize the choice later made by the French in establishing their fur trade route and its outposts. Like their Algonkian (Anishinaabeg) trading partners, the French found it best to steer clear of their European rivals—first the Dutch and, after 1644, the British (Wolf 1982, 161). The French connection was later inscribed in the naming of the route's sole rapids, located on the French River. Named "Portage des Recollets," referring to the Franciscan missionaries who regularly used it, it appeared on maps by Franquelin (1684), de Fer (1718), and Bellin (1755).

The French period in the upper Great Lakes, then, commenced with the French establishing their communication between Montreal and their initial economic and religious bases—Michilimackinac and St. Ignace, respectively—via the extant Indigenous route through Lake Nipissing. Their mission on Georgian Bay at Ste. Marie dans les Hurons was also accessed from this northerly route. Yet midway through the French period, their trading center was relocated from Michilimackinac to Fort Pontchartrain at Detroit—an aggressive territorial move that signaled a disruptive development in the upper Great Lakes maritime network. Moving furs and trade goods to and from Detroit put the French and the Anishinaabeg on a collision course with the British-Iroquois alliance that claimed the southerly route.

Cartography of the French Colonial Era (1616–1760)

The transformation of the St. Clair and Detroit strait, then, is a product of the French expanding their network of maritime transport zones to include not only the traditional Anishinaabeg route via Lake Nipissing but the route through Lake Ontario and Lake Erie and into Lake Huron as well. From the perspective of their Indigenous economic and military partners, this was a reoccupation of ancestral lands by the descendants of refugees (White 1991). As a result, the demographic landscape was highly dynamic, as peoples were in constant motion. At the same time, the French cognitive landscape was rapidly transforming as more extensive knowledge of landforms, shorelines, and interior lakes and rivers was added to their maritime taskscapes. By examining the resulting cartographic representations of the two alternative trade routes in chronological order, their underlying agenda may be seen as it played out on the landscape over the duration of the French colonial era.[2]

The earliest French map to depict the Great Lakes is Samuel de Champlain's unpublished effort of 1616. Both the northerly Lake Nipissing and southerly Lake Erie routes are present, but the former, which Champlain surveyed in person using an astrolabe, is the more accurate. Revised and published in 1632, it served as the model for subsequent refinements by Jean Boisseau (1643), Champlain himself (1653), and DuVal (1664). Their labeling of features reveals a greater preoccupation with the naming of Indigenous groups than with that of landforms or water bodies. This suggests a high degree of dependence on localized Indigenous partners—as informants, guides, translators, negotiators, and trappers.

The same is true of Nicolas Sanson's influential *Le Canada, ou Nouvelle France* (1656), which, together with sketches from Louis Jolliet, served Galinée well in his own travels some dozen years later. A detail showing both the northerly and southerly routes (map 3) illustrates the density and diversity of populations east of Lake Huron (labeled "Karegnondi"). The relative paucity of labels west of the Strait may be attributable both to lack of knowledge and to the depopulation occasioned by the Iroquois Wars. Sanson's map gives visual force to Michael Witgen's assertion that the presence of "an infinity of undiscovered nations" in the heartland of the continent made the Anishinaabeg indispensable to the fur trade (Witgen 2012, 20). At that time, both the Anishinaabeg and their language of Anishinaabmowin, particularly the Ojibwe dialect, were particularly well-established in the Great Lakes, functioning as a lingua franca among disparate nations, even the Iroquois (Voegelin and Voegelin 1964, 52; Wolfart 1988, 121).

2 This focused discussion of colonial mapmaking is necessarily brief. Brian Dunnigan's masterful *Frontier Metropolis* (2001) provides a lavishly illustrated survey of early Detroit as seen through maps and primary documents.

MAP 3. Nicolas Sanson, *Le Canada, ou Nouvelle France* (1656), detail. "Mont Real" appears near the right edge; "L. Nipissiriniens" (Lake Nipissing, top center) flows into an accurately drawn Georgian Bay. The group "Ariatoeronon" in the thumb of Michigan's Lower Peninsula is a variant of Atsistaeronon, the Huron name for the Mascouten. (John Carter Brown Library)

Sanson's depiction of the Great Lakes was closely followed by Francesco Bressani (1657) and François Du Creux (1660). The latter, publishing as "Creuxius" a history of Canada in Latin, perpetuated Sanson's naming of Lake St. Clair, "Lac des Eaux de Mer," now Latinized as "Lacus a[q]uarum Marinaru[s]."

In these early maps, numerous unnamed tributary streams line the transport corridor, as seen in the Sanson and Creuxius versions of Lake Erie. With Bernou (1675) and Franquelin (1684), several things began to change. First, named places—particularly inland lakes, tributary streams, islands, and portages—became more numerous as the French cartographers received reports from missionaries, explorers, and *coureurs de bois* (independent fur traders) taking a more active role in wayfinding, along both the northern (Lake Nipissing) and southern (Lake Erie) corridors. Franquelin's map of 1684 shows dozens of named features—rivers, inland lakes, villages, islands—radiating outward from Fort Frontenac, established on Lake Ontario a decade earlier.

Second, the names of occupying groups became correspondingly less numerous. In what is now southwest Ontario, the reason is obvious. Bernou shows group after group as "*nation detruite*" (destroyed nation). Franquelin labels Huronia "*Ancien Pays des Hurons*" (ancient land of the Hurons); the lands of the Petun and Neutrals are likewise identified in the past tense: "*Ou estoit la Nation du Petun*" (where the Petun Nation was). With their informants killed or scattered, the French produced maps that were more geophysical and less ethnographic, in effect.

The cartographers had at last caught up with the events of previous decades, as the ruinous Iroquois Wars had produced the abandoned landscapes witnessed by Galinée and Hennepin. In building Fort Frontenac, the French erected not only a bulwark against British incursion from the south but a platform from which to seek *rapprochement* with the ascendant Iroquois (Wolf 1982, 169). The northerly Lake Nipissing route was still evidently preferred for purposes of the fur trade, as it traversed more productive beaver habitat. But the southerly Lake Erie route through Iroquois territory was no longer marginal, being used chiefly for diplomacy, including pacification through the distribution of trade goods. Coronelli's map of 1688 depicts both routes to Michilimackinac with roughly equal accuracy but with little detail of the southerly route above Lake Ontario.

The Strait between Lakes Erie and Huron would soon prove pivotal in the continued shift to the southern route. In establishing Fort St. Joseph in 1686 near the present site of Port Huron, Duluth submitted glowing reports of the bounty of the Strait, which were echoed by Lahontan, who nevertheless abandoned the fort two years later, deeming its location strategically unnecessary (Duluth 1902; Lahontan 1905). These positive accounts doubtless helped entice the ambitious Antoine de Lamothe Cadillac, appointed by Governor Frontenac to command at Michilimackinac in 1694, to seek greener pastures to the south. With Cadillac's relocation of the French fur trade's Great Lakes hub, attention to mapping of the Strait in detail commenced. Cadillac's unnamed 1702 map of "Detroit Erié," as the Strait was then called (map 4), drew attention to the most strategic location on the Erie route. It was soon followed by Jean-Baptiste Couagne's *Nouvelle France* (1711). So detailed that it was classified by the French in the atmosphere of escalating tensions with the British, Couagne's work established a benchmark for subsequent cartographic efforts (map 5).

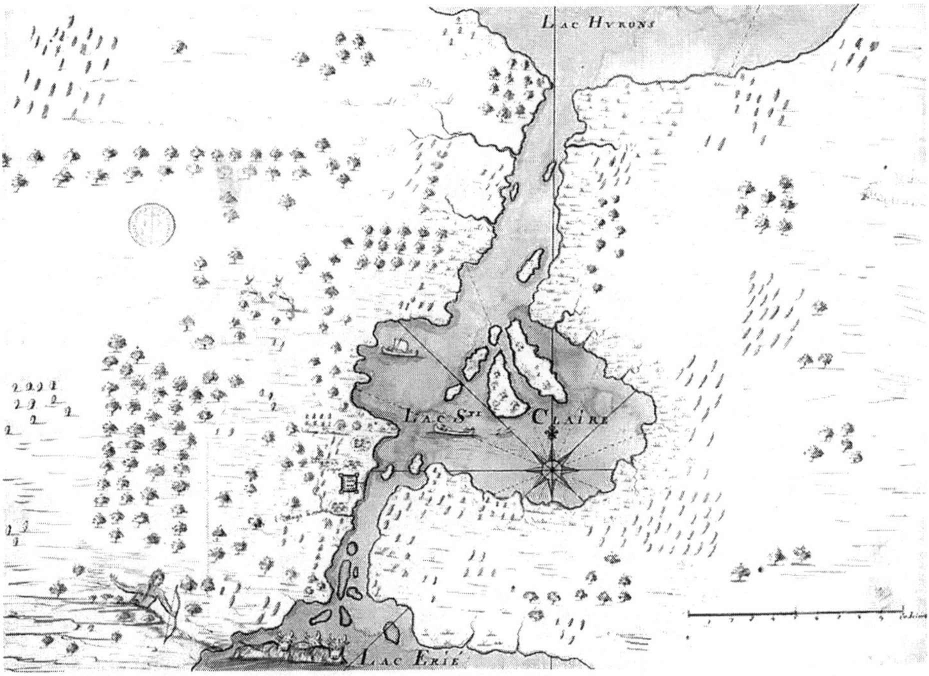

MAP 4. Antoine de Lamothe Cadillac, "Detroit Erié" (1702). Most of the major navigational features of the Strait are present, albeit often in rudimentary form, including the islands and channels of the St. Clair delta. Note the depiction of a sailing canoe in a recognizable Anchor Bay. (Wikimedia Commons)

The American-born Couagne introduced numerous and significant features, particularly tributary rivers. On the Michigan side, he locates the "Huron" (now Clinton), Rouge, Ecorse, "Raizin," and "Miamis" (Maumee). On the Ontario side, the Cedar and Canard are marked; what may be the Thames is unlabeled and has its mouth in the northeast rather than the southeast corner of "Lac St. Claire." Moreover, "les Mississagues," a village of "two hundred men" is depicted at the mouth of the westward-flowing river, suggesting that it may be a conflation of the Thames with the Chenal Écarté, a channel in the St. Clair delta. More significant, the delta itself is not depicted with any degree of accuracy. Instead, Lake St. Clair is shown uniformly studded with islets, simply indicating its complex but arbitrary navigation: all routes through the delta were passable by canoe, and all led either upstream to the main course of the St. Clair River and the Mississauga village, or downstream through Lake St. Clair to Fort Pontchartrain.

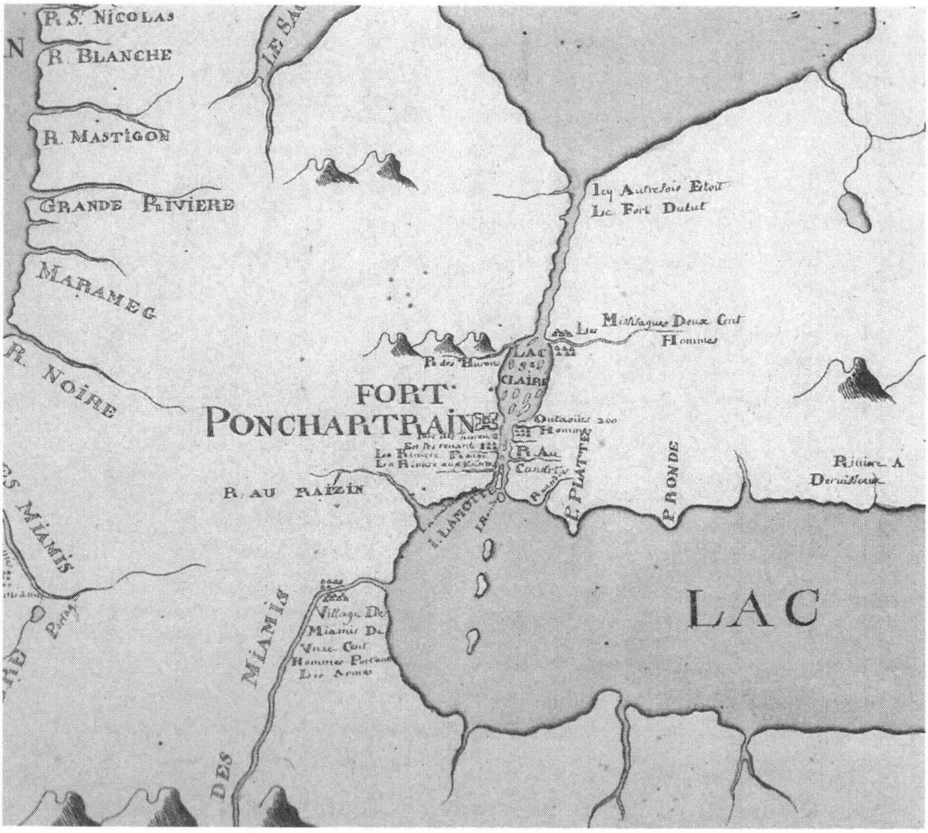

MAP 5. Jean-Baptiste Couagne, *Nouvelle France* (1711). Note the "Missisagues" at the mouth of an unlabeled river. (Bibliotheque National de France)

The high point of French cartographic representation of the Strait belongs to Sieur de Boishébert, commander at Fort Pontchartrain from 1730 to 1733. Upon his arrival at Detroit, he began a survey of the entire Strait, completing it in 1731 (Beauharnois 1906, 141). The result was unsurpassed for eighty-five years (map 2). The latitude of the entrance to the Strait was given as 42° 4′ N, which corresponds exactly to the mouth of the Detroit River, at a time when precision to within fifteen minutes of latitude was considered good. The St. Clair maritime landscape had assumed the shape of the taskscape that persisted into the modern era, including the main tributaries to Lake St. Clair and the St. Clair River. Above all, the delta was accurately represented, with the North, Middle, and South Channels; the Chenal à Bout Ronde; and the Chenal Écarté all present. Walpole, Squirrel, and Harsens Islands are identifiable, with the last showing the Mississauga village and labeled "Île de Nénehe."[3] Like Couagne's map, Boishébert's effort was submitted directly to the colonial authorities and appears to have been intended for official use only, as its features do not appear on subsequent commercial maps. As the French continued to use only small craft, the prospect of building upon Boishébert's work to determine the optimal deep-draft route through the St. Clair delta for larger vessels never came to fruition under French rule.

Ironically, the most influential cartographer of the closing years of the French period was Jacques Bellin. This was not owing to his accuracy—quite the opposite, in fact. In 1744, Bellin published his *Carte des Lacs du Canada*, showing all five Great Lakes with their modern names (map 6). The St. Clair system is dotted with sixteen tiny islands, arranged like peas in a pod. The Thames River, though nameless, is noted as "river we ascended 80 leagues without finding rapids" ("Riv. quon remonte 80 lieues sans trouver des saults"), which is precisely correct. On the other hand, two spurious features debuted as well: a large but fictional "Isle Philippeaux" in the center of Lake Superior and a phantom plateau ("terrain plus elevé") running the length of Michigan's Lower Peninsula. Those two features acquired a life of their own, persistently appearing on maps of North America for nearly a century.

The navigability of the Thames, on the other hand, was another matter. When he revised his map in 1755, Bellin's Thames was now labeled "unknown river said to be 80 leagues long *but full of rapids*" (emphasis added; Riviere inconnu qu'on dit avoir 80 lieues de course mais rempli de saults). Between the classified work of Boishébert and the seeming about-face of Bellin, were the French strategically withholding accurate information while spreading disinformation? In the aftermath of the British takeover following the French and Indian War, at least one Englishman would come to that conclusion.

Accuracy aside, the French colonial ideology, as reflected in its choices of what to represent in its cartography, called for access to Indigenous partners in the fur trade as well as to shipping routes to the Atlantic Seaboard via Montreal

---

3 The island may have been named for a Mississauga chief, or an inherited family name. Ferris (2009, 38n2) relates that a Chippewa named "Nangi" was said to be the chief of the "St. Clair community" during a land cession negotiation in the 1830s.

MAP 6. Jacques Bellin, *Carte des Lacs du Canada* (1744), detail, showing Thames River as "Riv. quon remonte 80 lieues sans trouver des saults" (river we ascended 80 leagues without finding rapids). (Wikimedia Commons)

(Jensen 2019, 19). In maritime terms, this meant transport zones along the interior rivers together with passages between the trade hubs along the Great Lakes. Jean-Fréderic Bernard's "Le Cours du Fleuve Missipi" (1737) graphically illustrated the shift of the preferred route from the north to the south. While both were present, a prominent dashed line followed the route from Fort Frontenac through Lake Erie, the Strait, and Lake Huron. West of Mackinac it split, one fork going to La Baye de Puans (Green Bay)—where refugees from the Iroquois Wars had relocated—and, by portages, into the Mississippi River. The other led to Fort Miamis (Chicago) and the Illinois River. All routes required portages: around Niagara, up the Ottawa River, into the Illinois. The shallow-draft nautical technology and maritime practice of long-distance travel by canoe thus rendered the hydrology of the St. Clair delta as unproblematic for a Frenchman of 1737 as it had been for Champlain in 1616—in effect, it was just another river.

In other ways, however, the French colonial transportation network was logistically strained. White calculates that the carrying capacity of the canoe-based system was unable to meet the demand for French manufactures by their Algonquian clients (White 1991, 135). The situation did not improve for the British when they took possession of Detroit in 1763, and immediately found themselves on the defensive. Pontiac's half-year siege failed in large part because the British were able to relieve their beleaguered outpost by water, using armed ships as floating fortresses. The urgent need to mobilize their maritime capabilities, both naval and commercial, in their newly acquired territory above Detroit became immediately apparent. To do so, they would need proper nautical charts. As Captain Gother Mann of the Royal Engineers wrote to Lord Dorchester in 1788, "Vessels sailing on these waters being seldom for any length of time out of sight of Land, the navigation must be considered chiefly as Pilotage, to which the use of good Nautical Charts are essential, and therefore much wanted" (Mann 1888, 36).

British Cartography in the Great Lakes (1684–1818)

The new masters of the Great Lakes began by using French maps that, by design, were not as precise as they might have been. Jonathan Carver, an agent in the fur trade, traveled extensively through Britain's new territory between 1766 and 1768 in search of the fabled Northwest Passage. In his memoir, he complained bitterly about the difficulties he encountered in traveling: "I knew many obstructions would arise to my scheme from the want of good Maps and Charts," he recalled, "for the French, whilst they retained their power in North America, had taken every artful method to keep all other nations, particularly the English, in ignorance of the concerns of the interior part of it; and to accomplish this design with the greater certainty, they had published inaccurate maps and false accounts; calling the different nations of the Indians by nicknames they had given them, and not by those really appertaining to them" (Carver 1781, ii).

Recalling Bellin's fictional "Isle Philippeaux," the phantom Michigan plateau, and the Thames's spurious "rapids," one must feel some sympathy for the frustrated entrepreneur: "Whether the intention of the French in doing this," Carver complained, "was to prevent these nations from being discovered and traded with, or to conceal their discourse, when they talked to each other of the

Indian concerns, I will not determine; but whatever was the cause from which it arose, it tended to mislead" (Carver 1781, ii–iii). Unfortunately, the British not only used French maps; they diligently copied them, errors and all, at least until the territory was theirs to survey. Thomas Kitchin's prewar 1747 map had drawn heavily from Bellin, as did those of Emanuel Bolton (1752) and Henry Overton (1754). Knowing this, the French in effect mobilized their maps as instruments of national security.

Upon occupying Detroit, the British did precisely what Cadillac had done upon his arrival: they began mapping their new possession. The difference was that the British, determined to use sailing ships, were initially concerned less with the shape of the landforms than with that of the submerged landscape. Lieutenant Jehu Hay reported in 1762 to his commander that "there is not enough water in Lake St Clair to carry the Vessels through to Lake Huron" and that two officers, Brehm and Robinson, had taken soundings with a weighted line. Hay noted that their results varied somewhat, which he attributed to "some roving Sand Banks" (Hay 1911, 165).

Their initial sketch covered the western half of Lake St. Clair, including what came to be known as Anchor Bay. There they sought refuge from strong contrary winds, anticipating its future navigational role (Campbell 1762). The soundings revealed the presence of bars across the mouths of the North and Middle Channels. The South, Bassett, and Chenal Écarté remained unsurveyed for the time being, the eastern portion of the sketch bearing the note "A deep bay of Rushes as far as can be seen." This appeared to confirm the observations of Robinson's colleague Diederick Brehm, who had attempted to survey the delta the previous November, and found the "eastern channel," evidently either the Bassett or Chenal Écarté, "losing itself in the rushes and froze, which obliged me to return back a larger channel" (Brehm 1883, 25).

As suggested by the sloop *Welcome*'s 1782 observation of war poles, by the time of the American Revolution, British warships were preferentially using the South Channel, naming it "the Ship Channel," but diverting course to Anchor Bay and the North Channel at need (*Welcome* 1779–82). Critically, the British Navy and its civilian surrogate, the Provincial Marine, carried the manpower to physically overcome the obstacles to using the shorter South Channel. Most merchants were not so fortunate, often using canoes to cover the entire distance from Montreal to Michilimackinac and Green Bay.

By 1781 they too felt the logistical constraints the French had experienced but on a larger scale. Besides high-value cargoes of manufactured goods, their Native allies in the north, as limited practitioners of agriculture, demanded food as the price of their allegiance. In that year, at the height of the American Revolution, a group of merchants in Montreal petitioned the governor, Sir Frederick Haldimand, for assistance: "This trade in which [we] are deeply concerned," they complained, "cannot be carried on without large supplies of Indian Corn and other Provisions with which your Memorialists have been usually provided from the Settlement of Detroit as it is impracticable to carry then from hence: particularly Indian Corn because it would require such an augmentation of Canoes with men to work them as to accumulate the expense far beyond any benefit they could hope to reap by the Trade" (Haldimand Papers 1892, 620–21). At the ragged fringe of empire, lengthy, attenuated supply chains were impractical either for diplomacy or commerce.

At the American Revolutionary War's end, the British, pressured by their fur merchants, refused to relinquish the Northwest Territories, nominally ceded to the United States under the Treaty of Paris in 1783 (Dunbar and May 1995, 88). Unless they had the means of keeping their Native allies faithful, however, the enterprise remained doomed. A more robust commercial transport network was needed, one sustainable by commerce, not simply naval might. This meant ships, not boats and canoes. An early map documenting the shift of the preferred shipping route from the South Channel to the deeper North Channel is that of British surveyor Thomas Smith (1809). Smith's remarkably accurate chart was titled *The Mouths of the River St. Clair, with the Islands and Channels ascertaining the main navigable waters which separate that part of Upper Canada from the United States* (map 7). Already the North Channel is identified as "The River St. Clair." This chart is the first to label Anchor Bay, the reason given as a note: "Here the vessels lighter to pass the Bar." The soundings show the bar as having ten feet of depth compared to the South Channel (identified as the West Branch of "Warpole Channel"), which shows six-and-a-half feet at the bar across its mouth.

A chart of Lake St. Clair produced in 1815 clearly delineated the narrow curving passage approaching the North Channel known as the Elbow. Crucially, its cartographer, Emeric Essex Vidal, appended the following to Smith's note on Anchor Bay: "These Waters have a periodic flux and reflux and the Soundings

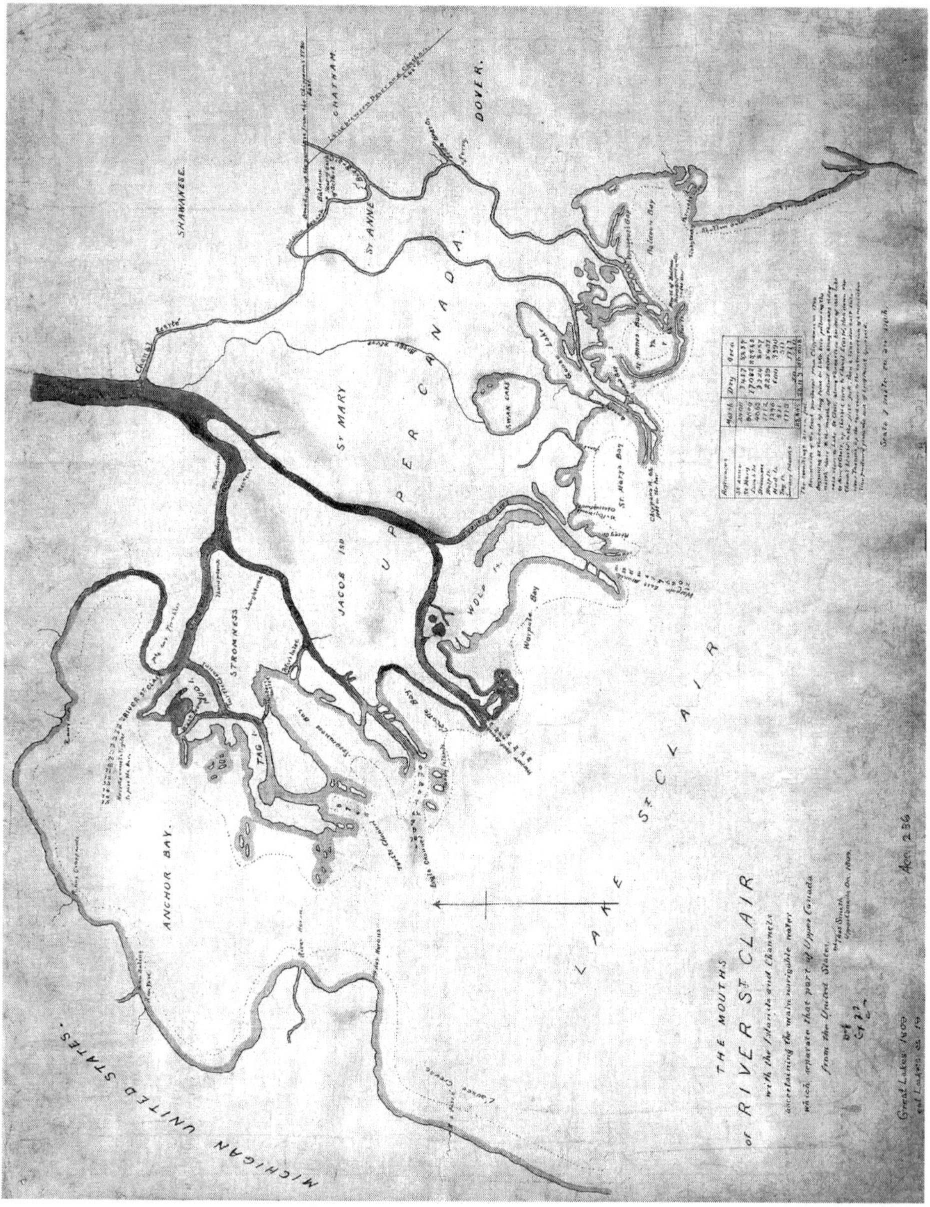

MAP 7. Thomas Smith, *Mouths of the River St. Clair* (1809). "Anchor Bay" is now labeled, and the entrance to the North Channel is marked "Here the vessels lighter to pass the Bar." The South Channel and its branches are labeled as "Warpole." Barely legible is the labeling of the North Channel: "River St. Clair, which divides U[pper] Canada from the U[nited] States." (Clarke Historical Library, Central Michigan University)

may differ from two to three feet" (Vidal 1815). Two years later, naval surveyor Henry Wolsey Bayfield updated Essex's rendering. The South Channel, which had long served the shoal-draft boat traffic, was now labeled "The Old Ship Channel," while the North Channel, with a minimum charted depth of seven feet, now bore the title "New Ship Channel." The shape of the Elbow was accurately charted and noted "This Channel is staked every Spring" (map 8). Bayfield's chart expanded upon Vidal's brief "periodic flux and reflux" remark, noting that "the vessels lighter to pass the Bar, on which the depth of water varies according to the seasons, and also on diff't years, to the amount of 2 or 3 feet." This bit of local knowledge, once generally known, would prove critical to navigation for decades.

The commercial interests, which had earlier been constrained by the inadequate carrying capacity of the French/Indigenous canoe-based maritime network, were now served by the surveying and marking of a natural route through the delta that could be followed by modest-sized sailing vessels—with skill, patience, luck, and often assistance. The political interests

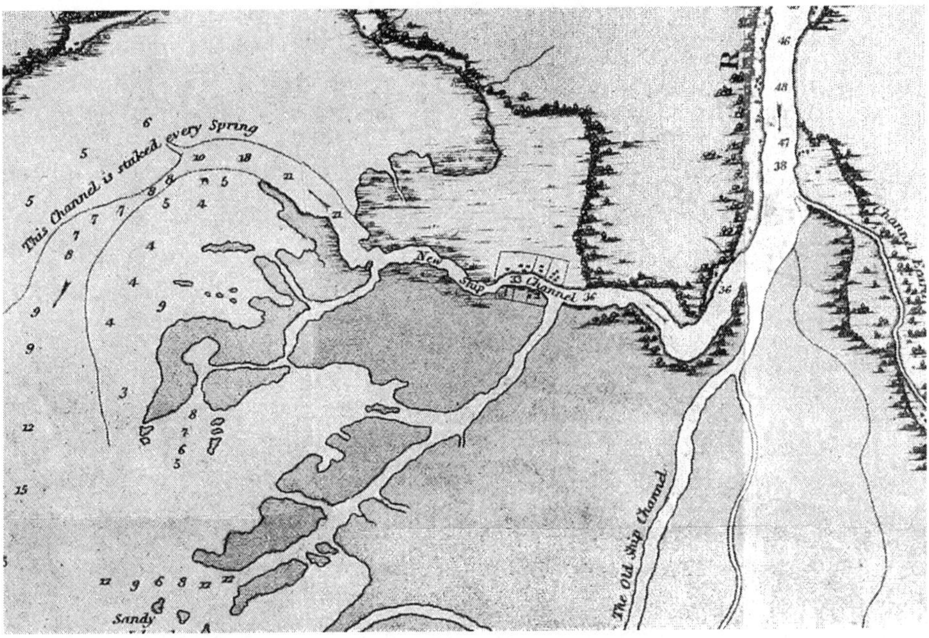

MAP 8. Henry Wolsey Bayfield, *Track Survey of the Lake & River St. Clair* (1817), detail. Note North Channel labeled as "New Ship Channel"; staking of the Elbow; ribbon farms along North Channel. (Great Britain, Admiralty, Hydrographic Office)

of Great Britain and the United States were served shortly thereafter by the 1821 issuance of the "plane chart" that accompanied the recommendations of the International Boundary Commission. In a departure from standard border determination practice, the American and British commissioners agreed to retain the designation of the North Channel as the official shipping channel yet recommended the natural course of the South Channel as the international boundary, where it remains substantially unaltered to the present.[4] From this point onward, the initiative in the cartography of the St. Clair system passed largely to the Americans, as it was driven by the hydrographic surveys of the Bureau of Topographic Engineers commencing in the 1840s.

With each successive survey, the colonial British mariners were better able to adapt both their behavior and their technology to achieve their social, economic, and military goals. Especially when combined with surviving ships' logs, our best evidence of their progress is in these maps and charts: not only their improving accuracy but their choice of what to represent and what to omit. French maps of the Great Lakes had devoted great attention first to the locations and names of Indigenous groups, thereafter to riparian routes to the interior. British mapping gradually replaced these details with more accurate representations of the location and shape of the open-water maritime corridor, as it impacted military and commercial interests.

American Maritime Cartography of the St. Clair Delta

A brief overview of early American cartography in the St. Clair system will suffice here, as maps will soon loom large as evidence of the physical transformation of the Flats in the mid-nineteenth century. With minor emendations, Bayfield's 1817 chart, or its 1821 iteration as the Boundary Commission finding, served as late as 1841. The following year, the Bureau of Topographic Engineers issued a new map of the delta based on extensive surveying of the mouths of all channels on the American side (map 9). The complexity of the

4 This deviation from the standard practice of placing the international boundary along the center of official waterways explains Doty's remark regarding Lauson's Island, "This Island is supposed to belong to the English." But for this exception, it would have.

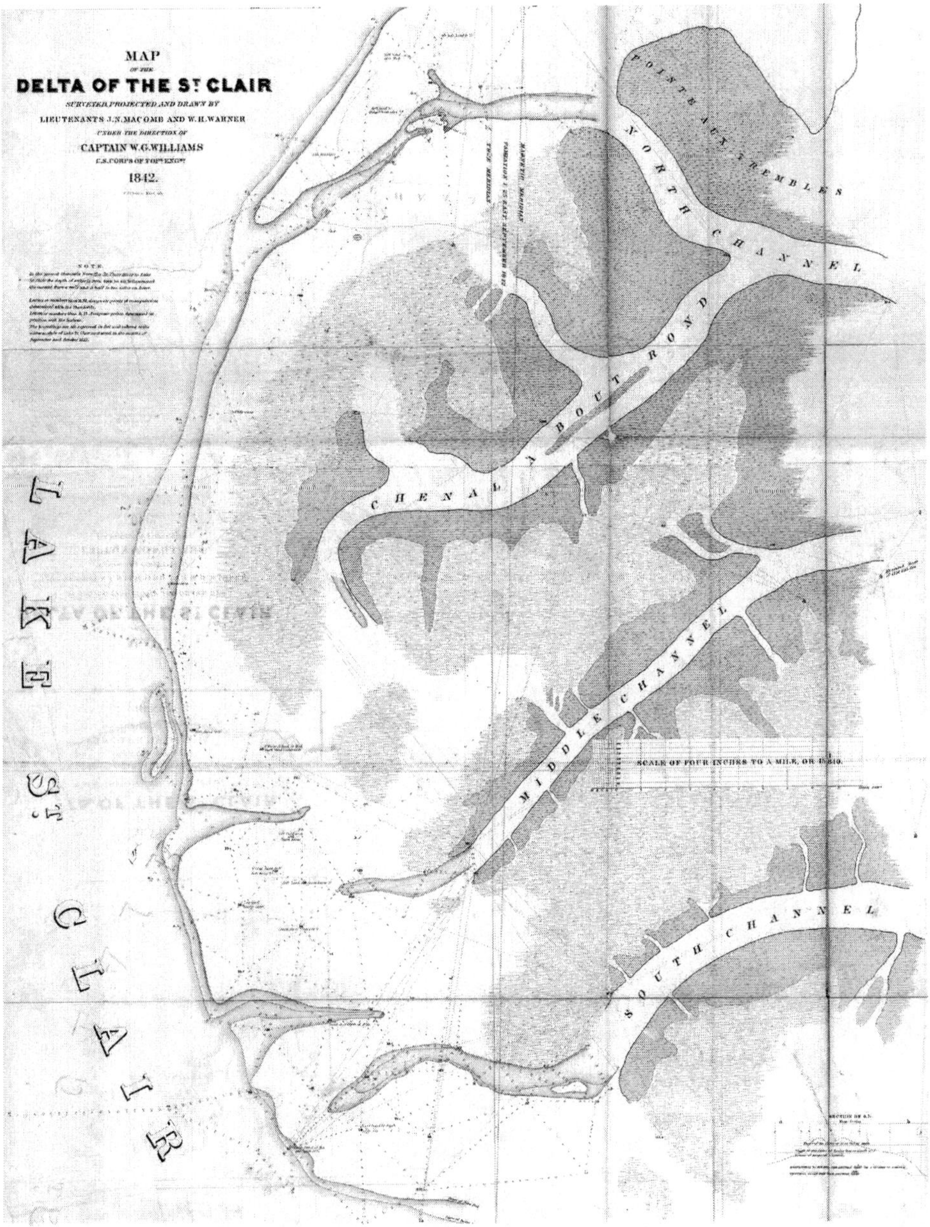

MAP 9. W. G. Williams, *Map of the Delta of the St. Clair* (1842). (Library of Congress)

Elbow's hydrology was laid bare, as was the true shape of the South Channel bar. Within six months, the Bureau had issued a revised plan for improvements to the navigation of the Flats, taking advantage of this new knowledge. Thereafter, cartographic efforts in this area were not merely descriptive but incorporated projected modifications: deepening, widening, straightening, and marking the extant channels and finally creating new channels altogether.

Representation as Placemaking

The ways in which each occupying group named and depicted the landscapes they created by their knowing, dwelling, and moving link these symbolized representations to the ideology that determined what was literally noteworthy, what constitutes a *place*. In the case of the precontact Indigenous population, the limited number of surviving names, even including those recorded or adopted by the French, prohibits generalization beyond the obvious: that affordances (good hunting, oak trees) or physical attributes (a kettle-shaped lake) were doubtless common. Elsewhere in the Great Lakes, certain places were named for mythic events. A distinctive landmark on the Lake Michigan shore, *L'ours qui dort* (the Sleeping Bear), appeared on Bellin's map of 1755 and was certainly in common French use from their earliest explorations of that area, having been acquired from Native informants. The same may have been true in the Strait, but that knowledge, and thereby an Indigenous sense of place, has apparently been lost, or at least obscured.

French naming and mapping reflect the ambiguity of their colonial enterprise. Forced in many ways to rely on their trading partners and religious converts, they blended Indigenous names (*Otsi-keta*, *Ganatchio*) and their own French "nicknames," as Carver termed them (*Huron*, *Cheveux Relevé*, *Erié*), with physical attributes (*eaux de mer*, *pointe aux chênes*) and gestures toward their noble patrons (Pontchartrain, Frontenac) and religious figures (Ste. Clare, on whose August 11 feast day the La Salle party entered the lake that now bears her name). The colonial French map is thus a bricolage of the expedient, the descriptive, the politic, and the pious. The apparent transition from an initial emphasis on locating Indigenous groups in the landscape, to subsequent naming and mapping of the landscape's physical features, suggests a shift in the ideology that invariably underlies the choice of what is represented. It appears that as the annihilation and displacement of Native peoples continued, French society—whether administrators, missionaries, colonists, or traders—came to prioritize the location of geographic features above what had been largely ethnographic data.

Considered strictly in terms of maritime transport routes, French cartographic practice reflected their nautical practice: coastal navigation, accessing inland rivers and lakes using portages—all using canoes and shoal-draft vernacular adaptations. In such a system, strict spatial accuracy was not essential. Instead, a detailed schematic diagram of the *connectivity* of the larger landscape served their colonial enterprise. Simply put, the affordances offered by the fur trade and the constraints imposed by the canoe and the astrolabe shaped the French cartographic representation (Taylor 1949).

The canoe, despite its virtues, ultimately limited the capacity of their transport network and contributed to their displacement by the British, who soon felt the pinch themselves as they extended their commerce deeper into the frontier. Accurate navigation by deep-draft vessels may have been compromised by poor charts, but their very ability to access the upper Great Lakes was constrained by the St. Clair delta. Coincidentally, the British takeover of New France occurred just as horologist John Harrison perfected his practical marine chronometer (1761), permitting accurate measurement of longitude. But it was the ancient and humble lead line—endlessly heaved and retrieved by the survey crews of Robinson, Brehm, Bayfield, and Williams—that opened the route through the Flats to commercial shipping, modestly at first, and with difficulties and delays while awaiting favorable sailing conditions at Anchor Bay.

There matters stood for a quarter-century, from 1817 to 1842, from Bayfield to Williams. Faced with ever-greater strain upon the transportation network of the Great Lakes, the emergent American hegemony in North America turned to cartography as a planning tool—the representation of a *potential* maritime landscape, a *future* place. Before turning to that watershed development, a review of seafaring—the practice of movement by water, will complete the overview of the four processes of maritime landscape formation.

6

Sweetwater Seafaring

Movement in the St. Clair Maritime Landscape

The St. Clair River is thirty miles long,
Heave 'er up lads, heave 'er high!
An' we'll set our canvas to this merry song.
Heave 'er up and bust her.
Up the river we'll sail on a towline breeze.
Heave 'er up lads, heave 'er high!
Astern the Flats, ahead the big seas.
Heave 'er up and bust her!
—"Heave Her Up and Bust Her" (capstan chanty)

Sometimes the best way to get through a hard, monotonous job is by singing. Capstan chanteys were work songs sung by sailors winding a heavy line onto a capstan—a vertical windlass with radiating push bars. It was located in the bow of a sailing ship, where it was used for heavy work: raising the anchor, hoisting sail, lightering cargo, or towing a ship upriver. As the sailors marched in a circle, each pushing a capstan bar, they kept time—and often vented their feelings—by singing. A popular capstan chantey was "Heave Her Up and Bust Her," referring to breaking the anchor loose from the bottom when preparing to get underway. While a chantey could have dozens of stanzas, the two above give a glimpse of nautical life on the St. Clair River as the Age of Sail gradually gave way to that of steam. Leaving Anchor Bay, the breeze was often contrary or simply too weak to propel a schooner upriver toward the "big seas" of Lake Huron and Lake Michigan. The "towline breeze" was a sarcastic reference to the practice of catching a tow upriver from a steam-powered tugboat, at least until the thirty miles of the St. Clair River were astern and the schooner could "set her canvas" in open waters. These few lines capture a transformational moment in a distinctive context, where sailors had learned to maintain their traditional practices by selectively taking advantage of new technology.

Seafaring as Practice; Seamanship as Identity

Seafaring may be viewed as the coordination of two actions, *propulsion* and *navigation*: making a vessel move under its own power and making it follow the intentions of the people aboard. While intimately related, the former emphasizes the relationship between humans and their conveyance; the latter, between humans and their taskscape. Changes in either action, whether by adapted practices or technological innovation, create disruptions that transform the Nature/Culture relation and thereby the maritime landscape itself.

Nautical practice emerges from the interaction of the *identity* of the mariner with the maritime landscape.[1] Given that the landscape is socially constructed, the identity of an Indigenous, French, British, American, or Canadian mariner will be conditioned by differing mentalities. These in turn relate to social criteria—affordances and constraints perceived in the maritime landscape. Social identity is performed, reproduced, and transmitted through the repeated process of purposeful movement by water—that is, seafaring. Accounts of occupying groups operating watercraft in the Great Lakes, particularly in the

1 In anthropological discussions of practice, it is virtually de rigueur to invoke Pierre Bourdieu and practice theory, usually with the result that the discussion becomes hopelessly abstruse. In the interest of simplicity and clarity, I will note here that Bourdieu's notion of *habitus* is here approximated by *identity*. His concept of the *champs*, as the immaterial field of social interaction, is here better served by the socially constructed yet agentic landscape itself (Costa 2006).

St. Clair maritime landscape, can shed light on the actors' social identities and how they operationalized the ideologies of their culture.

Indigenous Maritime Practice: The Versatility of Simplicity

Precontact burials in the Strait indicate that the region was connected to long-distance exchange networks, evidenced by artifacts of copper, mica, ivory, and marine shell (Halsey and Brashler 2013). By the outset of the historic period, Indigenous groups had long adapted their behavior to the Strait's locale. They had solved problems of procurement by water of the means of subsistence, whether gathering or growing foodstuffs, hunting, fishing, or trading. Ethnohistoric and archaeological evidence indicates that Indigenous peoples practiced open-water, coastwise, and inland navigation in the precontact period (White 1991; Cleland 1992). The long-distance networks of the Odawa ("traders" in Anishinaabmowin), the well-established portages along inland chains of lakes and rivers, the flight across Lake Michigan during the protracted Iroquois Wars—even the ritual observances of the Iroquois themselves at Springwells—all confirm this. The St. Clair River, with its abundant affordances and documented presence of anthropogenic landscape transformation, was already a key nexus in a trade network that stretched from Hudson's Bay to the Gulf of Mexico.

Indigenous maritime practice, then, involved the two principal components of seafaring stated above: propulsion and navigation. The former required strength, skill, and stamina, as it consisted primarily of paddling the canoe. This was no mean feat, especially in strong current, in severe weather, or over long distances. The exception to paddling was portaging across adjoining drainages or around obstacles. At these times, the canoe was typically unloaded and carried overland, but it could also be "lined through" shallows or spring floods using a rope and persons on shore. Notwithstanding Hennepin's anecdotal account of small sheets of birchbark serving as sails in a following breeze, wind was not systematically used for propulsion (Hennepin 1903, 37).

Navigational practice certainly included the use of landmarks, as suggested by such place-names as the Sleeping Bear, which would have been useful in either marking coastwise progress along Lake Michigan or making landfall upon crossing from the Wisconsin shore. It is certain that a form of dead reckoning was also used, as evidenced by accounts of Native-guided journeys projected or recorded in terms of the number of days of paddling (Karamanski 2017). It would be a great mistake, therefore, to consider the maritimity of the Indigenous inhabitants rudimentary or unsophisticated. Upon their arrival, the French explorers, missionaries, trappers, and traders were utterly dependent on guidance from the Natives, whom they ignored at their peril.

French Maritime Practice, 1679–1763: Adopt, Adapt

The route to European-style vessels and navigation practices on the upper Great Lakes was neither swift nor smooth. Sieur de La Salle's *Griffon*, the first decked vessel to sail the waters above Niagara, was a spectacular failure. Arguably its loss in 1679 was not due to being ill-adapted to the Great Lakes but because its occupants possessed neither the experience nor the respect that the inland seas demanded. Moreover, they compounded their lack of local knowledge by disregarding the warnings of their Native informants (Dunbar and May 1995, 37–38).

While the brief career of the *Griffon* may have culminated in some as-yet-undiscovered spot in Lake Michigan, its difficulties began in the St. Clair delta. As related by Père Hennepin (La Salle's chronicler), after sounding the river's maze of channels and sandbars, the French sailors were again stopped by the rapids at its head. There, a team of men hauling a towline along the shore finally allowed the *Griffon* to gain the open waters of Lake Huron. When applicable, then, *Griffon*'s sailors drew upon the traditional repertoire of European sailing technique: sounding a channel using a weighted line and hauling against a current. What their ocean-going experience would not have prepared them for was the sudden appearance of violent storms, particularly in the fall. They were most likely near the windward shore of northwestern Lake Michigan, where the opportunity to observe the oncoming weather and to shorten sail would have been brief.

For the remainder of their colonial period, in material culture and nautical practice, the French *voyageurs* adopted not only the Indigenous birchbark canoe but its world. An elaborate network of lakes and rivers, passages and portages, formed the physical and cognitive taskscape to which their Native partners' boats and practices had long since adapted. Large *voyageur* or "trade" canoes, as much as sixty feet in length, plied the routes between Montreal, Detroit, Michilimackinac, and La Baye (Green Bay), often in flotillas. The identity and nautical practice of the French *coureur de bois*, independent and entrepreneurial, were not unlike those of his Indigenous trading partners with whom he became frequently assimilated. Paddled, portaged, or pulled, his canoe traversed elaborate long-distance networks, exchanging furs from the hinterlands for goods from Europe.

In the Strait centered on Detroit, the world of the sedentary *fermier* was narrower and less venturesome. The French settlement pattern triggered an admixture of vernacular designs evolved from old-world archetypes, always within the local parameters of shallow draft and minimal requirements for launching and landing. Notable was the versatile flat-bottomed bateau, designed to be rowed, poled, or sailed and capable of being scaled larger or smaller as needed. These vessels perfectly complemented the ribbon farms, linking the farmer with local markets, where he could exchange his produce for supplies. His maritime practice, like his agriculture, linked him with his Frenchness, his colonial identity.

The constraints of the St. Clair River's natural landscape that necessitated these adaptations, the ones that had challenged La Salle—sandbars, narrow and convoluted channels, contrary winds and current—were thus overcome but at the price of limiting carrying capacity throughout the entire Great Lakes trade network. This bottleneck would not sit well with the British colonial ideology nor with the assertive identity of the British seafarer, accustomed as he was to the modes of propulsion and navigation that had gotten him across the Atlantic and, indeed, around the world.

Takeover on the Frontier: Britannia Rules the Lakes, 1763–1813

The resumption of European-style navigation of the waters above Lake Erie effectively began in the early 1760s with the occupation of Detroit by the British, the conclusion of the French and Indian War, and the onset of Pontiac's

Rebellion. During the siege of Detroit, two Niagara-built British ships, the sloop *Michigan* and the schooner *Huron*, broke through the attackers to bring supplies and reinforcements to the beleaguered outpost. Following the peace, the latter vessel, now renamed *Victory*, connected Detroit to Niagara (Porteous 1939, 90n). A sister ship, the schooner *Gladwin*, was placed under the command of Captain Patrick Sinclair, and provided regular service to Michilimackinac from its home port at Fort Sinclair (now St. Clair, Michigan; Carver 1976, 69). The connection from Detroit across the St. Clair Flats to Fort Sinclair still required transportation in the French fashion, by loading passengers and cargo onto canoes or shallow-draft bateaux plied by local *habitants* (Porteous 1939, 90; Carver 1976, 69).

These maritime taskscapes formed transport zones intersecting at transit points, where the transition from one vessel type to another entailed the unloading and reloading of cargo and passengers (Westerdahl 1996). Each transport zone (open water, coastal, estuarine, inland river) is dominated by a functional boat type, which comes to characterize that type of zone (Westerdahl 1992, 11). This sequence of transport zones, using ships linked by boats, created a transitional hybridized corridor that lasted for at least the first two decades of British rule. It was necessarily awkward, as attested by complaints of missed connections and lost or strayed boats (Porteous 1939). From his 1765 description of his route through the Flats to Fort Sinclair, it is evident that trader John Porteous's small fleet of bateaux followed the Old South Channel: the shortest distance but well-known for the sandbar at its mouth impeding larger vessels (Campbell 1762; Carver 1781, 150).

Movement toward a continuous ship-based transport corridor between Niagara and Michilimackinac was accelerated by the outbreak of the American Revolution. Although the upper Great Lakes were not initially an active theater of war, the British government responded to the potential threat to its lucrative fur trade and strategic route to the interior. To defend from attack by land, they built Fort Lernoult on the heights above Detroit where Pontiac had once positioned his besiegers. Their maritime defense included arming all merchant vessels operating under contract to the Crown and restricting all trade to those ships (Ericson 1969, 97).

The Provincial Marine, as this improvised navy was called, included the sloop *Welcome*, whose log has fortunately survived. Between August of 1779 and October of 1781, *Welcome* transited the Flats no less than ten times, clearing the bar at the mouth of the South Channel without incident in only three cases, one of which was downbound with an assisting current. All the other groundings required some combination of nautical practices: lightering, shifting cargo temporarily onto boats; kedging, propelling the ship by repeatedly placing its anchor at a distance using a ship's boat and winching the ship forward using its capstan; or warping, similar to kedging, where towlines were attached instead to trees or other objects on shore. A true emergency might require jettisoning the ship's ballast or cargo.

During its operations on the Flats, the *Welcome* assisted sister ships *General Gage*, *Felicity*, and *Wyandotte* in similar straits, in the last case careening—tilting the hull onto timbers—and using tackle to skid the little sloop across the bar (*Welcome* 1779–81). In two notable instances, after successfully freeing itself from the bar at the mouth of the South Channel, *Welcome* abandoned the attempt to cross and instead bore away northwest to chance the mouth of the North Channel. The entry for Tuesday, July 18, 1780, notes that "having miss'd the [South] Channel got aground—hove off and passed by [way of] the North Channel in 8 foot water."

This observation—that the North Channel route, while slightly longer, was apt to be more easily navigable—proved crucial when hostilities ceased. So long as Britannia ruled the waves of the Great Lakes by naval might, the square-rigged, full-keeled vessels of the Provincial Marine possessed the requisite crew power to muscle their way through the bottleneck at the Flats. The chief tactical virtue of the square-rigged ship with its many sails was that it was more difficult to disable in combat (Labadie and Murphy 1987, 27). In the competitive commercial environment that finally ensued in peacetime, however, both time and labor were costly. The labor-intensive process of maneuvering a square-rigger became prohibitively expensive. This was especially so in sailing the confined waters of the Great Lakes with their frequent changes of course and wind compared to the open sea, where a ship might hold its course for days on end.

Gradually, the cost-effective fore-and-aft schooner design prevailed but at a cost of its own. Between the belated British turnover of Detroit and Mackinac in 1796 and the return of war in 1812, an uneasy and short-lived peace settled on the Flats. A remarkable account from this brief interval features the British merchant schooner *Hope*, which ran hard aground in October of 1805 while trying to negotiate the treacherous Elbow at the entrance to the North Channel. It remained stranded for three days until assisted by an American vessel that graciously lightered it over the bar (Hughes 1895). Improved maneuverability alone did not guarantee success; sometimes the extra manpower was needed after all.

What made the North Channel route workable was Anchor Bay. Positioned in the northwest corner of Lake St. Clair, the aptly named bay benefited sailors in three ways. First, it offered anchorage during periods of calm or of winds from the north or east. At such times, sailing simultaneously against the current and a headwind became impossible. Second, its sheltered position was ideal for the process of lightering cargo into boats. Third, the confined waters of Lake St. Clair were prone to *seiches*—in Great Lakes usage, any sudden rise in the water of a harbor or a lake (Considine, 2008; Jensen 2019, 45).[2] In the case of Anchor Bay, this was produced by south or southwesterly winds, pushing the waters of the shallow lake northward into Anchor Bay and deepening the passage at the Elbow (Cole 1903, 13; Ibrahim and McCorquodale 1985). Such winds simultaneously created the two conditions that permitted fully laden ships to proceed upriver: enough water to enter the North Channel without grounding or lightering and the very wind needed to sail thence upriver—first east along the North Channel to the main channel at Pointe aux Chênes ("oak point"; present-day Algonac), then north toward Lake Huron.

This generally cemented the practice of commercial ships using the North Channel as the "New Ship Channel," which is indeed how it appeared on the Bayfield chart of 1817 (map 8). The South Channel, identified only as the "Old Ship Channel," showed the same soundings at its mouth as in Thomas's chart of 1809, six-and-a-half feet. The depth at the bar of the North, or "New Ship Channel," was now marked at seven-and-a-half feet versus Thomas's ten feet. This disparity may partially be explained by the notation that appears in the legend on the Bayfield chart: "The vessels lighter to pass the Bar, on which the depth of water varies *according to the seasons, and also on diff't years, to*

2 Champlain had noted the occurrence of seiches in Georgian Bay. His map of 1653 notes an ebb and flow (*flux et reflux*) in precisely the area where it could be expected in a west wind.

the amount of 2 or 3 feet" (Bayfield 1817; emphasis added). It may be that the British Admiralty chart office responsible for this wording was unfamiliar with the phenomenon of freshwater seiches and misinterpreted Vidal—and possibly Bayfield as well—in accounting for the difference of two-and-a-half feet between their two soundings of the North Channel bar. It is certainly true that the lake level varies seasonally and yearly as described by Bayfield. Vidal offers sufficient reason to presume, however, that local mariners were well aware that a southerly wind temporarily brought deeper water to Anchor Bay as well as a favoring breeze.

At the same time as they were gaining knowledge of the water's behavior, mariners were learning more about the shape of the bottom. Unlike his rendering of the approaches to the other, seldom-used channels, Bayfield's 1817 chart of Anchor Bay and the North Channel shows greater attention to bathymetric detail: soundings throughout the bay and a pair of contour lines outlining the Elbow, where the natural channel curves dramatically from north to southeast (map 8). By 1817, there had been a crucial advance in the navigational infrastructure: the Elbow, Bayfield noted, was now "staked every spring" in an effort to avert the fate that regularly befell schooners like the *Hope* in 1805 (Bigsby 1850, 299).

The growing ship-based commerce now using this route as the transport zone of choice created a need for such ancillary services. An opportunistic maritime industry developed at points of need, particularly in Anchor Bay and along the North Channel. Lightering cargoes, aiding grounded vessels, provisioning becalmed or storm-bound sailors, maintaining the stakes and buoys outlining the channel—these practices formed the nucleus of the localized maritime industry and its infrastructure that evolved in the Flats (Rogers 1955, 36). Summing up the repertoire of maritime practices employed by the British during their colonial period, those involving *propulsion* included

- the hybrid transport network, bridging the St. Clair delta using small craft;
- lightering vessels to cross the bars at the mouths of the channels;
- freeing grounded vessels by towing them off the bar with rowed boats;
- kedging off the bar by deploying an anchor from a ship's boat;

- warping against a current using a towline fixed to objects along shore; and
- utilizing weather conditions, particularly seiches, to enter the North Channel.

Practices involving *navigation* complemented the foregoing:

- surveying the mouths of the delta's channels to determine optimal routes
- marking and following the surveyed routes using regularly maintained stakes

Despite their best efforts, the British colonial maritime network, like that of the French before them, strained to keep pace with increasing demand. Bulk commodities like corn required larger vessels, and the critical choke point remained the St. Clair River and its delta. At times, scores of ships lay trapped in Anchor Bay or along the length of the river. Sailing upstream was slow and uncertain. The attendant delays, transfers, groundings, and collisions were costly.

The colonial British maritime identity, like the French, is twofold, divided along lines that are evidenced in the hybridized transport zones that developed along the Huron-Erie strait. Independent merchants like John Porteous, trading between New York and Mackinac, emulated the logistics of Indigenous and French traders, opportunistically buying or renting small craft as needed, transferring their goods when possible to and from ships of the Provincial Marine. Those aboard Crown or Provincial Marine vessels, by contrast, took their behavioral cues from the naval model, as evidenced by the survey reports of Robinson and Brehm and the logbooks of the vessels *Welcome* and *Hope*: mission-oriented, coordinated with military command structure, discipline, and resources.

Travelers' Tales: Maritime Practice in the Early Nineteenth Century

As Great Lakes shipping shifted from naval to commercial practice, the conditions faced by American and Canadian mariners continued to pose obstacles nearly as great as the opportunities afforded by the opening of the frontier to the west. At the outset of the nineteenth century, the maritime landscape continued to determine where and when one could move, as it had for decades previous. It is a commonplace to credit technology with revolutionizing transportation in the nineteenth century: the steamboat and the railroad in particular. For that revolution to succeed, however, a great deal had to be accomplished first by adaptations in practice, as mariners addressed the constraints of the St. Clair Flats with old and new tools and techniques. Navigation in the St. Clair maritime landscape began as inauspiciously for the American and Canadian mariners as it had for the British tars who repeatedly ran aground aboard the sloop *Welcome* four decades previous. A handful of accounts, spanning the decade between 1830 and 1840 highlight the evolution in nautical practice between the ages of sail and steam.

Virtually the entire behavioral repertoire of transiting the Flats under sail can be found in Chandler Gilman's 1835 journal entry for Sunday, August 30, 1835. A physician and attorney on a pleasure tour, he provides an account so authentic and vivid that it merits reading in its entirety:

> For awhile our "White Pigeon" flew over the waves of Lake St. Clair at a merry rate, before a favouring gale, but ere we gained the opposite shore, we experienced the fickleness of the changeful breeze; the wind hauled round, first abaft the beam, then abeam, then on our quarter, and finally near dead ahead. The schooner, however, was well calculated for beating, and hugged the wind closely. In this way we approached the mouth of the St. Clair river. Here the lake is very shoal, and the channel, in which there is only about nine feet water, very intricate. As we drew full nine feet, our advance was almost hopeless; though owing to a change in the direction of the channel, our course was not quite so near the wind. Captain N——, who is an excellent pilot, and familiar with every crook and turn in the channel, determined to make a bold push for the river;

he accordingly placed one of his best seamen, a fine stout Canadian, at the helm, and himself mounted the fore gaff to look out for the channel and give the word. A man was stationed at either quarter to heave the lead, and we advanced. The wind was heavy, so that we drove through the water very fast.

Before long we began to feel that the keel touched, and looking astern, could see the muddy water eddying round our rudder. Still, we kept onward. Every now and then the leadsman on one side or the other would sing out, "Six," and once "five half feet;" showing that his side was already out of the channel. Now we approach the Elbow; the Captain cries, "Luff! luff!" the man at the helm bent his whole strength to the tiller when, snap! It broke short, close to the rudder head. Of course the vessel was utterly unmanageable, and swung right across the narrow channel, pushing her stern deep into the mud. The Captain, who had flown to the deck, set about making a new tiller, and in an hour 'twas done. The anchor was now put out ahead, the vessel was lightered aft (she was too deep there), and finally they succeeded in heaving her off. We had the more occasion to rejoice at our escape as we passed the schooner—at anchor, taking in her lading from a lighter alongside. She had been aground three days, and after many fruitless efforts to get off, the captain was obliged to send to Detroit for a lighter. (Gilman 1836, 61–63)

Two years later one James Logan, a Scottish attorney, journeyed through the Great Lakes. His two trips through the St. Clair River typify the extremes that travelers might experience. Initially bound downstream aboard an unnamed steamboat, his passage was without incident, scarcely mentioned in his memoir. Returning upstream was a different story: aboard the schooner *Benjamin Barton*, he, like Gilman two years before (and Hennepin even earlier), recites the familiar litany of every problem that a sailing vessel could encounter: delayed by contrary winds, aground in the Flats, lightered by a hired boat, repeatedly becalmed. Finally, it was towed by a passing steamer, evidently the *General Gratiot*, which had commenced service on that route in 1831. Nearing the rapids at the entrance to Lake Huron, the *Barton* was struck by a downbound schooner, with considerable damage to its bow. Repairs were quickly made at "the village at the mouth of the Black River," today known as

Port Huron, indicating that an entrepreneurial maritime industry had sprung up at this site of cargo transfers—and collisions (Logan 1871, 70–72).

Opportunism was the watchword on the frontier and perfectly describes the birth of the towing industry. We may never know the identities of the first ships involved—the steamboat that did the towing, or the sailing ship that was towed—but it probably was not unlike the earliest documented case I have found, a decade after *Walk in the Water* brought steam navigation to the upper Great Lakes in 1820. The Massachusetts-born Anglican clergyman Calvin Colton, aboard the new steamer *Sheldon Thompson*, related his passage through the Flats on August 4, 1830, in his memoirs. Their approach to the Elbow was inauspicious: "About four o'clock, p.m.," he noted, "we found ourselves, hard upon what may be called, with the greatest propriety, the *Delta* of the river St. Clair, which discharges itself by about *fifty* mouths into the lake of the same name. The principal navigable channels are *five*" (Colton 1833, 60, emphasis in original). Apart from his exaggeration of the number of mouths, Colton rendered a detailed and insightful account of what followed once the steamer had freed itself:

> The rest of the night from nine in the evening, till four in the morning, was industriously occupied in running twenty-five miles to Fort Gratiot, having the double obstacle of a stiff current to stem, equal to a rapid, and a schooner in tow, which with us, was bound for the Upper Lakes. If this vessel in tow could not classically be called an obstacle, it was at least a grave Saxon *hold back*.[3] But nevertheless, as the master of the steamer was sure of our money, there seemed no objection in his mind to get a little more, for helping this weather-bound ship; although he had never stipulated with us for the privilege. And besides, if it was not an act of humanity, it was a kindness—it being understood, that vessels, upward bound, are often detained in this current, not only days, but weeks, before a strong south wind springs up, sufficiently strong to bear them into Lake Huron. (Colton 1833, 63–64; emphasis in original)

3 The derivation of this term is uncertain. It may refer to an impediment in Anglo-Saxon law, as to a marriage or other contract, applied facetiously by Colton, a cleric.

Also aboard the *Sheldon Thompson* that day was former New York senator James M'Call, on a mission from President Jackson to mediate a tribal dispute in Wisconsin: "Notwithstanding the strength of the current," M'Call wrote in his journal, "the steam Boat towed a Vessel of 50 Tons burthen into the lake, although the current is at a rate of 5 or 6 miles an hour" (M'Call 1892, 182).[4] It appears clear that the arrangement was informal and may by then have become routine practice, the captain of the *Sheldon Thompson* sensibly taking advantage of the occasion to do well by doing good.

Last, the American author Eliza Steele, aboard the steamboat *Constellation* in 1840, described the towing of two becalmed sailing vessels in the St. Clair River above the Flats: the brigs *Milwaukie* and *Rocky Mountain*. Noteworthy is her description of the towing arrangement: rather than rigging a towline astern, the steamer lashed its two companion vessels abeam along either side (Steele 1841, 94, 97). In the broad expanse of the river, the width of this arrangement evidently did not pose the problems that it would have in the narrower channels of the Flats and may, in the experience of the captain, have afforded a greater measure of control (Warner 1998, 50). Sailing vessels on towlines were frequently reported as veering off course, often resulting in collisions with passing vessels or even their own escort.

From such casual beginnings the towing industry soon escalated as more vessels, both sail and steam powered, began to crowd the Strait. Then as now, time was money, and soon a second generation of powerful, purpose-built tugboats capable of taking a string of several schooners from Lake Erie to Lake Huron in a matter of hours rather than days became a common sight (Barry 1973, 124; Warner 1998, 46). In time, a third-generation towing industry emerged as more seaworthy towboats, designed to push their barges the entire length of their journey across the open waters of the big lakes, proved cost-effective. The transition to "consort towing" by fleets of dedicated towboats and barges was complete (Dappert 2006, 26).

4 M'Call's journal entry illustrates the then-current practice of referring to sailing ships as "Vessels," and steam-powered watercraft as "Boats" (Warner 1998, 55n). This can be useful in interpreting contemporary documents, as seen in the passage from the *Democratic Free Press* of 1831 in the following chapter.

Despite the apparent paradox, steam power actually allowed sailing to remain cost-effective for decades due largely to the nature of the Strait. While rightly characterized as the greatest impediment to navigation in the upper Great Lakes, it is only eighty miles long in a maritime network of routes totaling many hundreds of miles. Once free of the Strait, a schooner, crewed by fewer than a half-dozen, could transport bulk commodities slowly but economically, leaving passengers and time-sensitive freight to the steamers. The symbiotic relationship that developed between sail and steam, centered at the former's weakest point, prolonged the Age of Sail on the Great Lakes into the early twentieth century—well beyond that of the saltwater sailing fleet (Lewis 2015, 361).

An additional localized maritime practice deserves a brief mention: a second hybridized transport zone developed in the Strait, this one linking the steamboat and the railroad. From railheads in Port Huron and Sarnia, purpose-built railcar ferries of the Grand Trunk Railroad system closed the narrow gap between southeast Michigan and southwest Ontario in 1879, a dozen years before the St. Clair Tunnel spanned the river in 1891, followed by a rail tunnel under the Detroit River in 1910.

Great Lakes commercial maritime practice emerges as inventive, entrepreneurial, improvisational, opportunistic—attributes associated with survival in a frontier setting and in a period of rapid change. Westerdahl offers a remarkable indicator of maritime identity—the occurrence of nautical terms in colloquial use within seafaring communities (Westerdahl 1994, 265). Witness the popular British writer Anna Jameson, whose fine ear for dialogue repeatedly caught the novel idiom of steam, even in reference to the Panic of 1837: "I was amused at Detroit," she wrote in her journal of that year, "to find the phraseology of the people imbued with metaphors taken from the most familiar mode of locomotion. 'Will you take in wood?' signifies, will you take refreshment? 'Is your steam up?' means, are you ready? The common phrase, 'go ahead,' has, I suppose the same derivation. A witty friend of mine once wrote to me not to be lightly alarmed at the political and social ferments in America, nor mistake the *whizzing of the safety valves for the bursting of the boilers!*" (Jameson 1838, 7; emphasis in original).

The American ascendancy in North America is inseparable from the concurrent Industrial Revolution, but it was not mere technology that made it possible (Cain and Hopkins 1980). The evolution of towing is clearly among the most decisive developments in Great Lakes nautical practice in the nineteenth century, but it did not occur in a vacuum, nor did it emerge full-blown. Many factors had to align before the landscape of the Flats was transformed from a scene of dozens of schooners lying impatiently at anchor to one of hundreds of tugs and their tows streaming up and down a broad shipping channel. In the next chapter, this presents itself as a scaled-up manifestation of the "cascade model of invention" (Schiffer 2010, 57), applied not simply to a solitary technological innovation but to an entire landscape.

7

A Cascade of Contingencies

The Disruptive Nineteenth Century

The Milwaukie and Chicago papers are urging the necessity of speedy action in regard to improving the navigation of the St. Clair Flats. The Chicago Journal *says: "The remarkable, irregular rise and fall of water in the lakes, apparently independent of prevailing winds, lead many of our oldest seamen to apprehend a continued fall of water till it comes down, on the Flats, viz: six feet. Should this anticipation be realised, it would cut off from all participation in the upper lake trade all the steamboats and sail vessels which we have hitherto been accustomed to welcome to our wharves." The delay and expense experienced by our mariners during the last season, in getting across these Flats, can scarcely be estimated. This is an enormous evil, and no time should be lost in devising and applying the proper remedy. The object sought is of national concernment, scarcely less important to New York and New England, than it is to Michigan, Indiana, Illinois and Wisconsin.*

—*Democratic Free Press* (Detroit), February 3, 1846

Disruption and Innovation: The Twin Engines of Invention

By the mid-nineteenth century it was obvious that no amount of local knowledge and patience could solve the problems posed by the St. Clair Flats. Necessity being the mother of invention, a unique and intricate sequence of innovations led to its transformation from a literal backwater to an industrialized international waterway. Driven by economic and political disruptions, together with innovations in nautical technology and maritime practice, the modernization of the Huron-Erie strait altered the entire Great Lakes maritime network. The trajectory of the process describes an arc of successive events connected by a relationship of *contingency*. Each development occupied a decisive historical moment, itself a product of preceding events and a necessary condition for those that followed. Collectively, they comprise the causal chain that fell into place, domino-like, to produce a transformative effect. Applied to seminal inventions of the Industrial Revolution such as steam power or the telegraph, such causally linked events have been likened to a cascade (Schiffer 2010, 141). As with those specific technologies, incremental solutions to large-scale problems within the maritime landscape stimulated diverse bursts of innovation that flowed, waterfall-like, into general use.

The worst problems of the Great Lakes transport system were all present in the Flats in deadly combination. Narrow, unstable, and poorly marked channels; unreliable propulsion; inefficient practices; lax navigational rules; and inadequate ship-to-ship communications led to innumerable groundings and collisions—all in a restricted space prone to blockages. No single innovation, however revolutionary, would be sufficient to transform the Flats into a safe and efficient commercial waterway. Piecemeal collectives of humans and things had to be conceived, invented, financed, tested, improved, legislated, mobilized, combined, attempted, proven, standardized, and accepted. Nothing short of a cascade—perhaps on this scale "avalanche" would be the better term—could provide the required momentum. Not surprisingly, decades sometimes passed before significant progress was achieved.

Unlike those of the preceding French and British eras, the ideologies driving the new processes of postcolonial landscape transformation were those not of imperialism and mercantile economics but of national expansion and industrial capitalism. The emergent North America of the first half of the nineteenth century was the scene of competing Anglophone nation-states. While an atmosphere of neighborly rivalry could stimulate progress, one of hostility could not. The strategic Huron-Erie Strait could assume its modern identity as an urbanized political borderland and multidimensional transaction zone if the risk of war were permanently eliminated.

Peace and Promise: The "Era of Good Feeling"

In the aftermath of the War of 1812, despite an atmosphere of lingering suspicion that pervaded both Washington and Whitehall, peace and prosperity characterized the Monroe presidency (1817–24). In this "Era of Good Feeling," as it was dubbed, two remarkable instances of Anglo-American cooperation occurred: first, the formulation of the Rush-Bagot agreement of 1817; and second, the work of the International Boundary Commission. Under the terms of the former, the waters of the upper Great Lakes were effectively demilitarized, with both powers held to a limited number of gunboats and shoreline fortifications. This political sine qua non was achieved largely on the strength of the personalities of the negotiators, the American Secretary of State Richard Rush and British minister plenipotentiary Sir Charles Bagot (Stevens 1989, 51; Fitzpatrick 1917, 13). Although tensions occasionally arose along the border, notably in connection with Canada's Rebellion of 1837 and the American Civil War, the pacified status of the lakes provided the conditions under which both commerce and migration could flourish (Blois 1838, 107).

The International Boundary Commission, created under the terms of the Treaty of Ghent (1814), fielded a total of four bilateral teams, each responsible for a portion of a line that would run from Passamaquoddy Bay on the Atlantic to Lake of the Woods, deep in the North American continent (Carroll 2001). For the team charged with the boundary from the St. Lawrence River to Sault Ste. Marie, the St. Clair Flats posed multiple challenges. The first was to perform an accurate survey in a marshy landscape that was not only confusing and changeable but hazardous to health. The second was to determine the "true" channel of the St. Clair River through its delta on the presumption that the boundary would follow the midline of that channel. As it happened, there was a third task—to convince both the British and the American governments to agree on the boundary they would propose.

Given postwar tensions, it is surprising that the Commission arrived at the conclusion that the boundary should run along the center of the South Channel (Carroll 2004, 89). As with the diplomats Rush and Bagot, the decision reached says much about the temperament of the agents on the scene. The American, Major Joseph Delafield, and his British counterpart, Dr. John J. Bigsby, were already acquaintances, sharing a passion for geology that likely figured in the former's recommendation of his colleague (Carroll 2001, 106). Their decision seems remarkable considering the then-apparent natural advantages of the North Channel and its status as the preferred, and presumptive official, navigational route by both British and American mariners. That outcome had seemed certain, given the labeling of the North Channel on Thomas Smith's 1809 chart as "River St. Clair, which divides U[pper] Canada from the U[nited] States" (map 7). Delafield appeared to concur in his journal entry for July 21, 1820: "The ship channel or best one," he wrote, "is West of all the islands, and next to the American shore," implying that the North Channel was not only the preferred shipping route but the international boundary as well. Observing the Elbow and its charting, Delafield allowed that "the channel is very circuitous, and marked out by stakes on either side" (Delafield 1943, 281; also Bigsby 1850, 299).

The physician Bigsby quickly formed an ill opinion of Anchor Bay—literally. His journal entry that began chapter 2 describes a likely case of malaria in the survey crew. Treated by Bigsby using "bleeding and other appropriate remedies," fortunately including quinine, the lieutenant recovered sufficiently for the party to quit the "pestilential spot" for an island across the South Channel, then called St. Mary's but now known as Walpole Island (Bigsby 1850, 298).

Whether Bigsby's account of the North Channel passage was sufficient to sway the British contingent toward allowing the Americans the "pestilential" islands west of the South Channel cannot be known for certain. There were at least two contemporaneous developments that, to an alert observer, might have suggested that the "Old Ship Channel"—that is, the South Channel, might one day become *the* ship channel again. One of these was the canal-building craze that had already swept Britain late in the previous century and by 1820 was poised to do the same in the eastern United States. Excavation of the Erie Canal had already begun in 1817. Its completion in 1825, and the addition of the Welland Canal in 1829, would remove the obstacle to navigation heretofore posed by the Niagara Escarpment. Conquering the Falls would thus place pressure on the St. Clair Flats as the sole remaining impediment to navigation between the Atlantic and Lakes Huron and Michigan. Access to the strategic frontier outpost at Fort Dearborn—the future site of Chicago, with its proximity to the Mississippi drainage—hung in the balance. Surely the enterprise and initiative that could overcome Niagara could open the existing channels of the Flats to proper ships. In such an atmosphere, anything seemed possible, including a canal through the Flats. However, unlike the Erie Canal, where propulsion relied on its towpath, that alone would not remove the remaining impediments to sailing—contrary winds and a strong current.

A second critical innovation would have been even more obvious to the Boundary Commission, as they themselves had not only seen the future but been aboard it. The first steamboat on the upper Great Lakes, *Walk in the Water*, had been launched in 1818, while the Commission was already at work. Delafield, aboard the schooner *Red Jacket*, describes posting his dispatches "on board the steam boat" on at least two occasions (Delafield 1943, 275). The implications inherent in a vessel that could make its way against a current, unaffected by contrary or absent winds, and that could follow a narrow channel precisely, not needing to tack or alter course to make headway, must have been abundantly clear. By offering the shorter and straighter route, the South Channel, once excavated to a passable depth, appeared destined to supplant the North as the route of choice. Were the South Channel to lie wholly within Upper Canada, the British could be held entirely responsible for its improvement and maintenance while obliged by treaty to allow the Americans its use.

Perhaps in anticipation of this foreseeable future, the commissioners deviated from accepted practice and recommended the centerline of the South Channel as the international boundary. In doing so, they bisected the delta into roughly equal halves. The conditions were now in place for the ensuing cascade of technological innovations and economic disruptions—and political doldrums.

Innovation: The Arrival of Steam

The steamboat *Walk in the Water*, first of its kind to visit Detroit in 1818 and to traverse the Flats the following season, was laid out along traditional schooner lines (figure 3), drawing 8′6″ of water. Lamentably, there appear to be no surviving official records or passenger accounts mentioning its transits of the Flats on its annual round trips to the Straits of Mackinac. This argues in favor of the trips having been uneventful, likely by careful timing and execution. Given the greater charted depth and marking stakes of the North Channel, it is likely that, like sail traffic, it used the "New Ship Channel" through Anchor Bay, being able to pursue its course more accurately.[1]

Like all early steamboats powered by as-yet inefficient and unreliable engines, *Walk in the Water* also carried a proper two-masted schooner rig. While this made it less dependent on a favoring wind for propulsion, it would certainly have benefited from the additional water depth in Anchor Bay provided by a fresh southerly breeze. The chief advantage of a steam-propelled vessel in a restricted channel, however, was its maneuverability. Given a well-marked channel of sufficient depth, a steam-powered vessel could reach Lake Huron in a fraction of the time spent by sailing vessels waiting for wind, water, or both.

The pressing issues for commercial shipping thus became the accurate surveying and marking of the shifting navigable channels of the Flats and the improvement of those channels, especially the shallow bars at their mouths. In the event, neither of these breakthroughs came quickly or easily. The United States government, overwhelmed by the demands of its rapidly expanding frontier, had not yet developed the organizational capacity to perform detailed hydrologic surveys on a grand scale. And digging a canal across dry land, while slow and arduous as in the case of the Erie and Welland Canals, at least did not pose the problems of excavating underwater. It was not until 1838 that the first

1 In his description of passing through the Flats aboard *Superior* in 1831, English barrister Godfrey Vigne makes it clear that the ship used the North Channel, noting that the islands were on his right (Vigne 1833, 139). *Superior*, built in 1822, was good-sized for her day: 346.4 tons, 126′6″ long, 28′8″ abeam, and drawing 10′6″—two feet more than *Walk in the Water*.

FIGURE 3. Steamboat *Walk in the Water* (1818–1921), first steamboat on the upper Great Lakes, by J. W. Stanton. (Wikimedia Commons)

of these issues was addressed administratively by the Bureau of Topographic Engineers (forerunner of the US Army Corps of Engineers), while another decade would pass before the challenge of open-water dredging had its key breakthrough (Larson 1981, 36, 50). Before that, a trio of developments served to disrupt the landscape of the Strait and to highlight the severity of the bottleneck at the Flats.

Disruption: The Opening of the Erie Canal

When the last of its eighty-one locks was completed in 1825, the Erie Canal literally opened the floodgates, both to trade and to migration. Its significance was well understood at the time by the ambitious young nation (Andrews 1853, 55). Suddenly the flow of settlers into the American heartland, together with the finished goods they demanded and the commodities they supplied in return, began to escalate (Sauer 1956, 65; Fuller 1916, 71). From a population of 9,000 in 1820, the Michigan Territory alone grew to 32,000 in 1830 and, following statehood in 1837, to 212,000 in 1840. Between 1837 and 1847, shipping through the Erie Canal increased by 150%, from 667,151 to 1,661,575 tons (US Bureau of the Census 1975). To accommodate this demographic and economic explosion, two innovations emerged—one in nautical design, the other in maritime practice.

Innovation: The Pivoting Centerboard

The Erie Canal brought more than a flood of settlers—it brought a novel ship design to the upper Great Lakes that substantially increased the carrying capacity of the St. Clair Flats in the decades preceding the arrival of the steam dredge. The notion was a simple one: if you can't deepen the water, make the ship shallower. Traditionally, this meant making the craft smaller in all its dimensions: length and beam as well as draft, with a resulting decrease in its volume and hence its payload.

The limiting design element was some form of keel: a projecting timber running the length of the hull that stabilizes the ship but at the cost of increasing its draft. As a ship moves forward in the water, its keel provides lateral resistance to prevent capsizing and a planar surface to keep it tracking forward efficiently, even in a crosswind. When operating in light winds, or when sailing downwind, the keel was less needed, even adding drag.

Realizing this, sailors and shipwrights had been experimenting for years with devices that could provide stability as needed. As the intellectual ferment of the Enlightenment matured into the technological explosion of the Industrial Revolution, novel designs began to appear. In his essay *Focusing on the Centerboard*, maritime historian Henry Barkhausen traced the origins and development of movable surfaces designed to improve the upwind efficiency of sailing craft. These devices fell into two types: those mounted outside the hull and those mounted inside. The former type—the *lee-board*, usually mounted in pairs amidships on either side—had been common in Dutch overseas shipping through the seventeenth century but by the eighteenth century was largely relegated to inland navigation along their canals (Barkhausen 1990, 5). Such a vessel was a good choice for the International Boundary Commission, charged with the survey of the Great Lakes. The *Red Jacket*, chartered by the American contingent, featured two large fan-shaped lee-boards that, when raised, allowed the schooner to negotiate waters as shallow as five feet.

The future, however, lay with an inboard design featuring a stout waterproof box, or trunk, installed amidships along the keel and open at the top and bottom. Through this sleeve-like opening, a retractable weighted centerboard could be raised or lowered as needed. In its earliest iterations, the board, then called a "sliding keel," was raised and lowered vertically. This arrangement survives as the daggerboard on recreational dinghies. It was the addition of a pivot, allowing the centerboard to swing in an arc within the centerboard trunk, that prevailed. With its centerboard fully retracted, and equipped with folding masts, a "canal schooner" could negotiate the four-foot depth and the low bridges of the Erie Canal while carrying a respectable payload. By the same token, a "centerboarder" could easily clear the bars at the mouth of either the North or South Channel of the St. Clair Flats.

This advantage was not lost on the shipbuilders that had begun to spring up along the St. Clair River in the early 1820s. In fact, the knowledge of this breakthrough arrived in advance of the canal schooners themselves. In 1824, the year before the Erie Canal opened, a builder named Gallagher launched the first centerboard schooner built in St. Clair County, the *St. Clair*, at Ward's Landing (later Marine City). Taking advantage of its design, its owner, Samuel Ward, in 1826 made the first downbound voyage from the upper lakes, through the Erie Canal, to New York (Andreas 1883, 432). The ability to clear the bar without lightering certainly improved efficiency. But so long as steamboats were few, and sailing ships had to wait for favoring winds, it seemed the Strait would remain a time-consuming obstacle to upbound shipping. The situation in 1830 had changed little since Father Hennepin's time as another man of the cloth, missionary Elisha Loomis, complained, "Still detained by unfavorable winds, I engaged a passage to Mackinaw in the Sch[ooner] *La Grange*, Capt. Dingy [Dingley], soon after my arrival here [at Detroit]. The vessel has been ready to sail only two days now and the wind is contrary. The current here is so strong that it is in vain to think of beating [tacking] up the river. So we must have patience" (Loomis 1953, 36). Fortunately for the virtuous reverend, deliverance was at hand.

Innovation: Birth of the Towing Industry

Numerous accounts confirm that the *Sheldon Thompson* towing incident, related in the previous chapter, soon became typical (Warner 1998; Lewis 2015). Within a year, the new steamer *General Gratiot* (figure 4) was hailed in Detroit: "It is the intention of the proprietors," enthused the local press, "to run her from this city to Mount Clemens, Fort Gratiot, River Raisin, Maumee &c. and to employ her also for towing vessels, [timber] rafts &c. A boat of this kind, and for these purposes, has long been wanted" (*Democratic Free Press* June 16, 1831, 2). From this it may be inferred that in 1831 the towing industry in the Strait was in its infancy. With the arrival of the *General Gratiot*, a new class of purpose-built vernacular watercraft emerged. While the Ohio-built *Sheldon Thompson* drew 9′4″ of water (and not surprisingly had found itself "hard upon the Delta"), the *General Gratiot* drew a mere 4′6″, less than the centerboard schooners it was designed to tow not just through the Flats but against the current of the entire Strait between Lake Erie and Lake Huron.

The further refinement of the screw- or propeller-driven craft (after which this class of vessel took its name "propeller") was a vast improvement in efficiency

FIGURE 4. Steamboat *General Gratiot*, built 1831 in Black River, Ohio. (C. Patrick Labadie Collection, Alpena County George N. Fletcher Public Library. Alpena, MI)

FIGURE 5. Propeller *Goliath*, built 1846, St. Clair, Michigan. Image: Robert J. McGreevy (C. Patrick Labadie Collection, Alpena County George N. Fletcher Public Library. Alpena, MI)

over the paddle-driven steamboat, permitting the practice of "consort" towing of several schooners or barges arranged in a line astern (Dappert 2006, 11). Towboats rapidly evolved as the pace and volume of shipping through the upper Great Lakes accelerated. The propeller *Goliath* (figure 5), first of its kind to be built in the St. Clair locale, typified what was to come: compact yet powerful, with twin screws driven by matched high-pressure engines. The trade-off was greater draft for propellers than paddle-wheelers. Before its 1846 launching could take place, another development would be required—one that would permit *Goliath*'s 9′ draft to maneuver more surely, if not altogether unimpeded, through the Flats.

Disruption: Captain Williams's Survey of 1842

Early nineteenth-century British surveys of the St. Clair delta display considerable accuracy in terms of key landforms: the shape of the shoreline, the islands, and the banks lining the North Channel. Their limited hydrographic data elsewhere, however, quickly proved inadequate to the challenges posed by new nautical technology. So long as the North Channel passage remained the preferred sailing route, field surveys focused primarily on Anchor Bay and the critical soundings of the Elbow. By comparison, Bayfield's 1817 rendering of the approach to the South Channel appears cursory (map 10). A single line of soundings projects directly from the mouth of the channel, encountering a bar at 6′ of water, compared to 7′ in the North Channel. As a result, the South Channel had remained the choice of shallow-draft mariners whose boats had no need of extra depth, benefiting instead from its shorter length. The ability of a steamboat to proceed directly upstream, even while towing schooners, revived interest in the more direct South Channel route—if it could be consistently transited.

In the absence of certain knowledge of its detailed structure, rumor and speculation—and a touch of larceny—flourished on the Flats. The *Milwaukee Advertiser* of July 6, 1839, announced,

> A correspondent of the *Detroit Advertiser*, in advocating an immediate survey of the lakes, mentions that one of our largest steamers was lately desirous of obtaining a pilot who was acquainted with the various

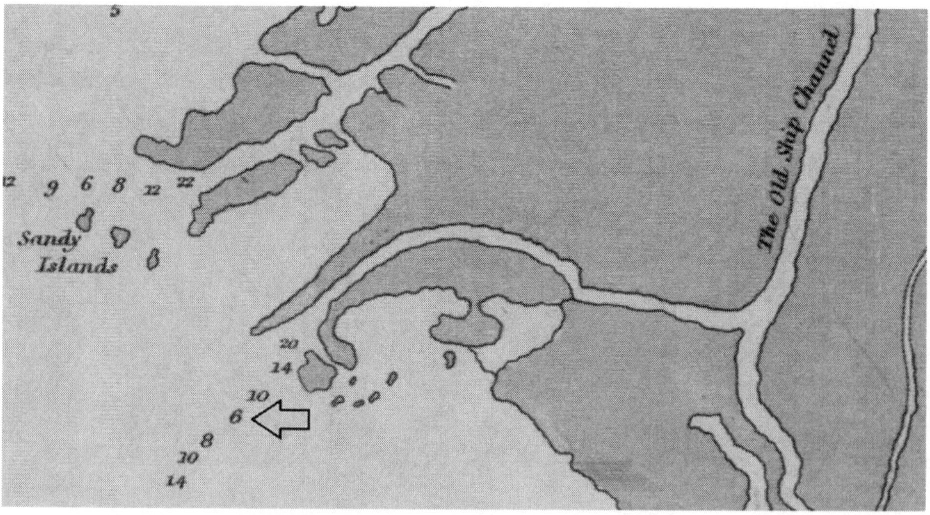

MAP 10. Mouth of the South Channel, Bayfield's 1817 chart of Lake St. Clair, detail. Note the single line of soundings proceeding directly southwest from the mouth of the channel. Arrow marks the supposed location of an obstructing bar. (Great Britain, Admiralty, Hydrographic Office)

> channels over the St. Clair Flats. One pilot said he knew of a channel having fourteen feet and another having 18 feet; but he asked a thousand dollars for showing it. The steamer *Great Western* offered $300 for a sight of the 14 and 18 feet channel, it is said. If there be any such channels it is highly desirable that they should be known. The only [i.e., North] channel now used has only nine and a half or ten feet in the shallowest point; and steamboats and vessel[s] of much draught have to exercise great care in the navigation of one or two miles over "the flats." Persons acquainted with Lake St. Clair express doubts of the existence of any such channels as that spoken of, but all concur in the opinion that an immediate and accurate hydrographic survey of the lakes is of great importance.

The challenge of revealing the submerged contours of the Flats was undertaken by an extraordinarily capable and visionary man, Captain William G. Williams of the Bureau of Topographic Engineers. While superintendent of harbor improvements for the southeast shore of Lake Erie, the hardy engineer had, in the winter of 1838–39, taken advantage of the lake's frozen surface to conduct a "geodesic survey" of the harbors of Buffalo and Black Rock, plotting an expansive system of reference points using triangulation. In a December 1841 report to his commanding officer Colonel John J. Abert, Williams proposed applying this method to the entirety of the upper Great Lakes, both the American and Canadian sides—commencing with "one point to which I beg leave to refer, as extremely important to the immediate interests of the commerce of the lakes—namely, the obstructions to navigation in Lake St. Clair" (Williams 1842a, 4). The following season, Williams conducted the first comprehensive survey of the American side of the delta, devoting equal attention to the North and South Channels.

In his initial report to Abert, Williams had advocated straightening the passage through Anchor Bay to the North Channel by dredging. His report of May 2, 1842, reiterated this position, urging the appropriation of no more than $20,000 to cover the cost of the work (Williams 1842b, 4). His chart of the North Channel had confirmed the complex hydrology of the Elbow (map 11), while that of the South Channel likewise revealed a bend of the submerged natural channel at its mouth (map 12). Where the current encountered the bar, its course was deflected first west-northwest, then southwest—a significant feature undiscovered by Bayfield's earlier, more cursory survey (map 10).

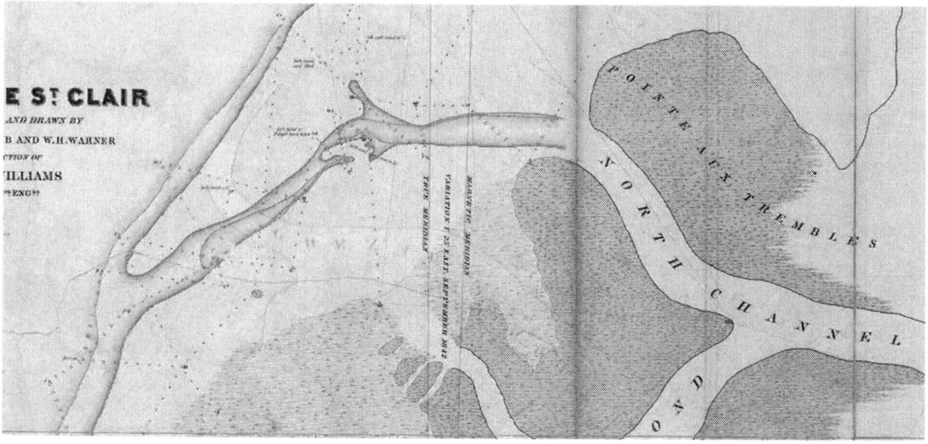

MAP 11. Mouth of the North Channel: detail of Williams's 1842 chart of the St. Clair delta, showing the notorious "Elbow." (Library of Congress)

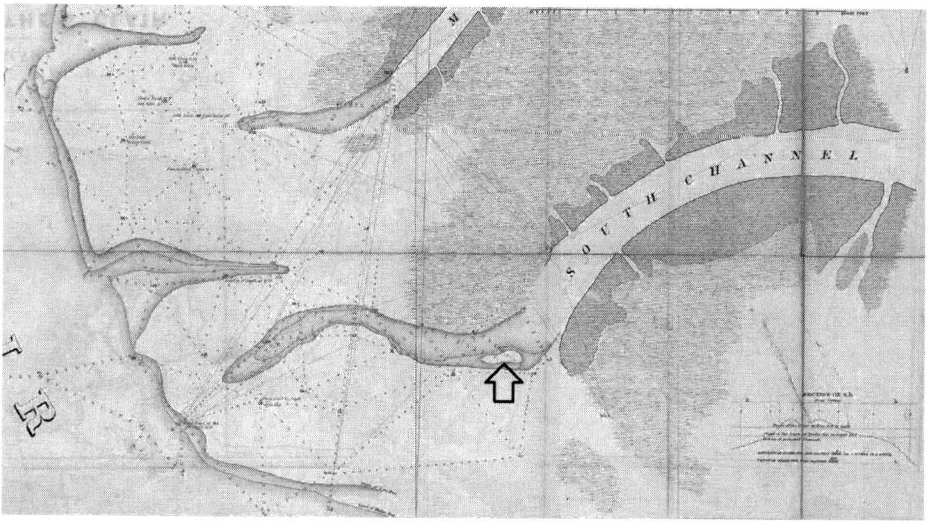

MAP 12. Mouth of the South Channel: detail of Williams's 1842 chart of the St. Clair delta, showing the curving natural approach to the South Channel. A comparison to map 10 shows how Bayfield's limited soundings missed this crucial feature by proceeding directly southwest, likely encountering the obstructing sandbar (arrow). (Library of Congress)

By December, Williams had switched his preference: "The north channel," he noted, "is the one which has been used by vessels; but it is very difficult, owing to a winding character. The south channel is that which I would recommend to be improved. It cuts off a distance of five miles, would require less excavation, and is in every respect more eligible" (Williams 1842c, 27). His revised rendering of the South Channel was submitted as an "Extract of a Map of the Delta of the St. Clair . . . with plans for its improvement" (map 13). He offered two options: the route labeled "A" on the chart simply followed the extant sweeping S-curve, while "B" drove straight through the apex of the outer bend to connect with a natural ravine. The second option would require more dredging but produce a straighter passage. In either case, the success of the project would depend on the technological ability to dredge a passage through the bar. Until that very literal breakthrough, no little amount of newsprint was expended in clamoring for a solution, as the commercial interests in Chicago, Milwaukee, and other nascent maritime communities along the upper lakes looked anxiously toward the delta and toward Washington, DC, where their fate, it appeared, was being decided as a matter of political gamesmanship.

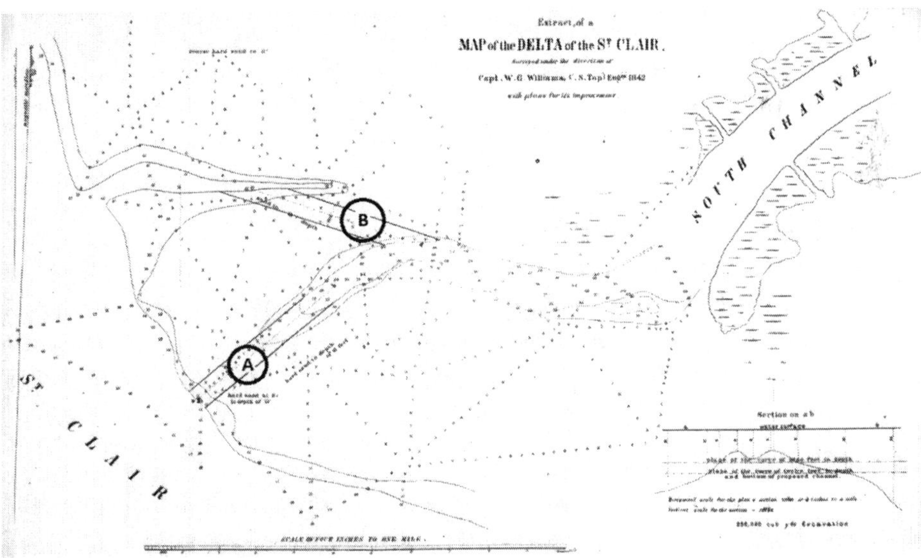

MAP 13. Plan for improvement of the South Channel: detail of Williams's revised chart (1842), proposing two options marked "A" and "B." Dredging of option "A" commenced in 1855. (Library of Congress)

Innovation: Mass Communications, Frontier Style

Although four centuries separate the invention of Gutenberg's printing press (1436) and Morse's telegraph (1844), the arrival of the two media on the American frontier was virtually simultaneous. Reports and rumors alike spread like wildfire in the charged environment of a commercial boom that depended on the health of the shipping industry. Once Williams's recommendations for the improvement of the Flats were public knowledge, the newspapers of the new Great Lakes cities became the vox populi of the commercial class. Much of our knowledge of this crucial phase in the transformation of the Flats from a place of doubt and danger to a safe and sheltered passage can be found in the pages of newspapers published between Buffalo and Chicago. The first issue that drew their attention was the need to know, almost on a daily basis, where the safe passages could be found—and if not improved, at least marked.

Innovation: Marking the Channel

The increase in the volume of shipping in the upper lakes was exacerbated by unusually low water levels in the mid-1840s. Repercussions were felt upstream, along the canals of New York: "If reports from Detroit may be credited," warned the *Jamestown Journal*, "the appropriation for the St. Clair Flats will be imperatively demanded. There are said to be but seven feet of water on the flats at the present" (*Jamestown Journal* April 24, 1846, 1). That same day, however, the *Milwaukee Sentinel* printed that "Capt. Allen, of the *Nile*, reports *nine* feet water on the St. Clair Flats. The *Nile* grounded for a while in coming up, but it was because she missed the channel, which has changed somewhat since last year" (*Milwaukee Sentinel* April 24, 1846; emphasis in original).

Clearly, if the channel was going to spontaneously change both its course and depth and dredging the St. Clair Flats, while "imperatively demanded," was not yet forthcoming, the private sector would have to look after its own interests. Just what those interests were, however, was a matter of perspective. The *Cleveland Plain Dealer* of May 14, 1846, reported that "the operation of staking out the channel of the St. Clair flats having been completed, we understand 8 feet 6 inches of water is the deepest channel that could be found. If this is so, it is evident most of our large class of boats and vessels will be obliged to light over." One week later, a reporter for the *Milwaukee Sentinel* noted that "the steamboat St. Clair now lying here [in Detroit], is to go upon the St. Clair Flats and aid in lightening vessels and boats over" (*Milwaukee Sentinel* May 22, 1846, 2). Already, a skeptic might wonder whether a local contractor had conveniently failed to mark the deepest passage, but there was worse to come.

The following spring, the *Cleveland Herald* announced, "it having been sufficiently understood from the course of the President, that the people have nothing to hope from the Government in the way of improving the harbors on the Lakes, and the St. Clair Flats," it fell to "private enterprise what belongs to the Government to do"—namely, "to mark out the channel so distinctly, that it may be passed in the night" (*Cleveland Herald*, March 17, 1847, 3). The stakes, financed by subscription, would be firmly set and topped with large painted barrels for added visibility. Perhaps shamed into action, Congress passed a lighthouse bill the following year, which included two lighthouses on the Detroit River and buoys for the St. Clair Flats (*Detroit Free Press*, August 24, 1848, 2). The buoys and their locations, described in an announcement by the Office of the Collector of Customs in Detroit dated April 2, 1849, made it clear in its references to the Elbow that the North Channel remained the preferred passage. The customs official, one C. G. Hammond, warned that "the expense of placing these buoys in position, and their value to the commercial interests, seem to justify the hope that Mariners will use all necessary caution to avoid their injury or displacement" (*Sandusky Register*, April 11, 1849, 2).

Alas, his words were not heeded, at least not at first. Perhaps this improvement did not sit well with the local operators engaged in the relief of grounded vessels: the following month, Hammond offered a $100 reward, to be paid on the conviction of offenders responsible for the disappearance of several of the new buoys "under circumstances inducing the belief that they were intentionally carried away" (*Detroit Free Press*, May 11, 1849, 3). Whether or not the miscreants were apprehended, Hammond's incentive and the righteous indignation of the shippers appear to have done their work. There were no reports of such incidents for exactly four years, when the issue resurfaced—with a pointed criticism of the local operators.

In the *Detroit Free Press* of May 5, 1853, Captain Alexander of the propeller *Bucephalus* reported under "Marine Intelligence," "Notice to boats and

Vessels crossing St. Clair Flats—In going up, the first stakes must be left one hundred feet on the starboard hand, where eleven feet of water will be found in the channel; but if left as has been the usual practice heretofore, of thirty or forty feet, only nine feet will be found. . . . If the Government pays for setting these stakes, why not let some disinterested man have the contract, and not one who makes towing and lighting over the Flats his only business—as there is one universal complaint from all who cross with large boats or vessels." Trusting private enterprise to look after its own interests was at best a two-edged sword, but relying on Washington had proven little better.

Innovation: The Steam-Powered Dredge

The federal government's obligations became the subject of endless newspaper stories, editorials, petitions to Congress, reports by the Topographic Engineers, and legislative bills during the period between the lake surveys of the 1840s, which exposed both needs and options, and the Civil War, which instantly diverted the Union's resources to the conflict. Once Williams's 1842 South Channel recommendation had become public, proposals for dredging took their place alongside those for marking the North Channel. As in the case of the stakes and buoys, inaction by the federal government led to private initiatives. When the *Milwaukee Sentinel* wrote on May 29, 1846, that "the government, we are happy to learn, has ordered the Steam Dredge, now fitting out in Erie Harbor, to Lake St. Clair, for the purpose of deepening the channel leading over the Flats," it failed to add that the dredge was merely on loan, and private enterprise was footing the bill.

The following year, Colonel Abert of the Topographic Engineers admitted to Congress that "the views of the general government upon this lake [St. Clair] having been limited to plans for improving the passage over the St. Clair Flats . . . surveys, plans and estimates have been made, but no appropriation has yet been granted. The pass over these flats is of extreme importance to the lake trade, and the embarrassment encountered there so serious, that during the course of last summer [1846], the Steamboat Association undertook, at their own expense, and with the use of the United States dredge boat, to open a passage of adequate depth over the flats; but their funds or arrangements were insufficient, and the work was abandoned" (Abert 1847, 42; also Larson 1981, 40). The failure of this effort to open a passage over what had been touted by Captain Williams as a relatively short distance, raises questions as to the nature of the South Channel bar, the effectiveness of the equipment used, and state of dredging technology at that time.

Continuing his report, Abert noted that, while unsuccessful, "the operations, however, developed an extremely interesting fact—that the flats were not a recent deposit, but consisted chiefly of an *indurated marl*. The removal of such a material is more difficult than the removal of recently deposited mud, and more costly; but the advantages in such an obstacle over a recent deposit are in the great probability that a passage, once opened, will remain open an indefinitely long period, requiring very little future work" (Abert 1847, 42; emphasis added). This echoed a comment made in Williams's initial report on the North Channel bar, where he opined that "the operation of dredging would be attended, I think, with success and permanent advantage. The marks of keels upon the bottom, where vessels have been dragged over the bar, are visible from year to year, showing a permanence in the character of the bottom, justifying every hope that the work once effected, would be lasting" (Williams 1842a, 4). This indicates that the bars across both the North and South Channels were composed of Abert's "indurated marl": a chalky clay-sand mixture of glacial sediments hardened by pressure from overlying depositions (Cole 1903).

Since the government boat had been capable of dredging the harbor at Erie, the bottom evidently resembled Abert's "recently deposited mud" more closely than the St. Clair delta. It would have employed the dredging technology of the time: a "bucket-and-ladder" design dating from mid-sixteenth-century Netherlands. A chain of scoops traveled along the length of a ladder-like suspended beam, its lower end winched into position along the bottom. The sediment thus raised was deposited into a waiting barge for disposal. Driven first by men on a treadmill, later by a team of horses, such "mud-mills" (*moddermolen*) both maintained the vital canals and provided dredge spoils for further dry land creation.

Characteristic of the Industrial Revolution, the British applied steam power to the device. In 1806, one Richard Trevithick mounted his invention aboard the gun brig *Blazer* (figure 6) for the purpose of "lifting mud at the entrance to the East and West India [Company] docks on the Thames" (Dickinson and Titley 1934, 81). A Scottish specimen of 1824, "at present employed in deepening the river Clyde, so as to admit of large vessels being brought up, does

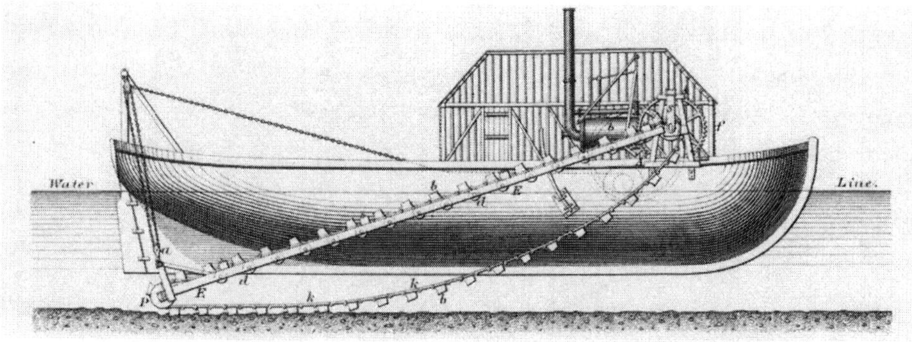

FIGURE 6. Trevithick's "Dredging Machine" aboard the *Blazer*, 1806. (Wikisource)

not differ so much in its construction from those employed in the Thames and Caledonian Canal" (*Glasgow Mechanics' Magazine*, September 25, 1824). Popularized during the British canal-building boom, the design crossed the Atlantic and entered the Great Lakes. As early as 1838, the removal of a bar at the mouth of the Clinton River was proposed to permit navigation by ships of up to eighty tons to Mt. Clemens, six miles upstream (Blois 1838, 329).[2]

A design adequate for "lifting mud," however, was insufficient to the task of carving a passage through the hardened clay of the St. Clair delta. A Great Lakes problem called for a Great Lakes solution. Abel Hawley of Milwaukee, a community with a vested interested in waterway improvement, was granted US Patent No. 5,743 on August 29, 1848, for his "Excavating Machine" (figure 7). It was a radical departure from the bucket-and-ladder design. Its single, heavy bucket showed promise of penetrating the dense clay that the scoops merely scratched, and removing it in substantial chunks. It was immediately put to the test on the Illinois and Michigan Canal which opened that same year, connecting Lake Michigan to the Mississippi drainage. Subsequent work on the Fox and Wisconsin Rivers and Milwaukee's harbor resulted in improvements

2 During the nineteenth century, registered shipping was generally reported in "gross tons," a figure derived by calculating the volume of the hull in cubic feet and dividing the result by thirty-five—the volume in cubic feet of a ton of seawater. Later in the century, as more accurate measures were standardized, both measures were usually given, the earlier being labeled "old style" tonnage and the newer, based on payload capacity, designated as "net" tonnage. For comparability, I have used "old style" throughout. While inaccuracies in individual vessels are inevitable, the trends indicated by the aggregated results are clear and reliable.

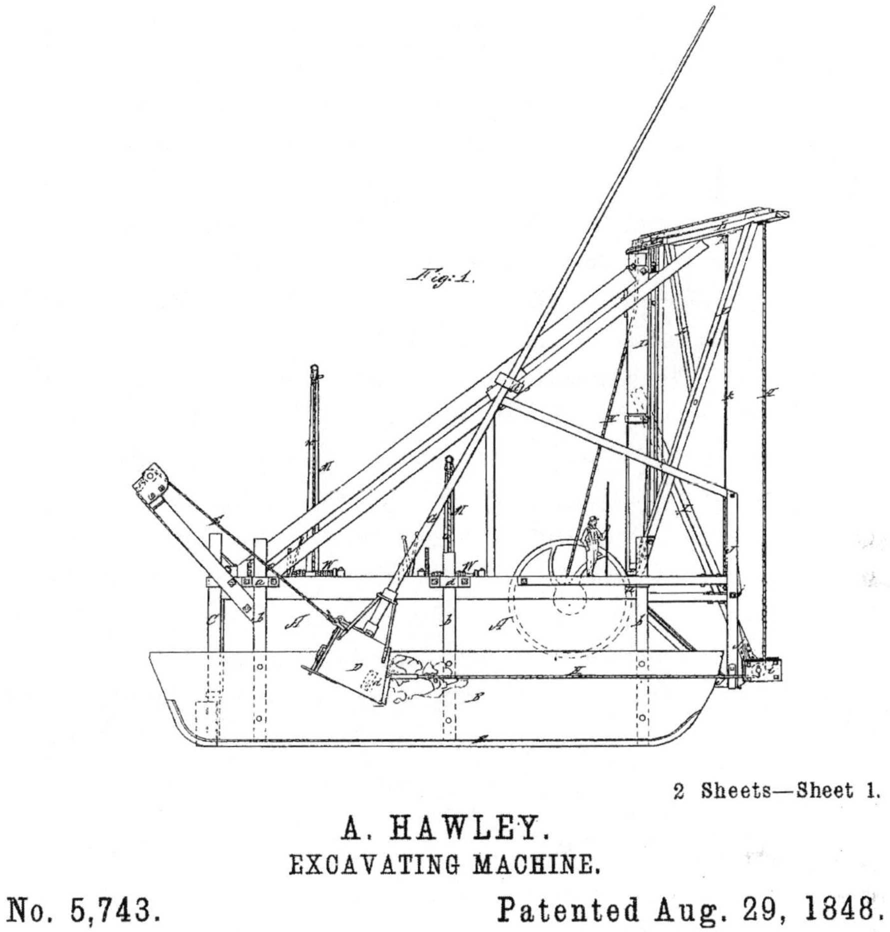

FIGURE 7. Hawley's "Excavating Machine," 1848. (US Patent Office)

to the design and a recommendation to Abert that the new device be tried on the Flats (Larson 1981, 50). In December 1852, Abert ordered a dredge to be built in Detroit by Hawley himself. Weather, labor disputes, and cost overruns delayed the work, but on September 1, 1853, Captain Augustus Canfield successfully tested the new device.

It was a victory, albeit a Pyrrhic one: the $19,500 spent to build the dredge had all but exhausted the $20,000 appropriated for the improvement of the Flats. In his annual report to Congress, Abert requested an additional $45,000 "for continuing the improvement of the St. Clair flats, Lake St. Clair: the importance of this improvement cannot be overestimated. The loss of time from lying around, and the expenses of towing and lightering occasioned by these obstructions, are very great and increasing" (Abert 1853, 12).

Abert's recommendations, incorporated into a comprehensive rivers and harbors bill of 1854, were vetoed by the South-sympathizing President Franklin Pierce as a benefit accruing primarily to Northern interests (Paskoff 2007, 103). Once again, the private sector stepped up. A delegation led by the Buffalo Board of Trade echoed the Steamboat Association of 1846: "As the General government has failed to furnish funds for the dredging of the St. Clair Flats, through the omission of the President to sign the bill passed for that purpose at the last session of Congress, it has become necessary that it should be done by private means and private enterprise" (*Detroit Daily Free Press*, April 4, 1855, 2). This new appeal elicited a shrewd response from the Congress: the committee would be allowed to use the government's dredge *if* they paid for its operation and upkeep. It seems a year of inactivity had taken its toll: "The first step to be taken preparatory to commencing the dredging," Lieutenant Colonel J. D. Graham understated, "was to repair the engine of this machine, which had suffered somewhat from its having been sunk under water. These repairs were made at the expense of the committee appointed by the delegates to act for them" (Graham 1856, 397–98).

Accordingly, the 1855 season got off to a late start in the latter part of July and ended in early October due to unseasonably stormy weather. Moreover, the civil engineer hired by the committee evidently had not read Abert's 1847 description of the bottom as hardened clay. Graham found it "more tenacious and more difficult than has heretofore been estimated . . . so that it requires the whole working force of the engine to drive the bucket into it" (Graham 1856, 398). Despite these setbacks, the new dredge, supplemented both by an idle government dredge requisitioned from Chicago and a pledge of financial assistance from the Canadian government, was able to make a cut to the projected depth of 13 feet but only half the projected width of 120 feet (Larson 1981, 53). At last, the technological means of radically transforming the maritime landscape lay within the reach of its new capitalist masters—but not quite within their grasp. The issues of politics and money proved at least as tenacious as the indurated marl of the Flats.

Interlude: Budgets, Vetoes, and the Prelude to Civil War

Contorted, narrow, and repeatedly obstructed—a description befitting the politics of improving the Flats as well as the delta itself, as the favoring political winds from earlier decades shifted inexorably toward the national catastrophe ahead. The "Era of Good Feeling" following the War of 1812 had fostered an atmosphere of opportunity and prosperity that drove the economic and demographic expansion of the newly admitted Great Lakes states. At the same time, this same prosperity widened the growing economic gulf between the agrarian South and the industrializing North, with which the Great Lakes states were economically and ideologically linked. Like other such projects, the improvement of the South Channel fell victim to regional squabbling. Politics aside, budgetary difficulties caused by the new nation's meteoric rate of expansion made these conflicts inevitable. In particular, the fiscal, logistical, and human resources of the Bureau of Topographic Engineers were stretched thin by the Mexican War (1846–48) at precisely the time when the clamor for the improvement of the Flats was reaching a crescendo.

Early presidential vetoes of internal rivers and harbors bills were ostensibly legalistic. John Tyler's message to Congress in December 1843 made it clear that the Constitution permitted only such "works in favorable and proper situations [which] would be found to be as *indispensably necessary in case of war* to carry on safe and successful naval operations" (Tyler 1843, 4; emphasis added). The following year he again vetoed a similar bill, which Congress overrode (Larson 1981, 41).

James K. Polk in turn vetoed a similar bill in 1848, reiterating Tyler's rationale for vetoing the River and Harbor Bill of 1847. Further, Polk resurrected the ideology of the prefederalist union—a "confederacy of twenty-nine States" as he carefully termed it: "The power to improve harbors and rivers for purposes of navigation," he wrote in his veto message, "by deepening or clearing out, by dams and sluices, by locking or canalling, must be admitted, without any other limitation than the discretion of Congress, or it must be denied altogether. If it be admitted, how broad and how susceptible of enormous abuse thus vested in the general government" (Polk 1848, 5). Arguing against such as a slippery slope, Polk exclaimed, "Where shall the exercise of the power, if it be assumed, stop?" Rather, he countered with a proposal consistent with a decentralized view of government, noting that while "no State shall, without the consent of Congress, lay any duty of tonnage," the converse was also true. With congressional consent, he argued, those states which stood to benefit could finance improvements through duties (Polk 1848, 6). The result was a further four years of stalemate. A brief respite came in 1852 when an appropriations bill signed by Millard Fillmore allowed work on the Flats to proceed, but by 1855 those funds too were exhausted.

In an 1853 report to the secretary of the treasury on North American trade and commerce, one Israel Andrews, American consul to Canada, summed up the frustrations of mariners, shippers, and federalists. In nearly a thousand pages of rigorous documentation, Andrews argued both passionately and empirically for federal investment in the nation's maritime infrastructure, reserving his strongest passages for

> the St. Clair flats, the greatest natural obstacle to the free navigation of the great lakes, with the exception of the rapids on the lower S. Lawrence, the Falls of Niagara, and the Sault Ste. Marie. These shallows lie nearly at the head of Lake St. Clair, about twenty-five miles above the city of Detroit. The bottom is of soft mud [*sic*], bearing a lofty and dense growth of wild rice, with a very intricate, tortuous, and difficult channel winding over them, in many places so narrow that two vessels cannot pass them abreast; nor is it possible to navigate them at night. There would be no difficulty whatever, and but a most trivial expense, as compared with the advantages which would accrue from removing this barrier, in dredging out a straight channel of sufficient depth to admit vessels of the largest draught. Nor is there any work more urgently and reasonably solicited from Congress by the men of the West, nor any more entirely justified by every consideration of sound economy and political wisdom, or more certain to produce returns incalculable, than the opening [of] the flats of the St. Clair, and carrying a canal around the Sault Ste. Marie. These improvements would at once perfect the most splendid and longest chain of internal navigation in the world, extending above two thousand miles in length from Fond du Lac, at the head of Lake Superior, to the mouth of the St. Lawrence river. (Andrews 1853, 192)

Deaf to Andrews's entreaties, the succeeding presidencies of Franklin Pierce and James Buchanan, both Northerners with Southern sympathies, brought the project to a virtual halt. While reiterating the same formal objections as Tyler and Polk, Pierce's 1856 veto of a bill to improve the Flats touched explicitly on the festering issue of regionalism: "It cannot be considered as a necessary means for the common defence," Pierce wrote, "and is subject to those objections which apply to other works designed to facilitate commerce and contribute to the convenience and local prosperity of those more immediately concerned—an object not to be constitutionally and justly attained by the taxation of the people of the whole country" (Pierce 1856, 1). Remarkably, with the support of Jefferson Davis, secretary of war and future president of the Confederacy, Captain Graham of the Topographic Engineers countered with a report to Congress on "the importance of the improvement as a measure of military defence of the national frontier" and Pierce's veto was overridden (Graham 1856, 396). Strange bedfellows, indeed.

Buchanan's veto of 1860 was a throwback to Polk, adding the technicality that by cutting the new South Channel entrance to an average width of 235 feet and a depth of 13 feet in 1858, the government had already accomplished its mission, and no further action was warranted (Buchanan 1860; Larson 1981, 65; Moulton and Thieme 2009, B.2.1). With the outbreak of the Civil War in the following year, the issue became moot. All dredging operations on the St. Clair River once again came to a halt, not to be resumed until 1867. The Union would be forced to fight with its maritime supply line to the Midwest perilously strained. Following the national paroxysm of the Civil War, the emergent American era saw capitalism triumphant: the Gilded Age, as it was called even then. Its cultural manifestation in the St. Clair Flats, to be discussed in chapter 10, is truly one of the most remarkable aspects of this entire saga.

Innovation: A Beacon of Hope

On the official 1857 navigational chart of St. Clair Flats, the following sailing directions appeared for the first time: "To enter the river by the South Pass: From the lighthouse at the head of the Detroit river, steer NE ½ N. for 20 miles, 'till you make the S. Pass Lighthouse, when in 15 feet water bring the Lighthouse and Beacon Light in range, steer on this range passing black spar Buoys No. 1 & 3 on the port hand and the red Spar Buoys Nos. 2 & 4 on the starboard hand till well up with red Spar Buoy No. 6 passing it close aboard on the starboard hand, when steer for the mouth of the river between red Spar Buoy No. 8 on the starboard hand & Day Beacon on the port giving a good berth on the port hand to black Spar Buoy No. 5" (US Bureau of Topographic Engineers 1857).

The minute details of this brief but dense passage reveal how the tide of man's control over the landscape was turning. An artificial path through the Flats had been made, requiring precise knowledge to negotiate it—knowledge transmitted through charts and texts. Three features are noteworthy. First is the inclusion of the South Channel, although the North Channel passage would continue to appear in commercial sailing instructions for another two decades (Thompson 1869, 89; 1878, 58; Barnet 1887, 111–12). Second is the use of a standardized system of buoyage that is still in use today: for upbound traffic, buoys kept to starboard are red and even-numbered; port buoys are odd-numbered (now painted green instead of black). Indeed, several of the buoys on the US Bureau of Topographic Engineers' 1857 chart have kept their number and position to this day, notably red buoy 6, across the channel from the Old South Channel beacon.

Finally, that beacon and its companion lighthouse were completed in 1859 as a set of lighted *range markers*, used by mariners to line up the narrow entrance to the channel by day or night. Upon reaching the beacon, the helmsman steered the buoyed course into the river. Those surviving structures, now automated and known locally as the Old South Channel Lights, thus mark a turning point, both literally and figuratively. After 1858, no significant work was done in the Flats until the end of the Civil War. When work resumed, it was far more ambitious and politically unopposed.

Given the evolution of specialized maritime practices and radical improvements in infrastructure, the resultant growth of the shipbuilding industry in the St. Clair locale may now be readily understood and appreciated. Advances having occurred in every type of vessel, whether sailed, self-propelled or towed, the choices made by shipbuilders reveal the dialectic between their traditions, technological options, local material affordances, and the constraints remaining in an evolving landscape.

8

Boat- and Shipbuilding in the St. Clair Maritime Landscape

Think of technology as congealed labor.
—Bruno Latour, *Pandora's Hope*

The story of Great Lakes watercraft development is the story of adaptation, evolution, and innovation. Each occupying group confronted its environment with a blend of its own traditions, local designs encountered, and emergent technologies. In a landscape as diverse, dynamic, and strategic as the Huron-Erie strait, localized patterns of construction, use, and loss repeatedly reveal the developmental processes at work, as builders sought to complement the landscape with the right tools for the job.

The materiality of watercraft is particularly seductive, especially in its aesthetics. Form usually follows function, and the appeal of such masterpieces as the birchbark canoe, the schooner, and the paddle-wheel steamboat lies in their graceful movement in a fluid medium. Nevertheless, the raison d'être of all nautical material culture, be it an anchor or an aircraft carrier, is to mediate between nature and culture—to emerge from the interplay of mission, materiality, and physical context as a functional instrument for advancing the social agenda. The ship is conceived and designed according to various mental templates and ideologies. It is then constructed, used, and disposed of within the complex set of social and physical constraints that comprise the maritime landscape itself (Gibbins and Adams 2001, 281). In making the case for a given watercraft as a social construction, it is necessary first to understand the mission its society sends it on. It then becomes a simpler matter to understand which watercraft got built, how they were used, and even why they were occasionally lost.

Such is the nature of the St. Clair locale that it posed distinct risks and hazards to navigation throughout the historic period. Equally true, however, was the abundance of resources it afforded to the maritime enterprise of boat- and shipbuilding, whether Indigenous or Euro-American. The interaction of these challenges and resources led to the development of highly adapted watercraft, built *in* and *for* Great Lakes maritime landscapes, particularly the St. Clair locale itself. Those which reflect localized traditions are termed *vernacular watercraft* (Meide and Sikes 2014, 115; Evans 2016, 9). Their conformance to a distinctive pattern of construction sets them apart in the eyes of local mariners and the maritime community at large (Evans and Smith 2016, 3).

So distinctive is the Great Lakes sailing environment that virtually any vessel built for use on its waters could arguably be termed vernacular. The regional evolution of consort towboats and barges (Warner 1998) certainly bears this out, as do the distinctive designs of the Mackinac boat (Barry 1973, 114–16), canal schooner (Barkhausen 1990), fish tug (Chiarappa 2005, 227–28), lumber hooker (Labadie and Murphy 1987, 34), and self-unloading bulk freighter (Lafferty and Van Heest 2009). Although access to the Atlantic Seaboard prevents it from being truly a closed system, the Great Lakes maritime network has historically operated largely as a world unto itself: "What was built on the lakes," avers maritime historian Bradley Rodgers, "generally speaking, stayed on the lakes" (Rodgers 2016, 205).

In his discussion of the origins of the steamboat, maritime archaeologist Jim Dolwick observes that "people, things and processes were blended together, dependent upon one another, exchanging properties and coming into conflict. As technological devices, steamboats consisted of an array of mechanical parts: steam engines, boilers, propulsion mechanisms, and boat structures; yet, they were also made up of more than just mechanical components. The inventor-entrepreneurs and builders brought together a vast array of people-and-things: artefacts, materials, skills, social and political organisations, natural resources, physical environments, scientific laws, economic forces, cultural preferences, places and spaces" (Dolwick 2008, 16). Dolwick's "vast array," combining cultural elements with affordances ("natural resources"), the landscape, and the environment ("places and spaces") recalls Jonathan Adams's list of seven elements as "interrelated constraints on the form, structural characteristics, appearance and use of watercraft" (Adams 2001, 301). Adams's network has already served to structure my approach to the formation of the landscape. Here it assumes its originally intended application to boat- and shipbuilding (figure 8).

From precontact times until the end of the nineteenth century, the St. Clair maritime landscape epitomized the totality of Adams's network. As a point of supply as well as of use, it offered an abundance of boat- and shipbuilding

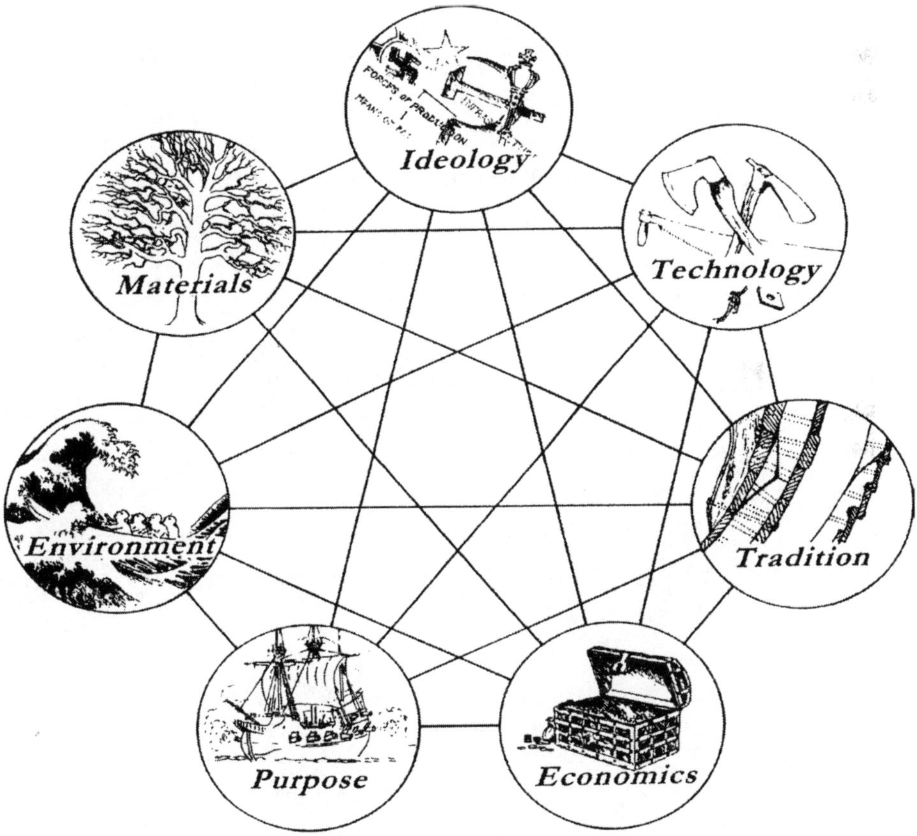

FIGURE 8. Jonathan Adam's network of the "interrelated constraints on the form, structural characteristics, appearance and use of watercraft." (Adams 2001, 301)

materials requisite for each occupying social group. As labor and capital flowed into the Great Lakes, it provided a challenging but profitable operating environment for which to design and build watercraft. It was only when the timber supply was simultaneously exhausted and rendered obsolescent by iron and coal that the St. Clair locale's role dimmed as a center of Great Lakes shipbuilding. The sections that follow examine boat- and shipbuilding during each of its five successive historical periods. As in the case of landscape formation, the mentality of the dominant occupying group sheds light on the decisions made by the builders.

Indigenous Boatbuilding in the St. Clair Delta

At the time of European contact, the Indigenous inhabitants of the upper Great Lakes used watercraft that were superbly adapted to the purposes of their makers and the conditions of their use. Their bark canoes, as vernacular watercraft, were most certainly reflections of localized technology and cultural traditions. So versatile and effective was the basic design that it has survived not only colonialism but modernity. A testament to a classic design is its longevity in use—none more so than the iconic birchbark canoe. Though its materials have changed dramatically, today's recreational canoe would be instantly recognizable and usable by Indigenous and colonial paddlers alike.

Across multiple transformations, the St. Clair locale's ecology posed a localized set of constraints, while simultaneously offering the requisite resources for dwelling and movement to each group that occupied it. For its Indigenous peoples, shelter, and boats chiefly required tree and plant species as well as hide and sinew, but as a nexus of a long-distance trading network, the Strait did not lack for lithic and copper tools.[1]

1 Grave goods found at Gibraltar's Cherry Island site (20WN898) and the Fair Haven's Riviere au Vase site (20MB3), while separated by some 100 km, display a remarkable similarity. Both burials feature a distinctive stag-handled square-bladed copper awl, assorted lithic scrapers, and chert drills—all perfectly consistent with a boatbuilder's kit, and both assemblages are datable to ca. 900 CE (Halsey and Brashler 2013). More work, hopefully including some experimental archaeology, would be needed to test this hypothesis, however.

Indigenous watercraft of the upper Great Lakes consisted primarily of bark canoes, with dugout canoes considerably less numerous, as their greater weight made them unsuitable for portaging and unmanageable in rapids (Lafitau 1977, 124). The deceptive simplicity of the canoe is not that of crudeness but that of elegance, as archaeologist Wilbert Hinsdale noted: "With his light bark canoe," he wrote, "the Indian could with ease overcome hindrances to freight-carrying boats, and by shouldering his canoe and baggage make a portage around rapids and other obstructions and set out on the waters beyond. By such means streams were followed to their sources, divides crossed, and voyages continued" (Hinsdale 1931, 7).

Canoes were also instruments of warfare, both by transporting warriors and occasionally engaging in naval battles, as during the wars between Ojibwe and Iroquois (Eid 1979). The advantage would have lain with the former. Lahontan in 1688 recorded, with considerable relief, that the birch canoes of his Ojibwe companions were far superior to those of a party of pursuing Iroquois. Entering eastern Lake Erie, he wrote, "we were secure from all danger, for the Iroquois Canows are so dull and large, that they cannot sail near so quick [*n'approchent pas de la vitesse*] as those made of Birch-bark. The former are made of Elm-bark, which is very heavy, and their form is very awkward; for they are so long and broad that thirty Men row in them, two abreast, whether sitting or standing, and the sides are so low, that they dare not venture 'em upon the Lakes, tho' the wind be very slack" (Lahontan 1905, 138). Joseph Lafitau, even less impressed, summed up the elm-bark canoes of the Iroquois as "constructed with all possible slovenliness and carelessness" while praising birch canoes as "masterpieces of native art" (Lafitau 1977, 126).

Stands of "canoe birch" (*Betula alba papyrifera*) were in effect a strategic resource, which flourished best in the north. Likewise, white ash, spruce, and white cedar, all required for the construction of birchbark canoes, were readily available in the Strait (Dodge 1914). A French report of 1718 described how the "Misisagué Indians" of the St. Clair delta "construct a great many bark canoes, which is a great assistance to them; they occupy them selves in this sort of work; the women sew the canoes with roots; the men finish them and make the [ribs] of these canoes, smoothen and floor (*varanguent*) them, and the women gum them" (Sabrevois de Bleury 1902, 370). A century later, Charles Trowbridge,

Cass's secretary on his 1820 expedition, described the construction in terms that suggest that it had not changed in the least:

> The construction of these vessels, so frail and yet so wisely used for the purposes of navigation on the Rivers of this Country, is such, that without the most extreme caution, the traveler is every hour in danger of losing his canoe, baggage and perhaps his life; for the Bark of which they are constructed is not more than 1/16 of an inch in thickness, and this is stretched over and then sewed to Beams or knees which are not more than 3/8 to 1/2 inch thick; between these knees (which are placed very close to each other) and the bark, are thin pieces of cedar wood, of the thickness of a quarter of an inch and length of ten to twelve feet, and arranged in such a manner as to join the edges, whereby the bark on the outside is prevented from yielding to trifling pressures. But the greatest strength of a canoe of this kind is in the gunwale (which is made of strong tough wood [generally ash] and well bound with watape [cordage made from spruce roots]) and the stiffening poles which are laid in the bottom of the vessel to support the lading, and prevent it from breaking in the waves. So that a canoe is equally strong and safe, whether laden or empty, provided it is not too heavily laden. (Trowbridge 1942, 137–39)

As late as 1826, Cass again assembled a flotilla of trade canoes to travel from Detroit to the western end of Lake Superior.[2] Thomas McKenney, Cass's companion, compared the canoe favorably to their becalmed schooner as a transport through the Flats, finding "this little bark, superior to the current, and even to the winds, in a place so narrow as this. Now we are stopped by the one, and baffled by the other" (McKenney 1959, 12–13).

Whether carrying wild rice, a war party, pelts, trade goods, or diplomats, in its design, construction, and use, the bark canoe articulated with each of

2 Cass's choice of canoes may not have been entirely dictated by their versatility and seaworthiness. Thomas L. McKenney, one of the Indian Department commissioners who accompanied Cass to the negotiations of the Treaty of Fond du Lac in 1826, noted, "It is somewhat remarkable, that in a sail vessel of any kind, the Governor suffers from seasickness most distressingly; but in a canoe, he is never sick" (McKenney 1959, 146).

Adams's septet of constraints, not excepting ideology. As noted by the French observer, the labor of their construction was divided along gender lines, presumably instantiating gendered social roles. Once finished, it was a powerful symbol of an ordered society, pervading Anishinaabeg culture. Two key officiants in the purification ritual for initiates to the *midéwiwin*, or Grand Medicine Society, were termed the *naganid* (bowman) and *wedaged* (steersman), as they respectively led and ended the procession of initiates entering the sweat lodge (*madodiswon*; Landes 1968, 54).

Technology has been described as "congealed labor" (Latour 1999, 189); it can with equal justice be viewed as congealed or embodied ideology, particularly in an object as purposeful and cohesive as a boat or ship.

Vernacular Boatbuilding during the French Period, 1640–1760

During the French and British eras, the complex sailing conditions of the upper Great Lakes were significantly different from the open waters of the Atlantic that had brought the colonists hither. Dynamic relations were created among at least three nautical traditions: ocean-going and coastal sailing ships; small boats used on European rivers and estuaries; and newly encountered Indigenous bark and dugout canoes. Each tradition sought niches in the diverse transport network. In time, distinctive vernacular boat and ship designs emerged and evolved as need dictated and opportunity offered.

While the colonial powers of Britain, the Netherlands, Spain, and France readily adapted to sailing conditions along the Atlantic Seaboard, traditional French open-water navigation did not fare so well as they penetrated the Great Lakes. Following the decisive fiasco of the *Griffon*, the story of French maritimity in the upper Great Lakes became that of small-craft navigation.[3] Explorers,

3 It may not be entirely true that the French never again attempted European-style navigation on the upper Great Lakes. In his travels on Lake Superior, trader Jonathan Carver in 1768 observed "part of the hulk of a very large vessel, burnt to the water's edge, just at the opening from the Straits of St. Marie's [Sault Ste-Marie] into the Lake" (Carver 1781, v). Carver's conclusion was that the French, "who always kept a small schooner on this lake while they were in possession of Canada" (Carver 1781, 134), had created a clandestine

fur traders, and missionaries alike adopted the canoe for the remainder of the French colonial era, gradually supplementing it with vernacular small-craft designs adapted from old-world models. Throughout most of their colonial period, the value of payloads of beaver pelts and French exchange goods were both sufficiently dense that large canoes, often mobilized in fleets, could sustain the transport needs of the fur trade in both directions (Lafitau 1977, 124; White 1991, 137). Critically, they were able to access the entirety of the maritime network. Maritime historian James Barry argues, "They were the only things that could navigate the rivers and be carried over the portages, and the fur trade could scarcely have existed without them" (Barry 1973, 28).

So long as river networks and their portages remained viable transport zones, the canoe provided a critical link in the overall Great Lakes maritime landscape. In the St. Clair delta, however, there were no portages, the critical constraint being the depth of the bars across the channel mouths. These conditions encouraged shoal-draft vernacular watercraft developed from old-world prototypes: "As time went on and the fur trade increased, the genius of the French evolved the *bateau*," observes maritime historian James Cooke Mills (1910, 34). Whether paddled, rowed, poled, or even sailed, the versatile bateau—originally developed along French rivers, coastlines, and estuaries—likewise flourished in frontier conditions of minimal shoreline infrastructure (White 1991, 211). These simple flat-bottomed boats could be built quickly and cheaply from hewn or sawed planks and fastened with pegs (Eldredge 1905, 700). Most of the early boats were doubtless small enough to serve the needs of an individual or two, but the design was scalable: "Some *bateaux* were of nearly three tons' burden," wrote historian James Cook Mills,

---

naval presence on Lake Superior. This wreck appears to have been that of a bark built by French entrepreneur Sieur de la Ronde Denis, in a failed attempt to develop a copper trade (Nute 1944, 160). At a reported forty-ton capacity, it was no inconsiderable vessel, which evidently never transited the rapids of the St. Mary's River. It is said to have been burned by the retreating French, if not by de la Ronde himself, on the cession of New France to the British in 1760. Historian Henry Howland thus qualifies the assertion that the Niagara-built British schooner *Huron* (1761), which played such a vital role in the relief of Detroit during Pontiac's Rebellion, was "the first decked vessel to plow the waters *of Lake Erie* since the days of the *Griffon*" (Howland 1903, 24; emphasis added), informed by his knowledge of de la Ronde's vessel, built and sailed solely on Lake Superior.

"and three or four men could propel one against a swift current of the streams by the use of oars and poles" (Mills 1910, 34).

With the addition of gaff-rigged sails, the larger bateaux evolved into the Mackinac boat, which, as its name suggests, took part in the coasting trade on Lake Huron and Georgian Bay (Mills 1910, 34). Cadillac's 1702 account of Detroit mentions such a scaled-up version: "I have also had a boat of ten tons burden built which will be useful for many purposes in the river" (Cadillac 1904, 137). This suggests that its design, while not suitable for navigation on open water, would serve for moving commodities, notably grain from the French ribbon farms along the Strait, to and from his mills at Fort Pontchartrain.

European-style shipbuilding depended on two key types of resources: first, timber that could be sourced locally; second, metal fittings, sails, cordage, and other manufactured ships' stores. The latter had been transported inland at no small effort and expense to build the *Griffon* just above Niagara Falls. The former, both hardwoods for hulls and conifers for spars, were only gradually cognized by early French arrivals to the upper Great Lakes, whose initial preoccupations were with furs and food. As early as 1679, the French were deeply impressed by the anthropogenic fruit orchards that lined the riverbanks rather than by timber-yielding species. Hennepin appended as an afterthought to his inventory, "The rest of the strait [above Lake St. Clair] is covered with forests, fruit trees like walnuts, chestnuts, plum and apple trees, wild vines loaded with grapes, of which we made some little wine. There is timber fit for building" (Hennepin 1966, 92).

Duluth's description of the forestation along the St. Clair River was likewise devoted first to trees that bore fruit and nuts: "It is a charming sight to see that River," he wrote in 1686, "bordered with an infinite number of apple-trees, with abundance of plums-trees of every kind, of Chestnut and Walnut trees, and the Hazel-bushes of France; and to find there the Vine, one of its finest ornaments, whose Grapes are fairly large and good. At intervals we come upon very large meadows, both dry and wet, full of grass that grows to the height of over three feet. They are broken only by fruit Trees, or by hard-wood timber of great height and of various kinds, such as the butternut and walnut, red and white Oak, Poplar, Basswood, Elm, Ash and Cottonwood" (Duluth 1902, 129). Cadillac's 1702 account was taken straight from Duluth's, his aim being to encourage French settlers in the fiefdom along the Strait that he planned for himself.

There is no mention by either author of the vast stands of white pine in the Lower Peninsula of Michigan, whose southern extremity lay along the aptly named Pine River, a tributary of the St. Clair. From the absence of interest in structural timber and naval stores, it appears that the earliest French perceptions of the local affordances were conditioned by their colonial pattern of living lightly on the land, not unlike their Indigenous trading partners. By the end of the French colonial period, however, *habitants* were exploiting the timber resources along the St. Clair River, albeit on a modest scale. A British description of the mouth of the Pine River in 1761 noted that "the inhabitants of Detroit had a sawmill at said creek and got all their boards and Pyn timber from it" (Brehm 1883, 25). Seven decades later, this modest French practice persisted. The American journalist Chandler Gilman, becalmed at Ward's Landing in 1835, observed, "At the wharf we found an old Frenchman, or rather French Canadian, busy bringing a raft of boards and smaller timber ashore" (Gilman 1836, 65).

It is likely that those boards had been milled a mere eight miles upstream at the Pine River and floated to Ward's Landing—the future shipbuilding hub that renamed itself "Marine City" only three decades later. It is also not unreasonable to infer that a number of those planks were used by the French descendant community to build the bateaux that long remained vital links to life on the Flats. Their simplicity transcends ethnicity, however: "Boatbuilding is not essentially ethnical in character," Westerdahl cautions. "It is often haphazardly and uncontextually applied, especially if it is not taking into account the question of function" (Westerdahl 1994, 267). The ability of flat-bottomed boats to negotiate the Flats served the needs of French settlers along the waterfront, then of British and American merchants moving goods and lightering schooners using punts. They survive in the recreational "jon boats" favored by local duck hunters, fishermen, and cottagers.

British Colonial Maritimity, 1760–1813: Boatbuilding

With the displacement of the French colonial empire by the British in 1760, European-style navigation resumed in the waters above Detroit with the arrival of the schooners *Victory* (built 1763) and *Gladwin* (1764). Both were full-keeled designs, built at Navy Island near Niagara in eastern Lake Erie, with a rather shallow draft of approximately seven feet. This allowed them to transit the preferred South Channel but not without some difficulty and risk. The hybrid route developed by the British called for the *Gladwin* to ply the waters from Fort Sinclair north to Michilimackinac, while boats transferred passengers and cargo to and from Detroit across Lake St. Clair and the Flats. The *Victory*, soon joined by other ships, carried the traffic between Detroit and the lower lakes. An extraordinary 1794 painting of the Detroit waterfront by a British lieutenant (figure 9) shows the elements of the system, each in its place. Small craft are shown in the foreground performing a variety of tasks: loading and unloading cargo using a pony-cart; fishing; moving cargo by sail, paddle, and oar. In the background, the square-rigged ships of the Provincial Marine lie at the King's Wharf with its warehouses for the king's stores. A more modest version of this scene would have played out at Fort Sinclair on the St. Clair River.

FIGURE 9. Edmund Henn, "A View of Detroit, July 25, 1794." Note the variety of vessels: canoes and bateaux in the foreground using the riverbank as a landing, while the square-rigged vessels of the Provincial Marine use the King's Wharf and warehouses (center background). (Courtesy of Detroit Public Library, Burton Historical Collection)

Throughout the period of British naval control of the Great Lakes, a militarized version of the hybrid transport corridor developed. Shoal-draft gunboats were mobilized for river duty, while ships of the Provincial Marine generally confined their operations to the waters below Detroit. Small craft had already proven their worth on the frontier. During Pontiac's 1763 siege of Detroit, "four batteaus made row-gallies," armed with swivel guns and grapeshot, protected the ships *Michigan* and *Huron* from raids while at anchor (Amherst 1931, 326). Thereafter the rowed gunboat became a staple feature of the British naval presence along the frontier. In his ill-advised campaign against the American-held fort at Vincennes in the Indiana Territory late in 1778, Lieutenant Governor Henry Hamilton left Detroit with a flotilla of forty-two *pirogues* and ten bateaux, including "a very large French one" carrying their sole artillery piece, a six-pounder cannon (Du Vernet 1908, 409). They made their way up the Maumee River, then portaged into the Wabash, taking the undermanned post at Vincennes without resistance. This served only to enrage the intrepid Colonel George Rogers Clark of Kentucky. His epic midwinter counteroffensive resulted in the recapture of Vincennes and Hamilton himself, who spent the remainder of the war in Virginia as the unwilling guest of its governor, Thomas Jefferson.

While Hamilton's gunboats were likely built along the Strait, it is not until the struggle for the Old Northwest in the 1790s that records show the British commissioning boats from the St. Clair locale (Hamil 1951). Following Anthony Wayne's victory at Fallen Timbers in 1794, British military operations were relocated. Detroit's Fort Lernoult and Fort Miamis on the Maumee River were at last surrendered to the Americans, as the British withdrew to Fort Amherstburg (now Fort Malden) in Ontario. To protect his northern flank, Lieutenant Governor John Graves Simcoe ordered a blockhouse and a fleet of six gunboats to be built at present-day Chatham on the Thames River, a navigable tributary of Lake St. Clair. Unlike the forested Michigan side, pine was not available nearby. Difficulties in obtaining the light, inexpensive, and easily worked timber forced the boatbuilder, one William Baker, to use local hardwood instead. The results were both too heavy and too expensive, and work was suspended before completion (Hamil 1951, 25). Chatham's career as a shipbuilding center was deferred by nearly four decades, when it would serve a commercial rather than military role.

British Shipbuilding in the St. Clair Maritime Landscape

The British occupation of erstwhile New France got off to a rough start with the 1763 uprising known as Pontiac's Rebellion. Instrumental in relieving the beleaguered outpost of Detroit were two ships, the schooner *Huron* and the sloop *Michigan*, sometimes referenced as *Beaver* (Howland 1903, 26). Both were built at Navy Island, just above Niagara Falls at the outlet of Lake Erie. At least a half-dozen ships were built there in the 1760s, including the schooners *Gladwin* and *Victory*, which carried the trade between Niagara and Michilimackinac (Howland 1903). Thereafter, Detroit shipbuilding eclipsed it for the remainder of its British occupation as maritime activity on the upper lakes increased.

Proximity to resources doubtless played a role. The British had been quick to realize the potential of the St. Clair locale's forests for the construction not only of buildings and boats but of ships. In 1767, the trader John Porteous, perhaps tired of struggling with small boats, remarked on the maritime potential upstream from the frontier town of Detroit: "Above F[ort] S[inclair] is a pinery from which D[etroit] & all the settlement is built, the timber being carried down on rafts. This swamp affords excellent pine & sufficient masts for any vessels" (Porteous 1767). The British began developing the site's nautical infrastructure promptly but gradually. In Jonathan Carver's journal for August 8, 1766, he noted, "Arrived at the block house [Fort Sinclair] commanded at present by Captain [Patrick] Sinclare [*sic*] who commands the vessel [schooner *Gladwin*] which passes and repasses from this place during the summer season with supplies of provisions for Michillimackinac [*sic*]. Very near under cover of this block house a small creek [Pine River] enters the [St. Clair] river in which the vessel is careen'd during the winter season" (Carver 1976, 69). The process of careening, whereby a vessel was beached and rolled first to one side and then the other, can be seen as a precursor to actual shipbuilding, as it allowed for regular maintenance of the hull—caulking seams, replacing planks, repairing frame timbers, and the like.

Three years later in 1769, one Alexander Grant built a single-masted sloop christened *Chippewa* at Fort Sinclair, site of the present-day town of St. Clair. It was rated at fifty tons and armed with four swivel guns (Anonymous 1888, 198–99). For years the little sloop was a one-off, an outlier in the pattern of shipbuilding in the Strait. Detroit was emerging as an "Atlantic *entrepôt*" handling the trade in ships' stores but not their manufacture. Iron fittings, cordage, and sailcloth were required under British colonial policy to be imported from the mother country and carried in the king's ships (Cangany 2014; Parkins 1918, 280). Transporting such bulky commodities by boat from Detroit across the Flats to the Pine River was an avoidable logistical issue. Detroit's advantages would also have included better access to skilled labor as well as greater security, first from Native unrest (recalling Pontiac) and within a few years, American rebels. Flammable stores of timber, tar, and pitch could certainly be better guarded at Fort Detroit than at remote little Fort Sinclair. In all, less expense and risk were involved in moving the timber to the shipyard rather than the reverse. Grant relocated his operation to Detroit, beginning with the sixty-six-ton sloop *Angelica* in 1771 and ending in 1790 with a second *Chippewa*, a schooner twice the size of its earlier namesake. Like Chatham three decades later, the isolated Pine River locale was forced to await a peacetime economy.

On the eve of revolution, the merchant fleet, like Fort Pontchartrain itself, was showing its age. Upon his arrival at Detroit in November 1775, British civilian governor Henry Hamilton surveyed the King's Shipyard and "directed the putting in repair of His Majesty's Vessels [i.e., the Provincial Marine] lying here." By that time Alexander Grant had built a half-dozen vessels there. A builder named Cornwall had launched another; finally, McTavish and McBeath's fifty-five-ton sloop *Felicity* brought the total to at least nine, with an equal number launched before the British finally left Detroit in 1796 (Hamilton 1908, 265; Anonymous 1888, 199).

When war came to the upper Great Lakes, Fort Sinclair and the upper Strait were far from the action. Rather, its principal role was as a strategic source of timber (Sabick 2004, 19). Following Governor Hamilton's failed venture at Vincennes early in 1779, Detroit was anticipating an imminent attack from the south by George Rogers Clark, now fortified with Hamilton's captured flotilla and artillery (Harrison 2014, 31). The log of the armed British sloop *Welcome* records that on May 27, 1780, the ship left Fort Sinclair on the Pine River with rafts of timber for Detroit's shipyard and likely its dilapidated stockade as well. Two weeks later, the sloop was back at Fort Sinclair, where two men were detailed on shore, "grinding the axes [and] making halves [hafts] for the same" for the felling of more timber (*Welcome* 1779–1782).

Peacetime brought glimmerings of hope for expanded commerce, and with them, attention to the St. Clair maritime corridor. In violation of the 1783 Treaty of Paris, the British maintained a firm hold on the fur trade and its posts at Detroit and Michilimackinac for another dozen years (Dunbar and May 1995, 88). The hybrid transport zone through the St. Clair delta, clearly the key constraint or limiting factor, had evidently outlived its usefulness. Lacking as yet the means to physically alter the landscape, the British turned to the two factors they could control: their vessels and their nautical practice. In neither area had there been technological breakthroughs. The former has been discussed already: such labor-intensive propulsion as warping and kedging, while suitable for warships, would not be cost-effective in commerce. The sounding and staking of the Elbow and the use of Anchor Bay for lightering or awaiting favorable conditions did not occur until the early nineteenth century. So too with the vessels: the centerboard and the steamboat were still nearly four decades in the future.

Until then the environment, technology, and economy were at mutual loggerheads. In his 1788 report on fortifications to Lord Dorchester, British engineer Gother Mann appended a critique of the navigation of the upper lakes, including British shipbuilding. His was an early voice advocating the use of schooners. The confined waters, he reasoned, favored the schooner as the design best able to sail to windward. As to their displacement, Mann recommended that "they should be from Eighty to One Hundred Tons burthen on Lake Ontario; and Fifty Tons burthen on Lakes Erie and Huron; but if not intended to communicate between these two Lakes, they may be then of the same size as on Lake Ontario" (Mann 1888, 37). Mann acknowledged that the navigation above Detroit was contingent on traversing the bar at the mouth of the St. Clair River, "through which there is a very narrow channel with not more than seven feet water, muddy bottom" (Mann 1888, 32). Mann recommended that vessels intended to traverse the Flats be smaller and lighter but not shallower. Against the latter, he warned, "it does not seem advisable, nor do I know of any good reason to continue the practice of building vessels flat bottomed, or to have very little draft of water, they are always unsafe, and many of the accidents which have happened upon the Lakes, have perhaps in some degree been owing to that construction" (Mann 1888, 37). The conundrum:

small, shallow vessels were effective but unprofitable; large ones were profitable but unsafe unless they were prohibitively deep.

Recalling that the eighty-ton *Gladwin*, built in 1763, drew only seven feet of water, while the sixty-ton schooner *Hope*, built in 1772, drew nine, Mann's recommendation favors the latter design. As if to prove Mann's point, the shallow-draft *Gladwin*, which had regularly traversed the Flats without incident, capsized with all hands in a gale on Lake Erie in 1768 after a career of only five years, owing to being poorly ballasted—a critical error for a hull of its design. The more seaworthy *Hope*, with its greater draft, had predictably run hard aground in the Flats in 1805. Yet it served a remarkable fifty-four years before grounding a final time in Lake Huron in 1826, with two lives lost. By that time, two wars had been fought, and the world had changed.

With the lifting of the repressive political and economic strictures of the colonial regime, the necessary conditions for a viable shipbuilding industry outside the Detroit area were in place: a pacified landscape; the freer movement of capital and of the manufactured goods needed to build and equip ships. Despite an abundance of resources, the commercial and military policies of the British motherland stifled local initiative. Instead, nautical technology was bound by naval tradition: costly square-rigged ships, manhandled through an environment for which they were ill-suited.

No wonder that when the constraints of colonialism were lifted, the abundant affordances of the St. Clair maritime landscape allowed it to thrive as a center of wooden ship production. Between 1824 and 1926, at least 781 commercial vessels were built in 16 shipbuilding communities there.[4] By

4 In restricting my study to commercial vessels only, I have omitted several classes of watercraft that did not impact the landscape on a significant scale or a long-term basis, such as private yachts, government survey boats, and lighthouse tenders. Much of the data for vessel construction, as well as loss and deposition (chapter 11) was drawn from the Great Lakes Maritime Database (GLMDB), hosted until 2018 at the University of Michigan, integrating access to multiple archives and special collections. It is continued by the Great Lakes Maritime Collection (greatlakeships.org) co-developed by Alpena Public Library and Thunder Bay National Marine Sanctuary. Among its digital holdings are the C. Patrick Labadie image collection. Also accessed were the Historical Collections of the Great Lakes (Bowling Green University); Dossin Great Lakes Museum; Milwaukee Public Library; the Brendan Baillod and David Swayze *Great Lakes Shipwreck* databases; the *Maritime History of the Great Lakes* compiled by Walter Lewis, William R. McNeil, and

comparison, approximately 600 such ships were built during the same period in Detroit and the downriver centers of Trenton and Wyandotte. The remarkable documentation of the industry permits a clear view of the choices made by shipbuilders in the ecology of the St. Clair locale within the burgeoning American and Canadian economies. It reveals the shifting tensions between materials and technologies, traditions and innovations in a competitive climate of industrial capitalism.

Postcolonial and Modern Shipbuilding, 1824–1926

Following the War of 1812, the Rush-Bagot agreement all but eliminated the British and American naval presences on the upper Great Lakes (Dunbar and May 1995, 138). The emergent capitalist economy no longer followed the British colonial model, where luxury commodities—furs—were exchanged with colonized Natives and immigrants for manufactured goods from the mother country. Continued largely as an instrument of government policy and often at a fiscal loss, the fur trade succumbed as well to changes in European fashion (White 1991, 485; Dunbar and May 1995, 143). Nevertheless, there were logistical similarities as westward expansion sent wave after wave of settlers into the receding frontier. There they produced such bulk commodities as timber, fish, grain, and minerals in exchange for the manufactures of the industrializing East (Woodford 1994, 52). The combined economic impacts of the Industrial Revolution and the Westward Movement on this new paradigm were rapid and dramatic.

The maritime imperatives of the expansive new capitalist economy were volume and profitability, as measured by speed, labor, infrastructure, and risk. The preceding chapter discussed the cascade of factors—political, economic, technological—that propelled the transformation of the Flats throughout the

Jack Messmer; the Father Edward J. Dowling S. J. Marine Historical Database (University of Detroit Mercy); and Wisconsin Historical Society Shipwreck Database (University of Wisconsin) as well as official vessel registries, both American and Canadian. The large-scale digitization and indexing of these records made the task of inventory, comparison, and analysis, while still daunting, something less than a life's work.

nineteenth century. The present section pursues how this transformation was manifested in the preeminent form of nautical material culture, the ship itself. Where, why, and how were ships built *in*, and often specifically *for*, the waters of the St. Clair maritime landscape? The following chapter complements this with a detailed examination of the physical transformation of the built environment of the Flats—landforms, water bodies, and infrastructure—that coevolved with local and regional shipbuilding.

The nineteenth century saw thousands of vessels launched on the Great Lakes, nearly all built of wood until its concluding decades. These ranged from bulk freighters and passenger steamers; through such smaller commercial craft as ferries, tugboats, and their consort barges; to small working craft like mackinaw boats, fish tugs, bateaux, punts, and canoes (Rodgers 2016, 205). Those latter craft were built informally, often at the point of use. The larger vessels, however, were produced in commercial shipyards. Once built, they were registered, taxed, insured, repaired, modified, lost, or scrapped—lengthening the paper trail of their usage patterns throughout the Great Lakes. This permits their analysis as indicators of shipbuilding and usage patterns over time.

Excepting the outlying sloop *Chippewa* (1769), commercial shipbuilding in the St. Clair locale began in the early 1820s, with a dozen sailing ships built within that decade in four locations: St. Clair (5 ships), Marine City (3), Mount Clemens (3), and Algonac (1).[5] Their average displacement was thirty-eight gross tons (figure 10), while their average draft was just under five feet (figure 18). Eight were two-masted schooners; the remaining four were single-masted sloops. All these patterns accord well with the recommendations of Gother Mann back in 1788: modest displacement, draft shallow enough to permit careful passage through the Flats, and the more maneuverable and economical fore-and-aft rig. Over time, some sixteen vessel types emerged from the shipyards of the St. Clair region in the century spanning the 1820s to the 1920s. Collectively, they comprise 781 vessels.

5 For the sake of clarity, I use the present-day names for communities that have changed their names, their boundaries, or both. Marine City furnishes a useful example that was discussed under toponymy in chapter 5: a merger in 1865 of Newport and Ward's Landing.

FIGURE 10. Average gross tonnage of vessels built in the St. Clair locale by decade, 1820s–1920s.

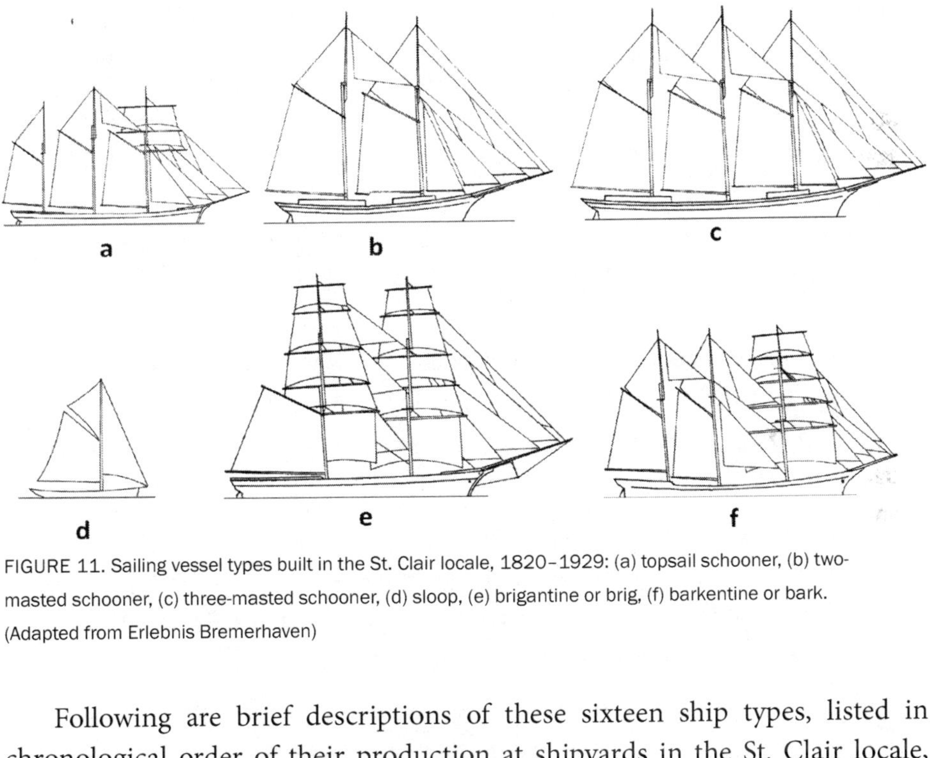

FIGURE 11. Sailing vessel types built in the St. Clair locale, 1820–1929: (a) topsail schooner, (b) two-masted schooner, (c) three-masted schooner, (d) sloop, (e) brigantine or brig, (f) barkentine or bark. (Adapted from Erlebnis Bremerhaven)

Following are brief descriptions of these sixteen ship types, listed in chronological order of their production at shipyards in the St. Clair locale, with the number of units produced there. Figure 11 gives schematic diagrams of six sailing vessel types; figures 12 through 17 offer pictorial examples of locally built specimens. Some, such as the barkentine, are distinctive in form; others—notably ferry boats, tug- or towboats, and barges—are highly variable in form but can be usefully grouped by function. In many cases, the historical terminology is imprecise; first, because a given vessel could fall into more than one category. A *propeller* (in form) employed as both a *towboat* and a *package freighter* (in functions) was a common occurrence, particularly in the early days of steam power prior to specialization.

Equally common was the alteration of a vessel's form or function during its service life. Schooners with retrofitted engines became steambarges or "screw steamers," while aging schooners, or steamboats with their engines removed, ended their careers as barges towed by propellers. A long-lived vessel was liable to have as many as a half-dozen incarnations, with attendant name changes. In compiling a database of ships built in the St. Clair locale, I have used the type (and name) under which a vessel was listed at the time of its initial launching, as this reflects both the original demand and the state of nautical technology as it relates to the landscape and its sailing conditions at that time.

- **schooner** (1821), 208 built. The earliest and commonest design, ideal for restricted sea room. Two or more masts, fore-and-aft rigged. The original British "topsail schooners" added square-rigged foremast topsails (figure 11a), improving downwind speed and upwind efficiency (Ericson 1969, 100). Faced with competition from steamers, midcentury schooners economized on crew size by eliminating the topsails (figure 11b), with larger specimens often compensating by adding a third mast (figure 11c). Centerboards were prevalent by the 1840s (Labadie and Murphy 1987, 27).
- **sloop** (1826): 15 built. Single mast, fore-and-aft rig with a single head sail or jib (figure 11d). Early specimens like the *Welcome* featured square-rigged topsails, similar to the foremast of a topsail schooner—likewise dropped to contain labor costs.
- **steamer** (1833): 57 built. Propelled by steam-powered paddlewheels. Unlike the stern-wheeler "riverboat," Great Lakes steamers were invariably side-wheelers (figure 12). The legendary *Walk in the Water* (1818) visited Detroit in 1820, continuing to Mackinac at least once in its brief 3-year career. Thirteen more years passed before a local shipbuilder launched *Lady of the Lake* at Mount Clemens. Steamers quickly dominated the profitable passenger trade, where a premium

was placed on speed, while sail remained economical for bulk cargo until the 1880s (Ericson 1968, 3).

- **ferry** (1839): 16 built. Any powered vessel serving as a maritime link in a land transport system, whether for passengers, railcars, or vehicles. Grouped by function rather than design, this class includes some of the largest vessels built on the Great Lakes.
- **brigantine** (1845), 9 built. Two masts, both square-rigged; also called a "brig" on the Great Lakes. Designed for naval combat, brigs with their numerous sails were more difficult to disable but required a large crew. Many brigs were rerigged as schooners for economical operation in peacetime (Ericson 1969, 101; figure 11e).
- **barkentine** (1847): 10 built. Three masts, only the foremast was square-rigged: locally known as a "bark." Like the brig, often rerigged as a schooner (figure 11f).
- **propeller** (1846): 56 built. Propelled by a steam-powered (later diesel) screw propeller. Versatile and powerful, often used for towing multiple sailing vessels, and for packet freight from the mid-nineteenth century onward (figure 13).
- **scow schooner** (1848): 122 built. Boxy, with a flattened bottom, square bow and stern, and simply rigged. Very quickly and cheaply built, and ideal for frontier ports, as it required minimal depth approaching the shore. Often converted to towed barges for moving bulk commodities like grain and lumber (figure 14).
- **steambarge** (1848): 98 built. The workhorse of the Great Lakes. Its combination of a schooner hull with a steam engine makes it the missing link between sail and steam in the Great Lakes (Rodgers 2016, 221). The design evolved in use, beginning with an aft pilot house, positioned directly over the steering gear. By shifting its pilot house forward and leaving the cabins aft, shipwrights around 1880 offered a long center cargo space above and below decks, often used for lumber. Commonly termed "lumber hookers," often doing double duty towing additional consort barges (Labadie and Murphy 1987, 34; figure 15).

- **towboat** or **tugboat** (1854): 69 built. A powered vessel used to move other vessels—sailing ships and later, dedicated consort barges. In common usage, *towboat* referred to a side-wheeler, while *tugboat* came to refer to compact, powerful propellers purpose-built for pulling or pushing one or more vessels. Also used as marine workboats for harbor work, construction, and salvage operations.
- **scow** (1858): 11 built. An imprecise catchall term for shallow-draft craft. Unlike a barge, it often had a minimal sailing rig, making it a scow schooner.
- **barge** (1861): 43 built. Unpowered, unrigged vessel designed to be towed or pushed. Many ships originally built as sailing vessels or steamboats ended their careers as barges.
- **schooner-barge** (1864): 29 built. Built on an efficient schooner hull but intended as a towed vessel with an auxiliary sailing rig.
- **excursion vessel** (1871): 3 built. Designed for passenger trade, especially day trips from urban centers like Detroit, Chicago, Buffalo, and Milwaukee (figure 16). While none of these early local specimens falls into the later "floating palaces" category, the Flats became the haunt for just such vessels, notably the Red Star and White Star lines, between the post–Civil War "Gilded Age" and the Great Depression.
- **package freighter** (1873) 8 built. Versatile propellers carrying a mixed payload: goods "packaged" in boxes, barrels, or bags on the lower deck; passengers in topside cabins. Their heyday was cut short by the proliferation of the railroad (figure 17).
- **bulk freighter** (1881) 28 built. Designed to carry bulk commodities (grain, lumber, coal, salt, sand, ore). Evolved from the steambarge, featuring a forward pilot house and aft cabins. Instead of a lower deck, bulk freighters featured large open central holds, accessed by deck hatches (Ericson 1968, 4–5). Most were wooden-hulled, with a handful of steel specimens built in the St. Clair locale before production shifted to Detroit area and Lake Erie shipyards. Today's enormous self-unloading "lakers" are their direct descendants (Lafferty and Van Heest 2009).

FIGURE 12. Steamer *Empire State*, built at St. Clair (1848). The largest steamboat on inland waters in its day, its stripped hull was repurposed as a dock in the Flats only ten years later. (C. Patrick Labadie Collection, Alpena County George N. Fletcher Public Library. Alpena, MI)

FIGURE 13. Propeller *City of New Baltimore*, built at Marine City (1875). (C. Patrick Labadie Collection, Alpena County George N. Fletcher Public Library. Alpena, MI)

FIGURE 14. Scow-schooner *Bertie*, under construction at Mt. Clemens (1896). Note the boxy hull lines and rig. With its centerboard raised, *Bertie* drew only four feet of water. (C. Patrick Labadie Collection, Alpena County George N. Fletcher Public Library. Alpena, MI)

FIGURE 15. Steambarge *Bessie*, built at Fair Haven (1880). Typical configuration: aft engine and cabin, a small emergency sailing rig forward, and a large cargo area—here seen hand-loading cargo—possibly barrels of lime. (C. Patrick Labadie Collection, Alpena County George N. Fletcher Public Library. Alpena, MI)

FIGURE 16. The excursion vessel *R. J. Gordon*, built at Marine City (1881), spent most of its twenty-nine-year career on Lake Michigan. (C. Patrick Labadie Collection, Alpena County George N. Fletcher Public Library. Alpena, MI)

FIGURE 17. Package freighter *Vanderbilt*, built at Port Huron (1871). The cabins indicate it carried passengers as well as manufactured goods. The arches, or "hogging trusses," kept the hull from flexing in heavy seas. (C. Patrick Labadie Collection, Alpena County George N. Fletcher Public Library. Alpena, MI)

Evolution of Great Lakes Shipbuilding in the Nineteenth Century

The shipbuilding industry that developed in the St. Clair locale may be understood in terms of Adams's network of seven elements affecting the building of ships:

- *Ideology, Purpose, Economics:* The Westward Movement became the expression of the ideology of Manifest Destiny. Waterborne movement along the expanding frontier, no longer exploratory or military, now served the purpose of exploitation through commerce and settlement. The resulting commercial fleet facilitated the flow of bulk commodities eastward to urban manufacturing and consumption centers, while manufactured goods and a shifting population flowed westward into the continental interior.
- *Technology:* Steam power was a monumental disruption that impacted every other facet of shipbuilding in some way. Steam powered the sawmills, vastly increasing both ship production and lumber shipping. Steam propulsion opened niches in the maritime economy for such innovations as bulk freighters, towboats, and consort barges. Steam dredges and pile drivers served in the creation of infrastructure, permitting larger vessels. The iron and steel industry likewise revolutionized shipbuilding. Improved metallurgy made for larger and stronger hulls and boilers alike.
- *Materials and Tradition:* Shipbuilders were entrepreneurial capitalists in a competitive market that was transitioning to steam, yet their early creations were fully rigged sailing vessels with sidewheels or propellers added on—not always gracefully or effectively. The simultaneous persistence and evolution of traditional ship designs were the product of the tension between the innate traditionalism of shipbuilders and the disruptive effects of steam. Wood was flammable and perishable, but as long as it remained abundant and cheap both as a structural material and as fuel, the St. Clair landscape continued as a locale for both shipbuilding and taking on firewood. Only when its supply was all but exhausted did wood cease to be a favored building material. By the end of the nineteenth century, wood had been supplanted by

iron and steel in the construction of ships and by coal in their fueling. Metal hulls were less limited in their structural options. From sleek passenger steamers to boxy but efficient bulk freighters, hull designs came to reflect the nature of their mission.

- *Environment:* The delta's natural channels, even with their worst obstructions located and reduced, continued as the major constraining factor influencing nautical design through the end of the nineteenth century. The centerboard schooner and the shallow-draft steamboat were responses to the unmodified environment. With large-scale dredging creating deeper, wider, straighter passages, the landscape of the Flats increasingly became a built environment, optimized for high volumes of navigation. Just as the dimensions of the Erie and Welland Canals had once dictated the dimensions of the canal schooner, in time the limiting factor in Great Lakes freighter design became not the St. Clair Flats but the Soo Locks.

While Alexander Grant's sloop *Chippewa* (1769) had foreshadowed the potential of the timber resources of the Pine River, some six decades would pass before it once again became the scene of actual shipbuilding. James M'Call, a US senator from New York aboard the steamboat *Sheldon Thompson* in 1830, wrote in his journal, "Stoped [*sic*] at Ward's landing [later Marine City]—miles above Lake St. Clair for wood . . . a fertile spot and I have no doubt in time will be a Village. *A Vessel has been built here in the last season.* Timber fine and Tall consisting of oak, Hickory, Maple, &c" (M'Call 1892, 182; emphasis added). The vessel was probably the seventy-ton schooner *Marshall Ney*, built by Samuel Ward, who gave his name to the landing.

The presence of sawmills served to catalyze the industry. Their distribution, even before the shipbuilding boom in the 1840s, indicated where the shipyards would develop along the river. The *Gazetteer of Michigan* for 1838 lists fifteen sawmills in the St. Clair locale, clustered in the areas of present-day Marine City (7 sawmills), St. Clair (5), Mt. Clemens (2), and Port Huron (1). Of the last, the author added that Port Huron "possesses excellent facilities for ship building, and furnishes an abundance of the best material, especially spars, for that business" (Blois 1838, 346). The lumber supply merely awaited the demand, which was not long in coming.

By the Age of Steam, southeast Michigan led the Great Lakes in shipbuilding, with the heaviest concentrations in Detroit and along the St. Clair River, where a "plethora of yards" had sprung up in the shadow of the seemingly inexhaustible timber stands (Mills 2002, 12). Those shipyards formed the nuclei of sixteen maritime communities along the Strait between Port Huron and Algonac as well as on the two major tributaries of Lake St. Clair: the Clinton River (Mt. Clemens, Michigan) and the Thames (Chatham, Ontario). This spatial patterning of shipyards, maritime archaeologist Anthony Firth argues, creates "a landscape of technological and financial innovation inhabited not just by shipwrights but by the whole of the soon-to-be modern population of the region"—that is, the maritime community (Firth 1995, 4). Of the total 781 commercial ships built throughout the St. Clair locale, nearly half (49%) were produced in Marine City (216 ships built) and Port Huron (168 built).

The dynamic between the natural affordances and constraints of the St. Clair landscape and the cultural demands of the Great Lakes shipping industry long favored the agency of Nature over Culture. Despite abundant building materials, ships could only be built so big and still navigate the Flats. Adaptive cultural practices, however—waiting for seiches, sounding, and marking the deepest natural channels—gradually ameliorated the situation. But it was the deepening of those channels, and finally creating new ones, that permitted more and larger vessels to transit the Flats (Jensen 2019, 45). This impact can be indexed by vessel draft. As historian Thomas Odle observed, "Until 1858 the draught of vessels built on the Great Lakes was determined by the depth of water in the North Channel of the St. Clair River" (Odle 1956, 3). In other words, until the engineers produced the technology to break through natural obstructions, it lay with the sailors and shipbuilders to make a countermove: the former by surveying, marking, and learning to navigate the Flats; the latter by building boxy shallow-draft centerboard schooners that could maximize their payload.

The initial response of the shipbuilders was a modest increase in average draft. Figure 18 shows an increase of 1.2 feet in the average draft of vessels built in the 1830s over those of the 1820s. This is the decade that followed the accurate charting and marking of the Elbow approaching the North Channel. It also saw the published observation of the effects of wind and current and the designation of Anchor Bay as a place permitting either lightering or waiting for favorable conditions. The average draft of 6.1 feet remained safely within the

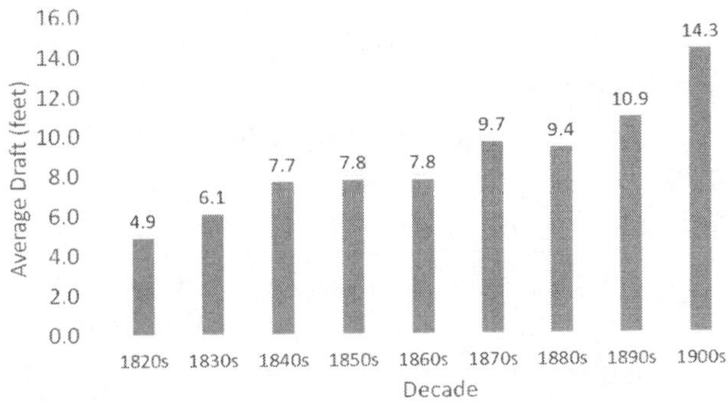

FIGURE 18. Average draft of vessels built in the St. Clair locale by decade, 1820s–1920s. Note the flat curve from the 1840s through the 1860s.

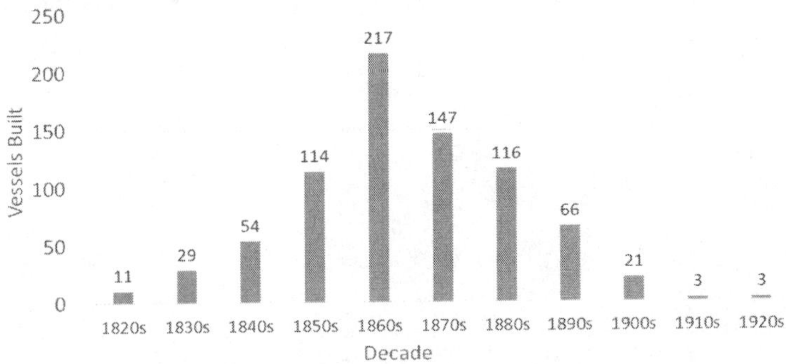

FIGURE 19. Vessels built in the St. Clair locale by decade, 1820–1929. Note the doubling of ships launched each decade between the 1820s and the 1860s.

charted minimum depth of the North Channel bar. Constrained in terms of gross tonnage and draft but blessed with seemingly endless forests, shipbuilders compensated with quantity: between 1820 and 1869, the number of ships launched in the St. Clair region doubled every decade, peaking around 1870 (figure 19).

The technological impact of steam power, both upon self-propelled steamboats and unpowered sailing vessels, formed a new paradigm in the 1840s around the disruptive practice of towing. Even prior to steam dredging, the combination of accurate charting of the natural passage over the South Channel bar and the ability of steam-propelled vessels to follow the deepest soundings directly up-current encouraged shipyards to increase their average draft to 7.7 feet. Following the initial dredging in the 1850s, the hiatus imposed by the Civil War put a stop to the improvement of the South Channel. This stagnation was reflected in a negligible average draft increase to 7.8 feet, which persisted for the remainder of the 1860s.

Following the Civil War, aggressive improvements of the St. Clair Flats beginning in 1871 triggered a significant increase in average draft to 9.7 feet (figure 18), from whence it continued to rise as the shipping channel through the entire Strait was progressively deepened (Moulton and Thieme 2009). This also permitted a corresponding increase in the average tonnage of new vessels (figure 10). The subsequent decline in number of vessels launched (figure 19) was due to a combination of developments: an increase in average tonnage per vessel, and the waning of the wooden ship industry in the region; ships became bigger but fewer (figure 20). These factors produced economies of scale, particularly in terms of labor: a large bulk freighter, it was estimated, could be manned for a mere eight dollars a day more than a medium-sized one

FIGURE 20. The Lester shipyard at Marine City, 1874. Shown under construction is the *V. H. Ketchum*. Laid down as a schooner but completed as a propeller, at 270′ it was the largest ship on the lakes when launched. It ended its days as an unrigged barge, burned on Lake Superior in 1905. (C. Patrick Labadie Collection, Alpena County George N. Fletcher Public Library. Alpena, MI)

(Woodford 1994, 53). But there were other nails in the wooden coffin, and they were made first of iron, then of steel.

Like the fur trade canoe of the previous century, the wooden ship had reached its structural limits. Vessels in excess of 1,500 tons became the swan song closing the nineteenth century. The 2,036-ton *Italia*, launched in 1889, marked the zenith of wood, while the 1,751-ton wooden bulk freighter *Alfred Mitchell* (1900) was the last of its kind built in the St. Clair locale. Once again, the 15.5-foot depth maintained in the Flats channels was the decisive factor. Owing to their greater strength, metal hulls weighed much less than wooden hulls of comparable displacement. Above 2,000 tons, a wooden ship could not pass safely or profitably through the Flats, while an iron ship of similar draft could carry 3,200 gross tons of freight (Griffin 1893, 821).

The "iron age" was itself brief: the future was in steel, and the future was being made elsewhere. Of 781 ships built in the St. Clair area, only ten were steel-hulled (figure 21). By the turn of the century, lumber companies had depleted the supplies of white oak and pine throughout the Great Lakes. While wood prices rose, steel prices fell, thanks to the newly adopted open-hearth process. Insurance rates too were lower for steel hulls: they lasted longer in freshwater with less maintenance, they were less prone to fire, and their drier holds were ideal for grain and other perishable bulk cargoes (Dappert 2006, 26; also Mills 2002, 3).

Canadian Shipbuilding

With its political partitioning and demilitarization, the prospect of war was all but eliminated from the St. Clair maritime landscape. As a commercial transport and shipbuilding zone, however, American barriers to lumber exports took the place of furs as a source of tension.[6] The lack of extensive pine stands

6 A brief incident was triggered in 1870, as the artificial St. Clair Flats Canal created an ambiguity in the international boundary. A lumberman contracted with a Canadian shipper to deliver a load of timber to the Canadian side of the Flats. Upon landing, the ship, its cargo and owner were seized by US Customs officials claiming they were on American soil and demanding a heavy tariff. A hastily improvised Canadian "gunboat" arrived on the scene with the Ontario Minister of Public Works aboard, evidently to enforce the

FIGURE 21. Launching the bulk freighter *North Star* at the Great Lakes Engineering Works in St. Clair (1909). One of the few steel-hulled vessels built in the waning days of the St. Clair shipbuilding industry. (Detroit Historical Society)

on the eastern side of the Strait was a constraint on Canadian shipbuilding, one which had been foreshadowed in 1794 by William Baker's difficulty in building proper gunboats at Chatham for lack of access to the lighter, more easily worked timber. While the Ontario shipyards continued to languish until the 1860s and thereafter never achieved the volume of their Michigan neighbors, the flourishing towing industry created an opportunity in the maritime transport system: a sudden demand for towboats between Lake Erie and Lake Huron. Schooners

position that the disputed landing was on the Canadian side. This triggered rumors in both the American and Canadian press that Canada had "seized the St. Clair Flat Canal." The *Detroit Free Press* of October 12 trumpeted, "The British Flag flying over the Works! And a Canadian Gunboat There to Maintain It!" In the wake of the War of 1812, the "seizure" of the Flats seems an apt instance of Marx's 1852 commentary on Hegel that history does indeed repeat itself, playing out first as tragedy, then as farce.

were still numerous, each liable to need assistance transiting the Strait. This in turn opened a specialized niche in the local shipbuilding industry.

Timber, being scarce in Ontario and now expensive to import due to American tariffs, was already a material constraint on the Canadian side. Moreover, a further political constraint had developed. The American government, protective of its own fleet, required American-registered vessels to be built in American shipyards and did not permit Canadian vessels to traffic between American ports (Griffin 1893, 831). Meanwhile, the American shipyards were producing increased numbers of ever-larger sailing vessels in the Strait. For the struggling Canadian shipyards, economic opportunity lay in expanding into the local practice of consort towing between the lakes. They began producing compact but powerful propeller-driven tugboats, requiring much less timber than the big schooners they towed and fitted with high-efficiency steam engines imported from Great Britain. The result was a symbiosis between the local Michigan and Ontario shipyards, as the former met the demand for inexpensive tonnage while the latter expedited the movement of those schooners through their most problematic and risky pilotage, the Strait itself, without running afoul of American protectionism.

A vernacular design developed. Tugs built for use in the Strait were characterized by two features: powerful engines capable of towing multiple sailing vessels between Lakes Erie and Huron and minimal draft to allow maneuvering in shallow water while freeing grounded vessels. The average draft of the locally built tugboat fleet was 6 feet (1.8 m), with only a single vessel drawing more than 7 feet (2 m). Tugs that operated exclusively in the Strait could forgo the deep-water performance and stability of long-haul boats that plied the open waters beyond. Of a total of 69 tugs launched in the St. Clair locale between 1854 and 1902, 29 (42%) were Ontario-built. For comparison, only 20% (153 of 781) of the total number of vessels of all types were Ontario-built. The Ontario ships were skewed toward steam (24%, or 82 of 335) and away from sail (only 14%, or 57 of 404). Ontario also supplied an outsized share of the versatile propeller vessels, which were likewise smaller yet powerful and often used for towing: 34%, or 19 of the regional total of 56. A similar proportion of purpose-built barges, 14 of 43 or 33%, came from Ontario shipyards. This last may be owing to a second timber-saving tactic: recycling. Opportunistic shipwrights, particularly in Sarnia, took advantage of the ready supply of wrecked, burned, or aging hulls, rebuilding and returning them to service as newly registered barges.

Shipbuilding and the *Longue Durée*

From its very inception, boat- and shipbuilding in the St. Clair locale was adapted to the local environment and its sailing conditions. Throughout the *longue durée* from European contact until the end of the nineteenth century, the maritime landscape's environment and materials—problematic sailing conditions and abundant timber, respectively—remained relatively constant. In each of the historical periods, by contrast, social and cultural shifts occurred: from subsistence to colonial mercantilism to industrial capitalism. The result in each case was a distinctively adapted nautical material culture—vessels and their associated technology—that reflected the identity, traditions, and maritime practice of sailors and shipbuilders alike.

By the late nineteenth century, the technologies of steam power and metal hull fabrication had, in a series of disruptive innovations, shifted the preponderance of agency away from the environment and given it to the industrialized American and Canadian nation-states. In the process, the unique alignment of affordances that had led to the rise of the St. Clair locale as a center for shipbuilding was eclipsed. The newly emergent steel cities arose where iron ore, coal, and labor could be brought together by water, rail, and road. The lasting significance of the Strait as a critical transport zone, however, was only beginning to be realized. As its constraints to movement were minimized, the significance of its geographical positioning at a natural crossroads became all the more obvious. The next two chapters examine the physical transformation of the maritime landscape of the St. Clair Flats: first, into the world's busiest commercial waterway; then, into a recreational mecca nostalgically poised between a bygone frontier and an industrial urban future.

9

The Transformed Maritime Cultural Landscape

By last mail, orders from the Engineer Department reached the engineer office in charge of our river and harbor improvements, directing General Cram to discontinue all operations he may have commenced upon the present crooked old channel of St. Clair Flats, and to make the necessary arrangements for commencing work upon the proposed new channel without delay. Under this authority, given by the law, General Cram proposes to abandon the present crooked route, and make a straight ship canal from the mouth of the pass, directly across the flat into the lake, which will be only one and a half miles long, thereby saving one mile at least, and have a depth of thirteen feet below the lowest stage of water, and a width of 300 feet between its banks.

Such a canal would allow sail vessels, under a fair wind, to pass without being towed day and night. General Cram says, "Very few channels of commerce present such a constant stream of passing vessels as seen during the season of navigation in the channel of the Flats. In October 1866, a gentleman of veracity informed me, that while he was detained in coming through, he counted one hundred vessels in the crooked portions of the channel at one time, struggling to get through, and that the jam near the lighthouse was fearful."

—*Chicago Tribune*, March 20, 1867

Throughout the historical period in eastern North America, a persistent objective of each successive dominant culture has been the optimization of maritime transport zones between the Atlantic Seaboard, the Great Lakes, and the rivers beyond. The clear trend is toward ever-increasing range, scale, and diversity of movement; the increase of access to exploitable resources; and the reduction of obstacles. There is scarcely a development in the processes of knowing, representing, dwelling in, or moving through the St. Clair regional maritime landscape that is not, by accident or design, contributory to the long-term phenomenon of *connectivity*. The cascade of incremental developments throughout the pivotal nineteenth century marked a tipping point in the shifting balance of agency that had been slow to develop, then jogged forward by a series of crises and disruptive innovations. Having analyzed maritime practice and nautical technology—seafaring and shipbuilding—it is time to examine the cumulative effect of human agency on the environment itself, as modern society increasingly shaped its maritime landscape with powerful new tools.

The Erie Canal had opened in 1825, followed by the Welland Canal in 1829, yet it was not until 1842 that the notion of dredging to improve the passage through an existing waterway was seriously discussed. Why? The British and Americans had both been building canals since the latter half of the eighteenth century, while the Dutch had been at it far longer. Technological difficulties aside, it may be that while the maritime system of the upper Great Lakes had reached its capacity, the benefits of improvement did not yet outweigh the costs. The massive increase in shipping during and following the Civil War, however, exposed the cracks in the system. The rising rate of shipping accidents in the Flats alone suggests that safety and efficiency were declining. Counting only incidents within the entire St. Clair system that resulted in a sinking, in the decade of the 1830s there were only two; in the 1840s, six. In the 1850s, there were twenty-one, and in the 1860s, thirty-one (figure 22).

Bureaucratic inertia, logistical hurdles, and the Panic of 1837 can all be blamed for delaying the actual execution of improvements to the Flats. But the dearth of early calls for the physical improvement of the ship channel, however ineffectual, is noteworthy. It suggests that the constraints posed by the St. Clair Flats had not yet progressed to the point where merely marking the best natural route was no longer seen as adequate. The leap in vessel losses in the 1850s and 1860s vividly shows that progress, when it arrived, came at a price.

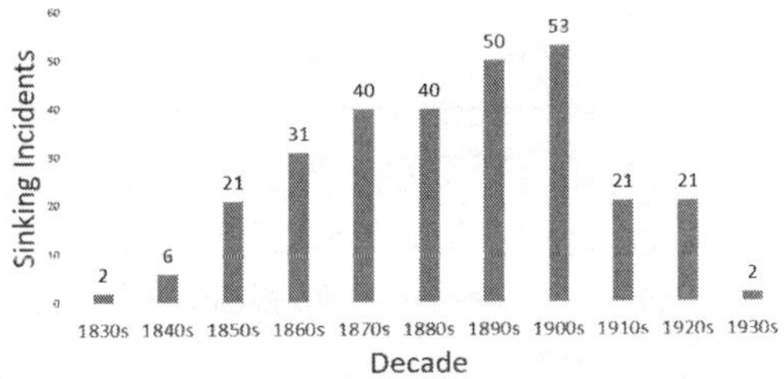

FIGURE 22. Count of sinkings in the St. Clair locale by decade, 1830s–1930s. Note the dramatic reduction as twentieth century practices and technologies were adopted.

Aftermath of the Civil War: Work Resumes

The shortcomings of the limited pre–Civil War dredging (map 13) had been painfully apparent to burgeoning upstream cities like Chicago, whose *Tribune* enthusiastically reported the recommendation of General T. J. Cram of the Topographic Engineers for abandoning the "present crooked route" approaching the South Channel using range markers and buoys and dredging a direct approach. As calculated by Cram, the construction cost of a straightened canal would be $428,754 (Cram 1867, 58). Offsetting this outlay, Cram calculated that the yearly costs for "towage, pilotage, grounding damages and collisions is nearly $500,000." The new canal would thus "pay for its whole cost in less than one season of navigation" (*Chicago Tribune* March 20, 1867).

Unlike prewar efforts, the work progressed uninterrupted by budget cutbacks and presidential vetoes. In the spring of 1869, the *Detroit Post* of March 20 ventured a cautious sigh of relief, noting "five dredges with their appropriate scows and tugs, together with three pile drivers and all the incidental machinery are now on the ground and in complete readiness for work." Calling for the needed appropriations from Congress, it concluded, "this is a purely national work, and let no exertions be spared which will tend to ensure the early completion of an improvement whose value is incalculable." As the work neared completion in the summer of 1870, the local press reported that "the scene presented at the canal is one of great activity. No less than six steam barges are employed, five steam pile drivers, three tugs and a large number of scows, while three hundred men are engaged in the work, and with their families, who also have their homes upon the dock already built, quite a little town is to be seen" (*Detroit Free Press* July 29, 1870, 2).

In 1871 the much-anticipated "St. Clair Ship Canal" opened, ending the thirteen-year hiatus occasioned by the Civil War. Like his predecessor Captain Williams, Cram reckoned that the current in the dredged passage would keep it clear without further maintenance. In this age of optimism, Cram was a man of his time; he was, however no visionary: "In this revised report I have estimated for the dredging in the proposed canal to give us a depth of 13 feet below the stage at which we found the water in our recent observations. This, I think, will give *a canal deep enough for all time to come*" (Cram 1867, 58; emphasis added). Instead, within a year of its opening the churning propellers of towboats, squeezing past each other, eroded the embankment, even where reinforced by a wooden dike. Schooners under tow, yawing into the shallow margins of the canal, exacerbated the problem, especially when they grounded and had to be pulled off. Parts of the canal were promptly reduced from 13 to 11.5 feet (Larson 1981, 82). Nor was the mere act of straightening the entrance a panacea. The Ship Canal merely led the way to more of the "crooked old channel" upstream. Continued collisions and groundings, particularly in the "Southeast Bend," where the natural channel bends westward, prompted continual dredging, marking, and the removal of obstructions—among them numerous wrecked and abandoned vessels.

The Modern St. Clair Corridor Takes Shape

In their 2009 report to the International Upper Great Lakes Study, Army Corps of Engineers archivists Ralph Moulton and Scott Thieme compiled an exhaustive *History of Dredging and Compensation: St. Clair and Detroit Rivers*, presented as a timeline from 1852 to 2005, where every official cubic yard of dredging has been accounted for (Moulton and Thieme 2009). In its details, it shows how successive impediments along the entire Strait between Huron and Erie arose and were addressed. In the process, the entire river and its infrastructure of channels, harbors, and landings were optimized for deep-draft transport. The adage "the nail that sticks up the highest gets pounded down first" applies here, as the location of the shallowest and narrowest spots in the Flats that constituted the pinch-points for shipping, altered with each season of dredging and bank stabilization. The effects of the ongoing transformation may be seen in nautical design and maritime practice, as indicated by shipbuilding patterns and waterborne shipping, respectively.

By the turn of the twentieth century, the Lake Carriers Association, citing the persistent delays and obstructions caused by overcrowding, had effectively lobbied for widening the St. Clair Ship Canal through the creation of a second canal parallel to the 1871 cut (Lydecker 1900). Construction began in the 1904 season and was completed in 1907, with each channel measuring 150′ wide by 18′ deep (Moulton and Thieme 2009, B.2.6). Resembling a modern divided highway, one channel was designated for upbound traffic, the other for downbound, in an effort (not always successful) to minimize head-on encounters. A reinforced dike separating the canals was created by dumping dredge spoils between two creosote-treated wooden retaining walls, which were then planted with willows and grasses to prevent erosion. Like the original retaining walls, the dike required continual maintenance, especially when the canal was deepened to 20′ between 1915 and 1924, undercutting the original pilings. In 1935, the problematic (and rotting) dividing dike was removed, producing a single channel 700′ wide and 25′ deep. The bottleneck now shifted upstream to the Southeast Bend, immediately above the Ship Canal, where the tight radius of the turn created a blind corner. Numerous collisions attest to the inadequate sight lines, maneuvering room, channel markings, and ship-to-ship communications of the day. Of the innumerable collisions and near-collisions that took place in what was now the most dangerous stretch of the Strait, at least eleven resulted in sinkings between 1870 and 1905.

By the 1940s, it had become clear that the enormous ore freighters built to use the newly expanded Soo Locks between Lake Superior and Lake Huron could not safely traverse the curves of the Southeast Bend, thus jeopardizing a strategic resource on a par with the Soo Locks themselves. The dredging in 1960–62 of the "St. Clair Cutoff" provided a nearly straight passage from Algonac to the open waters of Lake St. Clair (map 14). With constant maintenance, the Strait has achieved a dynamic equilibrium between the entropic forces of Nature and the energy invested by industrial maritime Culture and serves to this day as a crucial international waterway—by most accounts the world's busiest. The

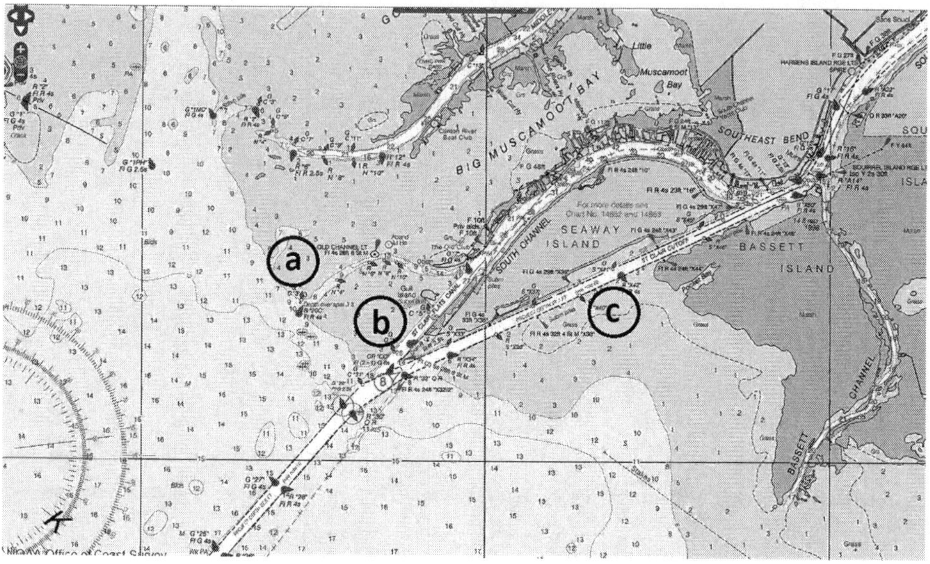

MAP 14. The South Channel today. From left to right: (a) the original channel (1858), note "Old Channel Lt" and "Abdn LH": the original beacon and lighthouse, respectively; (b) the St. Clair Flats Canal (1871); and (c) the St. Clair Cutoff Channel (1962). (NOAA Chart 14853)

abandonment of old transport zones for the creation of new ones has implications for regional landscape archaeology. The benign neglect of key features of older routes—Anchor Bay, with its once-staked Elbow; the lighthouses of the original South Channel cut, now adopted by a local preservationist group; the Southeast Bend—creates a horizontally dispersed historical landscape of accessible and interpretable remnants. Despite a popular textual metaphor of a "palimpsest," the Flats maritime landscape does not truly conform. Rather than being overwritten, these superseded—even neglected—features might be better thought of as "marginalia." And as every student of manuscripts knows, the margins are where the most revealing details are to be sought.

Transformation and Ship Design

So long as the depth of the South Channel route was less than that of harbors and canal locks, Great Lakes shipbuilders were constrained by the passage through the Flats. Generally, the dimensions of commercial ships coevolved with those of the St. Clair waterway. To be sure, there were a few spectacular outliers, such as the grain carrier *Chauncey Hurlbut*, built in 1873 by the Simon Langell shipyard at St. Clair. Despite drawing over twenty-one feet, it is recorded as having repeatedly traversed the Flats, albeit running aground at least once. In fact, the outcome of such oversized ships forcing their way through the Flats was a contributing factor to the prompt silting-up of the Ship Channel, forcing continual dredging and widening. Each improvement to the channel encouraged larger vessels, which in turn strained the entire shipping network at its weakest point. The dialectic between the transport zone and the ships that used it was one of each continually pushing the performance envelope of the other. Bulk freighters grew not only deeper but longer, to the point where the radius of the Southeast Bend of the South Channel became the limiting factor for freighter traffic, especially overtaking or oncoming encounters.

Transformation and Waterborne Commerce

The combined effects of the transformed waterway, evolving ship design, and maritime practice produced a reduction in the operating constraints of larger vessels. This is seen in the volume of shipping passing through the Strait. In a report to the Treasury Department on Great Lakes commerce, political economist George Tunell posited that the tonnage recorded passing through Detroit could serve as an indicator of commerce through the entire Strait (Tunell 1896a, 243). Figure 23 places Tunell's post–Civil War annual data alongside comparable pre–Civil War tonnage from the Census Bureau. Comparing figures 18, 19, and 23, it is evident that during the latter decades of the nineteenth century, increases in the average draft and in the number of vessels built in the St. Clair locale reflected a trend throughout the Great Lakes and were manifested as a marked increase in shipping tonnage passing through the Strait.

Despite competition from the railroads for local freight and passenger traffic, Tunell concluded, the lake carriers held a decided edge in the movement of four bulk commodities: iron ore, coal, grain, and lumber, which collectively

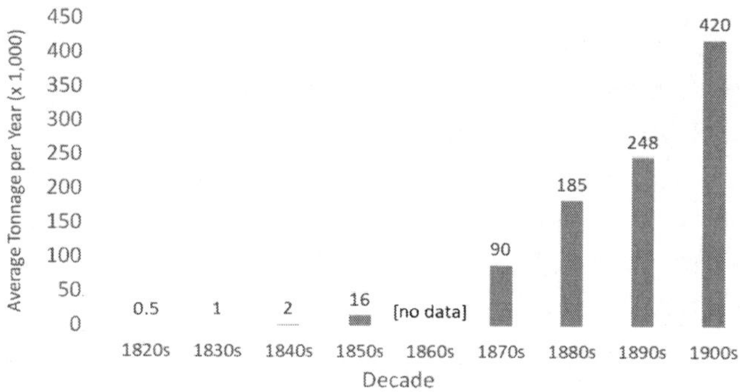

FIGURE 23. Average tonnage of shipping through Detroit by decade, 1820s–1900s. Data for the 1860s are incomplete due to the disruption of the American Civil War. (US Bureau of the Census 1975; US Bureau of Topographic Engineers; Lake Carriers Association)

accounted for nearly all the long-distance shipping on the Great Lakes (Tunell 1896b). Between 1867 and 1891, a contemporary study noted, the cost of shipping a ton of iron ore from Escanaba, in Michigan's Upper Peninsula to Lake Erie ports fell from $4.25 to just 84 cents, while a bushel of grain shipped from Chicago to Buffalo fell from 15 cents in 1860 to 2.5 cents in 1891 (Griffin 1893, 819). This suggests that deep-draft ships like the *Chauncey Hurlbut* were ascending the St. Clair River unladen, reducing the risk of grounding while proceeding upstream, then using the current to assist them in their downbound passage when fully loaded.

The uses to which the transport zone of the Strait was put by the maritime community were now skewed strongly toward moving raw materials and agricultural products from the Midwest to markets in the East. Not so with passenger traffic: long-distance movement was largely taken over by the railroads, while shorter water routes, especially between cities from Buffalo to Chicago, became increasingly dominated by a new type of watercraft: the dedicated passenger steamer. These came to include the "floating palaces" that catered to a new clientele—city-dwellers seeking a day's respite from the new industrial centers that now lined the lakeshores, including Detroit.

Transformation and Route Preference

As an indicator of the mindset of Straits mariners, regularly published official and commercial editions of sailing directions shed light on the shift in route preferences as the landscape was modified. In the two decades following the opening of the first dredged section of the South Channel in 1857, the North Channel route remained the option of choice for nontowed sailing vessels. As the proportion of ships that were either self-propelled or towed increased, and concurrently with improvements in the South Channel, route preference shifted. The order in which the North and South Channel routes are listed and the details of their description reflect this shift.

The 1857 publication of the official chart for the St. Clair Flats featured directions for approaching both the North and South Channels, or "Passes," in that order. The South Pass instructions, however, added detailed instructions for approaching the newly dredged section, using the numbered buoys and the alignment of the new lighthouse and its beacon (US Bureau of Topographic Engineers 1857). Thereafter, commercially published sailing directions regularly incorporated the latest enhancements—additional or lighted buoys, precise distances, and bearings.

The first edition of T. S. Thompson's commercial guide, *Coast Pilot for the Upper Lakes* (1859), lists the North Channel route first yet skeptically hints at its decline. Approaching the Elbow, it advises "leaving all the red stakes to starboard and black to port (*if there are any*), until in the St. Clair River, north channel" (Thompson 1859, 56; emphasis added). Directions to enter the St. Clair River "by the south pass or channel" are comparatively elaborate, noting that "this channel is under improvement, and will be dredged to 14 feet water." Mariners were advised to use the traditional lead-weighted line to sound their course through pilings marking the dredging area until they reached fifteen feet of depth in the river (Thompson 1859, 56). The following year, new aids to navigation were in place at the mouth of the South Channel: ten color-coded and numbered buoys replaced the pilings as guides. The official government Light-House Board description of the South Channel approach now began, "As you enter the channel between buoys Nos. 1 and 2, bring the light towers in range and run for them, until abreast of red buoy No. 4; then port gradually"; yet it concluded, "when abreast of black buoy No. 5; starboard gradually and run 100 feet from *two pine trees* stationed on the curve 50 feet from the channel bank, above which you are in St. Clair river" (US Light-House Board 1860, 3; emphasis added). Despite state-of-the-art buoyage, the days of navigating by "the Plum Bush" were yet not so far distant.

Thompson's second edition still listed the North Pass first and in unchanged form. The directions for the South Pass, meanwhile, grew ever more detailed, as additional sets of range lights marked each bend, indicating that mariners were now regularly risking the South Pass at night—formerly an almost unheard of practice. Again, not all landmarks were official or formal. Approaching Algonac, the pilot was advised to "keep in mid-channel until the *two log houses on the Canada shore* are in range"—that is, lined up with each other (Thompson 1861, 54; emphasis added). That last instruction—and evidently the two log houses—remained in succeeding editions until the fifth (1869), which noted in passing that the North Pass had not been staked since 1860. Concluding the section, Thompson anticipated "the new cut or channel over the St. Clair Flats," marked at its entrance by two lighthouses, would constitute an improvement "of incalculable benefit to the sailing community, also to merchants and owners of vessels" (Thompson 1869, 89).

Thompson's optimism notwithstanding, the opening of the straighter St. Clair Ship Canal in 1871 was no panacea. If anything, it too was a victim of its own success, soon strained to capacity. The constant churning of passing traffic threatened the stability of the narrow passage: "It is asserted that the St. Clair Flats ship-canal is a failure," complained the *Chicago Daily Tribune* of November 16, 1877. "The long, expensive cribs, filled in with earth and planted with willow trees in the hope that their roots would hold the soil against the action of the water, fail to answer the expectations of the engineer who planned the work. There is a constant heavy expenditure of money to stop these chasms. Singularly enough, the old [South] channel, dredged out twenty years ago, and left with nothing above water to mark the course but buoys, is as deep as ever, and shows no sign of filling up." Accordingly, Thompson's sixth edition (1878), while omitting altogether the North Pass, first listed the South Channel's "Old Cut" of 1858, followed by directions for the new Ship Canal (Thompson 1878, 58).

As evidenced in sailing directions, with each successive hydrologic or infrastructural modification of the Strait, commercial shipping migrated cautiously to the new route. Directions using expedient wayfinding markers like pine trees and log cabins gave way to private or commercial initiatives like stakes and painted barrels. These in turn were supplanted by standardized aids to navigation, installed, maintained, and charted by government agencies. The knowledge and cultural reproduction of this information likewise evolved from transmission within the closed society of mariners to its promulgation in official and commercial publications. As practices became codified, disseminated, and adopted, the carrying capacity, efficiency, and safety of the transport corridor increased. Seen in the *longue durée*, the trend in route preference through the Huron-Erie strait was away from the natural features of Anchor Bay and the North Channel, requiring behavioral adaptations (waiting for wind and water depth, lightering) to a built environment made to conform to societal demands.

Transformation and Dwelling: Patterns in Settlement and Population

From its outset as a trade route in the historical period, the Strait offered its dwellers economic opportunities, beginning with the Mississauga, who bartered fish and furs for French goods at Detroit. Difficult navigational points typically create a concentration of maritime activities where sailors require services—support, guidance, hospitality, and safety. Residents might be recruited into such ancillary maritime activities as pilotage, or the maintenance of routes with navigation markers from lopsticks to lighthouses. These form the nucleus of what Westerdahl terms "*maritime transport enclaves* or *niches*: the concentration along certain transport zones of activities associated with transportation, building, maintenance and management of ships" (Westerdahl 1994, 267; emphasis in original).

Historically, the first such enclave along the Strait was Fort Sinclair, later the town of St. Clair, where five critical activities came together in space and time. First, it became the transshipment point along the route between Detroit and Michilimackinac, where boats transferred their cargo to and from the *Gladwin* schooner. Second was the defensive function served by the fort; third, the access along the Pine River to vast stands of timber; fourth, the maintenance, storage, and later, the building of ships. Finally, it became a refueling station for wood-burning steamers bound for Lake Huron. All subsequent enclaves that developed nearby offered some combination of these activities.

Between the decennial censuses of 1850 and 1900, the population in the four principal Michigan maritime communities in the St. Clair locale underwent its most dramatic transformation. The village of St. Clair began as the largest of the four with a population of 1,722 in 1850, leading Port Huron by 153 souls. A half-century later the factors that had contributed to the rise and prosperity of St. Clair had all but vanished. After reaching a modest peak of 3,792 in 1880, its wood supply ran out—for local shipbuilding, for fuel, and for milled lumber—and the population declined accordingly to 2,543.

Meanwhile, Port Huron evolved into a robust transport enclave, first as the northern terminus for towboats picking up and discharging their consorts through the Strait. This prompted the development of the full suite of maritime support services. With the arrival of the Grand Trunk Railroad at Sarnia in 1859, the Port Huron-Sarnia locale became a rail transshipment hub, first by ferry, then in 1891 by a tunnel under the river. Until joined by the Michigan Central Railway Tunnel in 1910, the St. Clair Tunnel offered the only continuous rail service across the Strait (Barnett 2023, 18–19). The net result was a twelve-fold increase between 1850 and 1900, from 1,569 to 19,158.

Between these extremes, Mount Clemens, like Port Huron a county seat and administrative center situated at the intersection of water, rail, and roadway corridors, diversified its timber-based economy with manufacturing, agriculture, and a popular mineral spa (Magee 1980). The result was a five-fold increase, from 1,297 to 6,576 persons in 1900.

Marine City struggled as it clung to the last vestiges of the shipbuilding industry, transitioning from new ship construction to dry docks specializing in repairs and barge conversion of the aging and dwindling wooden fleet (Griffin 1893, 831–32). Between 1850 and 1900, it grew only fourfold, from 913 to 3,829 residents. In the intervening century, its local economy has diversified with the addition of the Morton Salt Works, US Steel, an Edison power plant, and recreational boating—all predicated on its location at the confluence of the Belle River with the St. Clair waterway. As with the ribbon farm, access to the river was a facilitating factor in successful dwelling in the maritime landscape but no guarantee of prosperity.

Perhaps the most remarkable development in the process of dwelling was the settlement of the archipelagoes that embraced the Middle and South Channels. The urbanization of Detroit and its Great Lakes sister cities in the post–Civil War era created a demand for leisure that transcended lines of social status and income. Lumber barons and day laborers alike took to the water, often rubbing elbows on the booming fleet of excursion vessels that radiated outward from Buffalo, Cleveland, Detroit, Milwaukee, and Chicago. Nowhere was the transformation more dramatic than in the St. Clair Flats, or as it came to be known, "Michigan's Venice."

10

From Tocqueville to Tashmoo

The Golden Age of the St. Clair Flats

In his journal for August of 1831, Alexis de Tocqueville described his journey north aboard the steamer *Superior*: "We embark at 2 o'clock. Shore of Detroit. Land low and cultivated. Many houses. Lake Saint Clair. In the evening dancing on the bridge. American gaiety." Two days later, he wrote from Fort Sinclair:

> At 1 o'clock I go shooting in the marshes on the other side of the river Saint Clair. First we go to the fort. In the forest on the way the sound of a savage drum. Some cries. We see coming eight savages stark naked except for a little loin cloth. (6 children, 2 men). Besmeared with dyes from head to foot. Hair bristling, lots of ends falling in queue behind. A wooden club in hand, jumping like devils. Beautiful men. Dancing for fun and to get money. We gave them a shilling. It is the War-dance. Horrible to see. What a degradation. (Tocqueville 1959, 143)

Adventures in the Liminal Zone: The Social Origins of a Recreational Landscape

As in so many other respects, Tocqueville was a man ahead of his time. In his telegraphic style, the astute observer of American culture captured the experience of a recreational visitor to the St. Clair locale, a full half-century before it became an everyday occurrence. The genteel social amenities of traveling by steamboat; sightseeing at the now-superfluous military relic; hunting for sport; and finally, the ambiguous "degradation" of being entertained by Indigenous identity performance—all are there. The emergence of an entire facet of the St. Clair Flats—that of a recreational mecca on the edge of a tamed wilderness—is a postscript to the prescient Frenchman.

Tocqueville was not alone in recording his impressions of this same voyage. A fellow traveler, the barrister Godfrey T. Vigne, Esq., wrote, "The 'Superior,' as she was called was, I think, the most comfortable steamer I had yet entered; her upper deck, about one hundred and twenty feet in length, was of great width [beam was 28′] and afforded an excellent promenade" (Vigne 1833, 137). Vigne likewise praised "the morass opposite the fort [Gratiot] which abounded in wild fowl of all kinds," while "the unbroken and interminable forest, with which [the riverbanks] are covered, contains more game than any other part bordering on the lakes, being less frequented by hunters" (Vigne 1833, 140).

The notion of a local pleasure cruise in the Detroit area had a few antecedents and coincides, not surprisingly, with the arrival of steam. Were it not for a bit of rough weather, the pleasures of exploring Lake St. Clair by steamboat might have been chronicled a decade earlier. Awaiting the departure of his delegation, boundary commissioner Richard Delafield joined a social party aboard the steamer *Walk in the Water* on its inaugural visit to Detroit. On the Fourth of July 1820, they "proceed into Lake St. Clair, but on account of threatening showers put about and run down the Detroit River, toward Malden," the erstwhile British fortification, where they enjoyed an excellent dinner, cotillions danced to a military band, and numerous toasts and gun salutes, all amid "great mirth" (Delafield 1943, 277).

Considering Delafield's British colleague Dr. Bigsby's description of the delta as "pestilential" (Bigsby 1850, 298), it is not surprising that the reputation of the Flats was slow to change. In doing so, the Flats actually capitalized on its frontier image, seen already in Tocqueville, as an encounter with the untamed. Calvin Colton, an American journalist and politician, described his 1833 departure from Detroit—again by steamboat—in a paean of clichés-to-be: "The passage over Lake St. Clair, in a day of such unrivalled physical glories, in such a company, on just such an expedition, leaving the regions of civilization behind us, and just about to plunge into the regions of barbarism—or rather, flying from a world, violated by the track and by the hand of man, into a world of virgin waters and into a virgin wilderness—all vast, and their proper character inconceivable, except by actual inspection; such a passage might well make an apology for the indulgence of some trifling ingredients of poetry and romance" (Colton 1833, 58; emphasis added). It is that concluding word—romance—that betrays Colton's aesthetic nostalgia. In time the Romantic Movement faded, but like other ideologies before it, it left its mark on the Flats.

From Pestilential Swamp to "Michigan's Venice"

The assimilation of the Flats as a recreational space by the burgeoning population of Detroit marks a distinct new transformation, one unrelated to its original role as a transport zone. Once its chief hazards to navigation had been mitigated, urban dwellers, transcending (at least for the day) divisions of income and class, de-marginalized the Flats, adding it to the social landscape. Detroit newspapers touted the egalitarian pleasures of the new class of vessels catering to "tourists and excursionists" (Dixon 2002, 11–12). The transport zone that had first developed as a corridor for commodities became the venue for an array of recreational activities. The earliest of these were illustrated by Tocqueville—the rustic amusements of passengers to Port Huron and beyond. While the dining and dancing took place at first aboard ship, others were situated in the landscape itself—hunting, fishing, gawking at the performances of the "savages" (perhaps with a wink on both sides). These earliest chroniclers, however, were still primarily engaged in the process of *movement through* the landscape. The picturesque *habitants* and savages, as providers of these aesthetic experiences, were the dwellers. The Flats was still a liminal zone to be traversed and not yet a destination in its own right.

This began to change in the post–Civil War period, as a small vanguard of the growing capitalist class in Detroit took to the water to seek respite from the increasingly crowded city not only on nearby Belle Isle (erstwhile Hog Island) but farther afield. Spearheaded by banker William A. Butler, a group of affluent Detroit sportsmen in 1872 founded the St. Clair Flats Hunting and Shooting

Club (later known as "The Old Club"), near Butler's ornate Victorian Gothic cottage at the mouth of the Old South Channel (Dixon 2002, 20, 42). Unconsciously mimicking the age-old seasonal round, sporting hunters and fishermen gentrified the subsistence pattern of *habitants* and Natives. These in turn monetized their role as guides, selectively providing access to their knowledge and ancestral landscape to paying outsiders. Within a few years, fashionable sportsmen's clubs had sprung up along the route of the now-daily steamboats, which plied the cultural borderland between civilization and a putative wilderness. As the clubs became more elaborate and influential, the seasonal rustications of their members were noted in the Detroit society pages.

In the wake of the exclusive clubs came affordable resort hotels catering to the working class, by the day or the week. The first of these was the Star Island House, developed in 1874 as a destination by the Star Line of excursion boats. Day tourists disembarking from the Port Huron boat, recounts Flats historian Michael Dixon,[1] "could spend the day fishing and have a fresh fish or frog leg supper before catching the evening steamer back to Detroit" (Dixon 2002, 45). In an 1895 feature on "Michigan's Venice," the *Detroit News Tribune* exclaimed, "And still the crowds come and come. Is there no end to them? Has the whole population of Detroit chosen this special day to go to the Flats? No, this is only a fair sample of every Sunday morning in summer; this is the Sunday crowd" (*Detroit News Tribune* August 18, 1895). By 1896, passenger and excursion boats made no fewer than a dozen stops at clubs and resorts between Lake St. Clair and Algonac (map 15).

None exemplified the Flats' new identity better than Joe Bedore's place, originally a simple log cabin that grew into a quaint and comfortable tourist hotel (Dixon 2002, 64–67). In the rotund figure of the French Canadian Joe Bedore, the image of Colton's hospitable but indolent *habitant* (Colton 1833, 61) was reborn as the soi-disant "King of the Flats," a beloved local character: guide, host, sage, and droll raconteur (figure 24).

A third class of recreational dweller in the Flats landscape was the seasonal cottager: "Every bit of land that thrusts itself out of the lake," observed travel

1 Michael Dixon's three-volume collection of images and reminiscences, compiled and republished in 2002 as *Life at the Flats: The Golden Era of the St. Clair River Delta* (Mount Clemens, MI: Mervue) is a treasury for this period in the history of the Flats.

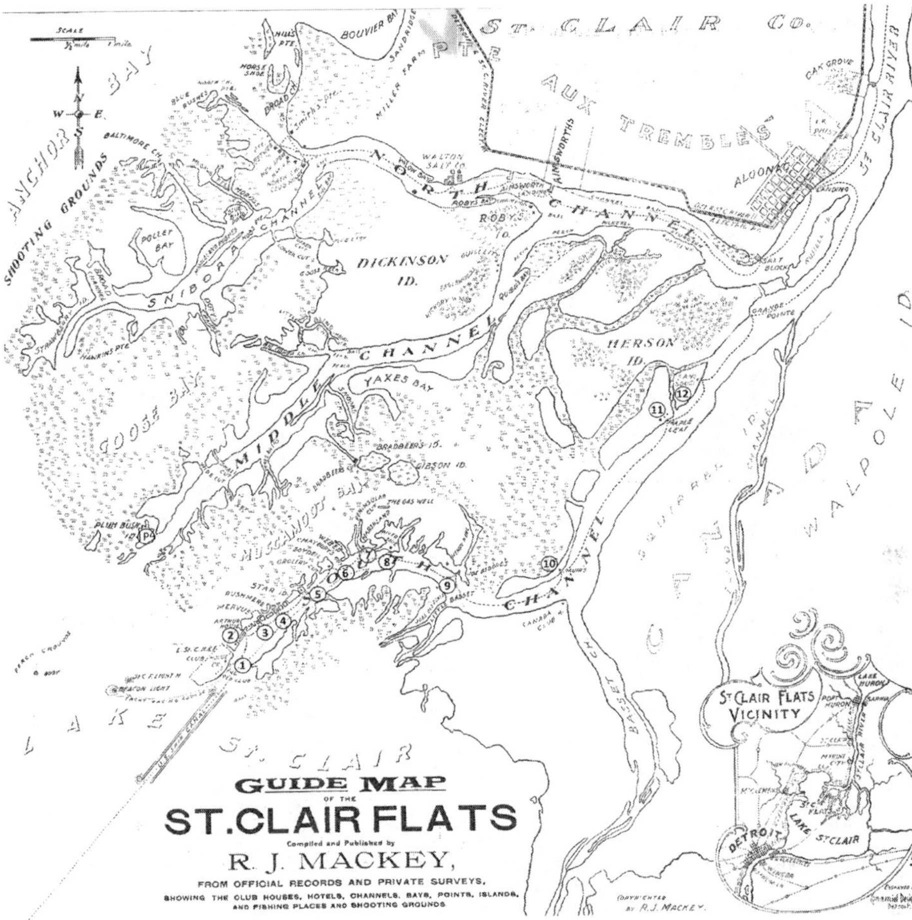

MAP 15. Detail of R. J. Mackey's *Guide Map of the St. Clair Flats* (1896), showing the stops between Lake St. Clair and Algonac, including the Old Club (1), Star Island (5), Joe Bedore's (9), and Tashmoo Park at San Souci (12). Note "Plum Bush Island" (P), center left. (Detroit Historical Society)

writer James Oliver Curwood, "is lined with summer cottages and lakeside inns" (Curwood 1909, 85–86). "There must be thousands of them in this American Venice," echoed fellow journalist Stuart L. Douglas. "It's most extraordinary for a big steamer to be loafing along here among all these cottages. You could toss the traditional biscuit from the deck and hit a happy householder in the eye almost anywhere" (Douglas 1906, 614).

The amphibious nature of the numerous islets—emergent wetlands that were occasionally submerged—created a corresponding legal liminality, as

FIGURE 24. Denizens of the Flats during its golden age. Left, resort proprietor Joe Bedore; right, the Private Club Girl. Details from "The Flat Dwellers at Michigan's Venice," a satirical article by cartoonist Fred C. Nash. (*Detroit Free Press*, July 23, 1905)

the federal government's Boundary Commission inventory of landforms had omitted them altogether, while the State of Michigan laid claim to the Flats as swampland. Into this literal and legal morass stepped (or waded), the "squatter," claiming that such improvements as driving pilings and building a shack upon them constituted homesteading (Andreas 1883, 220). Douglas's "happy householder" had often made something from almost nothing (figure 25). Joe Bedore had begun as just such a squatter, recollecting "that time when I drove a few spiles and threw up a little dirt and made up my mind I'd stay" (Dixon 2002, 64). Even the venerable and privileged Old Club was briefly scrutinized, at one point ordered by the state to vacate. Some cases dragged into the early twentieth century (Jenks 1912, 85; Dixon 2002, 158–59). Generally, titles obtained through "squatter's rights" were upheld, with Michigan claiming ownership of the remaining unimproved wetlands of the delta, thereby securing recreational opportunities for the general public (Rogers 1955, 40).

OH, JOY!

FIGURE 25. Newspaper cartoon satirizing the Flats squatter circa 1900. Note the flat-bottomed bateau in the foreground. (Dixon 2002, 156)

Social Reproduction of Class in the Recreational Landscape

As social groups coalesced in the St. Clair Flats recreational landscape, four modes of maritime dwelling developed:

- Sportsman's clubs, catering to the well-heeled and well-connected, the exclusive Old Club and the Canada Club being the archetypes of the hunting and fishing variety. The latter was on the Canadian side, leased from the Walpole Island First Nations (map 15). These were eventually joined by a handful of yacht and boat clubs, notably the North Channel Yacht Club on Dickinson Island, which likewise began as a shooting club.
- Resorts offering the public a variety of recreational amenities, minus the exclusivity of the private clubs. This social reproduction of the

urban class structure was not lost on the local newspapers, where both the "great unwashed" and the pretensions of those who arrived by private yachts rather than by excursion boats were fair game as objects of satire (figure 24). The pinnacle of this proletarian phase of the Flats' golden age was Tashmoo Park (figure 26), built in 1896 on Harsens Island by the White Star Line as a stop for their popular daily runs to Port Huron. It was complemented by its namesake: the steamer *Tashmoo* (figure 27), launched in 1900, among the fastest and best-appointed of the "floating palaces" (Stone 2015, 182).

- Private cottages, which ran the social and architectural gamut from Butler's Gothic getaway to "Jones' Rest" (figure 25), often remaining within family ownership for generations.
- A mixed bag of public recreational venues apart from the resorts: public parks; commercial marinas; state-owned wildlife refuges, wetlands, and boat launches. In this category may be included First Nations hunting areas on the Canadian side, accessible to the public only with a permit and Native guide.

FIGURE 26. The dock at Tashmoo Park, 1905. On the left is the bulk freighter *City of Rome*, recently sunk in a collision with the steamer *Linden*, with two lives lost. (Library of Congress)

FIGURE 27. The palace steamer *Tashmoo*, flagship of the White Star Line, circa 1905. (Wikipedia)

Through a variety of modes, and by all walks of life, the maritime landscape of the St. Clair Flats had undergone a sea change, as it were, to be more fully integrated into the social landscape of the Strait region centered on Detroit/Windsor. Extending the influence of the modern period from the political, commercial, and technological realms into the social sphere constituted a further shifting of the balance of agency away from Nature/Wilderness and toward Culture/Civilization. The Victorian worldview entertained a complex relationship with Nature, simultaneously romanticizing rusticity as a virtue while congratulating itself on its own sophistication. The Flats, marginalized from colonial times as a nuisance at best and a danger at worst, came to embody the nostalgic aspect of the former frontier outpost: Detroit's Playground, Michigan's Venice. Historian James Cooke Mills acutely observed this interplay at work in Tashmoo Park in its heyday: "Here all is not art, neither is all nature" (Mills 1910, 235).

By the end of the nineteenth century, conservation historian Roderick Nash writes, "the average citizen could approach wilderness with the viewpoint of the vacationer rather than the conqueror" (Nash 1982, 143). An aestheticized wilderness was now a thing to be "enjoyed from a comfortable distance"

(Neumann 2007, 1956), marketed as a vanishing commodity or recreational amenity rather than the risk or threat it had connoted to the pioneering colonialists. In the Flats, this was nowhere more dramatically symbolized than by the Walpole Island First Nations just across the water from Tashmoo Park.

Writing a mere fifteen years after Tocqueville, the famed Massachusetts poet William Cullen Bryant, on a tour of the Great Lakes in 1846, might easily have been peering into the future of the Flats when he wrote of Mackinaw Island, "To some, the savage visitors, who occasionally set up their lodges on its beach, as well as on that of the surrounding islands, and paddle their canoes in its waters, will be an additional attraction. I can not but think with a kind of regret on the time which, I suppose, is near at hand, when its wild and lonely woods will be intersected with highways, and filled with cottages and boarding-houses" (Bryant 1851, 302). The grandchildren of the "savages" that had lent a frisson of the exotic to Tocqueville's 1831 journey provided just such an attraction for the tourists at Tashmoo Park, dancing and selling handmade souvenirs (Mills 1910, 235). Such performances of tribal identity and lifeways, easily stereotyped as commercialization at best and degradation at worst, nonetheless served to preserve both the traditions and the social cohesion of the Walpole Island First Nations through stressful social and economic times (Nin.Da.Waab.Jig 1987, 81).

The Twilight of "Michigan's Venice"

The accidental sinking of the *Tashmoo* and its subsequent scrapping in 1937 marked a turning point toward the end of the "Michigan's Venice" era, one that was further sealed by the closing of Tashmoo Park itself in 1951. These nostalgically fraught losses mark the further evolution of the Flats. The big palace boats were able to hang on for a time, even in the face of rising competition from the personal automobile and the expanding road system, but aging fleets were expensive to maintain, let alone replace (Stone 2015, 226). Their lingering attraction had been a relaxed day spent in a genteel atmosphere—an amenity prey to economic conditions, particularly unemployment and depression.

The passing of the golden age of the floating palaces in the early decades of the twentieth century has been attributed to the rise of the automobile and improved roadways (Stone 2015, 224), with the Great Depression dealing the resorts a blow from which they never fully recovered (Rogers 1955, 39–40; Woodford 2012, 8). In a sense, however, it marked the maturing of the regional landscape, its population, and their relationship. The twin illusions of frontier and wilderness had outlived both their utility and their credibility.

While there remained a niche along the Strait for amusement parks and excursion boats, it was filled by Bob-Lo (a corruption of Bois Blanc, the erstwhile Odawa island it occupied). Lying in the Detroit River just off Amherstburg, Ontario, the park opened in 1898, served by a pair of ferries, the *St. Clair* and *Columbia* (Livingston 2008, 22). By the time of its closing in 1993, it too had been rendered obsolete by enormous operations like Ohio's Cedar Point, easily accessible from Detroit and Toledo by car. As with biological evolution, economic niches open and close, alternately promoting and punishing technological specialization.

At the outset of the historic period, both people and goods had moved on the lakes in the same way and in the same vessels at the same time, whether they were in canoes, bateaux, schooners, or even the earliest steamers. This situation persisted until the continental interior had been sufficiently populated, and its resources sufficiently exploited, that specialized forms of transport became viable. The package freighter, catering to the movement of both people and goods, occupied a niche where versatility in a time of change was an evolutionary asset. Eventually, however, each type of movement evolved along its own path. The shipping of commodities became the province of the bulk freighter, and package freight traffic largely went to the expanding rail network. So too with long-distance passenger traffic: the floating palaces carried neither cargo nor westward-bound settlers. Travel by rail between the eastern and midwestern cities outstripped waterborne travel in both speed and affordability.

In the maritime landscape of the St. Clair Flats, the processes of both movement and dwelling were progressively decentralized and democratized. While neither excursion boats nor resort hotels vanished overnight, the rising proportion of cottages led to a proliferation of small personal boats, from fishing skiffs and outboard runabouts to cabin cruisers. Unlike the big steamers, these could take their owners directly to their dwellings. The relationship between the two types of watercraft was analogous to that between the railroad and the automobile. There is more than meets the eye in the observation that the Model

T killed the big excursion boats—their gasoline-powered nautical equivalents were accessories to the deed. The irony lies in that the St. Clair locale led the nation in producing the instruments of the big boats' demise.

Recreation as Industry

With a ready consumer market, skilled labor, and the means of industrialized production close at hand, it is no wonder that the St. Clair region became to the recreational boating industry what Detroit was to the automobile. Beginning in the 1920s, three of the greatest names in modern wooden boatbuilding had their origins there: the popular Chris-Craft brand in Algonac, the high-performance Gar Wood in Marysville (Mollica 1999), and the luxurious Hacker, "the Steinway of wooden boats" in Mount Clemens (Barry 2002). In one sense, they followed the Detroit auto boom by a couple of decades; in another, these maritime communities merely revived a local industry that was over a century old—much older if one considers that among the skilled workers in Chris-Craft's Algonac plant were Anishinaabeg, crossing the river from Walpole Island each day (Nin.Da.Waab.Jig 1987, 86; Martin 1971).[2]

This was particularly true during the Second World War, when there was both a manpower shortage and a need by the military for highly maneuverable, shoal-draft boats that could be built quickly and cheaply—precisely the qualities that had traditionally distinguished the boats of the St. Clair maritime landscape. Moreover, wooden hulls, once a liability, were once again an asset, being less likely to trigger magnetic mines. Chris-Craft produced at least 243 wooden landing craft in its Algonac plant under contract to the US Army (figure 28) and served as the testing facility for an additional 12,000 boats built at its larger Cadillac and Holland, Michigan, plants.[3] With Gar Wood contributing an additional 188 units, and Hacker a limited run of high-speed picket

2 When Tecumseh's bones were reinterred at the memorial on Walpole Island, his mahogany coffin was made in the Chris-Craft plant by Anishinaabeg craftsmen.

3 In all, some 13,000 wooden boats, mostly landing craft and patrol boats, were built by Chris-Craft. Company tradition maintains that the first landing craft to hit the beaches of Normandy on D-Day were made by Chris-Craft (Reynolds 2019).

FIGURE 28. Wartime advertisement for Chris-Craft circa 1943, showing its personnel landing craft LCP(R) in action. (Detroit Historical Society)

boats (Barry 2002, 100), the St. Clair locale's boatbuilding industry was briefly remilitarized, albeit for combat on distant shores.

The peacetime economy of the 1950s produced all the conditions for the St. Clair locale's new role as a workingman's playground: unionized jobs with both high wages and leisure time, expanding roadways encouraging the beginnings of suburban sprawl, affordable powerboats, and hundreds of square miles of freshwater perfect for recreation of all sorts. The associated infrastructure provided through the public sector comprised buoys and aids to recreational navigation, dredged channels, public access boat ramps, shore fishing piers, and the services of the Coast Guard and its Auxiliary. Commercial facilities and services included numerous marinas, boat and yacht clubs, boat showrooms, repair shops, marine hardware stores, sail lofts, bait and tackle shops, and innumerable waterfront eating and drinking establishments. A multibillion-dollar economy developed around recreational boating in the Strait, with its epicenter at Lake St. Clair.

Perhaps the zenith (some might say the nadir) of recreational boating in the St. Clair locale is known as the "Jobbie Nooner," an annual celebration of "boats, booze," and other alliterative pleasures. Hailed as the "Mardi Gras of the Midwest," its origins are apocryphal but point to an incident in June of 1974, when a handful of boat-owning auto parts contractors ("jobbies") took off work early on the Friday before the summer factory shutdown.[4] The resulting spontaneous party in the Flats, aided by publicity both positive and negative, can draw as many as 4,000 boats and 10,000 participants to the shoals surrounding Gull Island at the mouth of Big Muskamoot Bay (Ferretti 2010)—only one mile (but considerable social distance) from the Old Club, where it all began exactly a century earlier.

Over the span of the nineteenth and twentieth centuries, the trajectory of the St. Clair Flats into the social fabric of the greater Detroit maritime landscape becomes clear. From an initial state of liminality and risk, it proceeded to industry and commerce, thence to privilege and exclusivity, and finally to

4 It is probably no coincidence that the original Jobbie Nooner was a mere five years after Woodstock (1969), as elements of mass-market tribalism characterize both. An "authorized definitive history" of the Jobbie Nooner based on interviews with its founders may be found on the Jobbie Crew's website: https://jobbiecrew.com/.

accessibility and inclusion. In the latter interval, an era of genteel mass transportation by floating palaces had waxed and waned, while utilitarian small boats had evolved from their various utilitarian functions to recreational applications ranging from family boating and sport fishing to racing and waterskiing.

With this latest transformation, the St. Clair maritime landscape has witnessed a *longue durée* of nearly four centuries during which hundreds, if not thousands, of watercraft and their contents were created, used, lost, destroyed, or abandoned. A substantial number have passed from the systemic context of usage to become part of the archaeological record. The following chapter turns from what was built in the shipyards to what was left behind—on uncharted sandbars, in deadly "ship traps," along crowded channels, in waterfront "boneyards" and maritime dumping grounds—all the places and ways that a vessel can come to grief.

11

Archaeology of the Submerged Landscape

The real challenge for a ship archaeologist is therefore to identify and select relevant contexts for the interpretation of the wrecks and from that construct narratives that are not only scientifically credible but also have relevance to modern society and ourselves.

—Johan Rönnby, "Maritime *Dureés*"

What Lies Beneath

This chapter takes a different look at the relationship between the maritime community, the maritime environment, and the ship itself. The foregoing survey of shipbuilding measured social intentions and nautical technology against available resources and environmental operating conditions, as determinants of what got built and used. By contrast, a survey of shipwrecks measures those relationships at their breaking point.

Of the landscape features discussed thus far, only a handful remain in place: the Old South Channel Lights (now protected and automated), the first St. Clair Ship Canal (its wooden retaining walls long gone), the pilings of some of the original resort docks. To the maritime archaeologist, this expansive landscape presents a sort of horizontal stratigraphy, where the past is arranged not in vertical layers but as a patchwork of marginalized activities and their associated material culture. Much more, however, has been razed and built over: Fort Sinclair and its careening platform, the sawmills and shipyards all along the St. Clair and Pine Rivers. Few significant infrastructural features of the built environment from previous cultural landscapes may truly be said to have passed unscathed into the archaeological record.[1]

Not so with ships, however. True, of the 781 locally built ships analyzed in chapter 8, none remain in service. A handful—at least eight—are known to have wrecked in the St. Clair locale, beginning with the schooner *Emily*, built in St. Clair in 1826 and capsized four years later on the Flats with the loss of seven lives. But these few were joined by many more from all over the Great Lakes, as recently as 1934. In the intervening years, most wrecks have either succumbed to the processes of scattering and decay or have been intentionally destroyed as obstructions to navigation. Those that remain are mute evidence of a specific ship's unique career—which, with effort, can be made to speak.

The Meaning of a Shipwreck

Every shipwreck represents a failure—the failure of a ship's captain to shorten sail in a sudden squall, of a helmsman to follow his course in a blinding fog, of an unattended boiler to hold together under too much pressure, or of an aging wooden hull to make one last trip. As with all archaeology, repeated behavior creates patterns wherein we look for the causes and effects that result in the deposition of material culture. In the complex St. Clair maritime landscape where the nature and loci of risk have shifted over time, the nature and loci of failures have done the same. This was particularly true in the dynamic

1 Fort Sinclair was assigned site number 20SC58 in 2002 by the Michigan State Historic Preservation Office (SHPO). Excavations to determine the exact location of the fort were made in 1970 (Mayhew 2003, 158–59) and in 1974 but have been ruled inconclusive. Two shoreline sites on Lake St. Clair are currently the subject of archaeological surveys: St. Felicity Parish, a mission church from the early 19th century; and Belvidere Village, a shoreline community on Anchor Bay. Both were inundated in the late 1850s, evidently as a consequence of the dredging of the South Channel mouth, which increased the flow rate into the lake.

nineteenth century, as new nautical technologies and practices coincided with economic, demographic, and political stresses to the maritime transportation network of the Great Lakes. Although the failure resulting in a wreck is seldom overtly deliberate, learning the identity and career of a wrecked vessel allows us to trace the intentionality behind its voyage and the events and context of its loss (Törnquist 2013, 26).

In the case of a bulk freighter known as the *John N. Glidden*, the purpose of its fatal voyage was much like those of the preceding quarter-century: to deliver iron ore from Lake Superior to Cleveland, Ohio. On October 9, 1903, however, its trajectory intersected with that of the propeller *Empire City* and its tow, the barge *Magna*, cargo unknown, "steaming swiftly" against the current at the St. Clair Ship Canal's mouth. The turbulence of their passing altered *Glidden*'s course, the steel hull of the barge shattering the bow of the wooden freighter (figure 29). The Buffalo Evening News takes up the story:

> As a result of the sinking of the propeller JOHN N. GLIDDEN by the barge MAGNA in the St. Clair Flats Canal, navigation in the Detroit River was practically put to an end. The propeller sunk to her decks diagonally across the channel in the canal at the Lake St. Clair end. A channel 75 feet wide remains between the stem of the boat and the east pier, but the current is so strong as to make it perilous for vessels to try to make the passage and from present indications navigation will be tied up for at least a week. When the accident occurred, the GLIDDEN was bound down the canal with a cargo of iron ore. The steel propeller EMPIRE CITY was steaming swiftly up the canal with the barge MAGNA in tow. In passing the GLIDDEN the suction of the EMPIRE CITY drew the GLIDDEN into the tow line and the barge crashed into it, splitting it open to the pilot house. The GLIDDEN went to the bottom instantly. Assistance was immediately sent to the scene of the blockage and tugs have been ordered to assist vessels in passing the wreck. A large fleet of vessels has already accumulated on both sides of the obstruction waiting to pass. (Buffalo Evening News, October 10, 1903)

The aging *Glidden* was beyond repair. The bow section was soon hauled away and its engines salvaged. The following spring a commercial demolition

FIGURE 29. Bulk freighter *John N. Glidden*, port side of shattered bow, looking southeast across the St. Clair Ship Canal, October 1903. (Dossin Great Lakes Museum)

crew took a week, and a ton of dynamite, to remove the rest to parts unknown or at least unreported (*Buffalo Evening News*, April 18, 1904). At that point, the *John N. Glidden* faced a second loss—its identity, transformed from a ship with a history into a statistic. Of 287 vessels that have been documented as having sunk in the St. Clair locale in the century between 1830 and 1934, more than half were raised and returned to service. At least 129 (45%), including the *Glidden*, were reported as total losses. Of those, less than a quarter (n = 30, 23%) have been reliably identified. At every remove from their working careers, these ships are stripped of their identity. The annals of Great Lakes shipping disasters are filled with ships' names without known wreck sites, while the navigational charts are dotted with wreckage sites without names. The *Glidden* was a casualty on the former list, its legacy merely a further comment on the ongoing risks of crossing the Flats in 1903 and the cost of doing business on its overcrowded waters. Only archaeology could bring it back.

The St. Clair Maritime Archaeological Record

As with the material degradation over time of the wrecked vessel itself, so too with its biography: its birth, career, and death. As Oscar Törnquist wryly notes, "Posing socially relevant research questions to a pile of planks is not done without some effort" (Törnquist 2013, 26). The storytelling potential of ships and their loss suggests a few "socially relevant research questions" regarding the landscape in which they were lost or abandoned. As events fixed in space and time, shipwrecks can serve as evidence of developments in the process of *movement* in maritime landscape formation.

As assemblages of multiple sites within a locale, their patterns of loss and deposition shed light on environmental cognition, risk management, evolving maritime practices, and advances in nautical technology. This is best done when the identity of the wreck and the career of the vessel are linked. The best-case scenario, then, is to pose socially relevant research questions to piles of old planks *and* piles of old documents. In the St. Clair locale, the dating of both piles begins in the mid-nineteenth century. The earliest documented shipwreck, the little schooner *Emily* capsized and driven ashore in the Flats in 1830, has vanished without a trace. The oldest surviving site of a known vessel is the brigantine *Saltillo*, wrecked in a collision near Sarnia, Ontario, in 1853.

In his seminal monograph *Maritime Archaeology*, Keith Muckelroy (1978, 158) schematized a processual approach to long-term wreck site formation (figure 30). While highly summarized, it represented a major step toward appreciating the nature and extent of the transformative processes, natural and cultural, at work from the moment a vessel ceases to operate as a means of transportation. Expanded and formalized by Gibbs and Duncan (2016), the ongoing processes of removal ("filtering") and rearrangement ("scrambling") rebut the notion that a shipwreck represents a frozen moment—the popular but flawed "time capsule" analogy (Goggin 1960, 353; Nutley 2008; Rodley 2012, 383; Arnshav 2013, 145). At each step of removal from a sinking incident, a substantial portion of the knowledge of what happened may become degraded, fragmented, disassociated from its object, or lost altogether—not that an anonymous wreck or a disassociated ship biography is without value, even in cases that resist our best efforts to reunite the two.

As the wrecks in the St. Clair locale occurred during the nineteenth and early twentieth centuries, virtually every total loss created a substantial paper trail, allowing meaningful analysis of temporal, spatial, and causal patterns. The aggregated details of these individual vessels and incident profiles permit their collective analysis as a database (Murphy 1983) using such key parameters as the properties of the vessel (vessel type and its mode of propulsion at the time of loss), nature and location of the incident, and on fortunate occasions, its passage into an archaeological context as an identified shipwreck site (Price and Richards 2009).

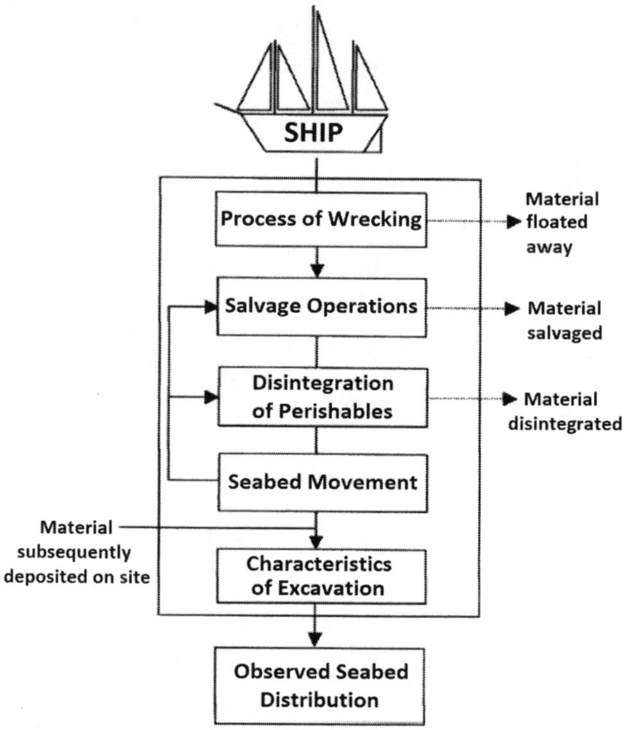

FIGURE 30. "Flow Diagram Representing the Evolution of a Shipwreck." (Adapted from Muckelroy 1978)

Ship Losses in the St. Clair Maritime Landscape: A Typology

Since waterborne shipping was and remains the lifeblood of the Great Lakes maritime economy, incidents of all types were reported, like the demise of the *John N. Glidden*, with the aid of the telegraph in the newspapers of the port cities that sprang up along their shores in the nineteenth century. The audience of interested parties included ship owners, manufacturers, merchants, investors, insurers, and above all, the families of the crews. Even such everyday occurrences as groundings, strandings, and minor collisions were frequently but not unfailingly reported. Total losses generally resulted in additional confirmatory documentation, principally insurance claims and surrendered registrations.

I analyzed the documentary records of incidents where one or more vessels were reported as not merely damaged or briefly grounded but having sunk or been driven hard ashore within the St. Clair locale: Lake St. Clair, the Flats, and the St. Clair River. Such reports, combined with the registration renewals required of commercial vessels, provide the data needed to determine which vessels experienced a sinking, its cause, and its approximate location. In all, 287 vessels meet these criteria and formed the documentary sector of my shipwreck database. Of those, a majority of 158 were reported as subsequently refloated and repaired, salvaged, removed, or demolished as hazards to navigation. The remainder of 129 vessels were abandoned, inaccessible, or only partially removed. These represent vessels with significant remaining wreckage that may have been allowed to pass into the archaeological record.

Turning from the piles of documents to the piles of planks, there are at least 95 known wreckage sites in the St. Clair locale. Of these, only 30 sites can be reliably identified with a specific vessel. This yields a 23% sample of the 129 total losses: a respectable sample for purposes of hypothesis generation and testing and perhaps a few tentative conclusions (Staniforth 1997). Since an exhaustive account of every shipwreck is out of the question, the best use of these fragmentary records and fragmented vessels is to relate them to the landscape and its transformation over time. Even an anonymous wreck has something to say about its resting place. With enough pieces of the puzzle in the right places, fitted to what we know from place-names, diaries, charts, and shoreline sites, the big picture is liable to clarify. Each unique event addresses broader questions and processes of change (Gibbins and Adams 2001, 281). Considered as failures, wrecks mark boundaries: the limits of the performance envelope of such social activities as communication and trade, technology and practice.

Relating the documentary record to the archaeological record yields four classes of archaeological records:

- Class A. Documented incidents resulting in the sinking or wrecking of a vessel, whether temporarily or permanently (n = 287).
- Class B. The subset of Class A incidents where the vessel was reported as a total loss and not recovered (n = 129).
- Class C. Wreckage sites in the submerged landscape (n = 95), including both officially charted (n = 74) and confirmed but uncharted sites (n = 21). A cautionary note: a single vessel loss

may result in multiple wreckage sites, as occurs with separated hull fragments and debris fields.

- Class D. Wreckage sites in the submerged landscape (Class C) that may be identified with specific Class B vessel records with varying degrees of confidence (n = 30).

Patterns of Sinking and Vessel Loss

All these classes have their usefulness. At a minimum, temporal and causal patterns of vessel sinkings may be sought in Class A, as most reported incidents provide not only the *when* but also the *why*. On a timeline of sinkings, fires would be expected to increase following the advent of steam, while a decrease in capsizes would correlate with the decline of sail. As the St. Clair corridor contains numerous points of reference, it is frequently possible to identify the *where*. On June 27, 1905, the bulk freighter *City of Rome* collided with the steamer *Linden* just off the dock at Tashmoo Park. Both ships sank to the bottom, and two lives were lost. Within days, both had been raised and were soon back in service, but photographs and documents survive as indicators of the risk posed by a large dock protruding into a busy stretch of the South Channel (figure 26). Certain features became notorious for specific types of incidents: the Elbow for groundings, the Southeast Bend for collisions, the wharves along the St. Clair River for fires sparked by closely packed wooden steamers firing their boilers.

Tracked over time, causal and spatial patterns of loss indicate the impact of changes in nautical technology, maritime practice, and the maritime landscape itself on the interplay between increasing the volume of commercial shipping and risk factors inherent in both the culture and the environment. Both the number of sinkings in the St. Clair locale (figure 22) and the tonnage of shipping through Detroit (figure 23) increased in the decades between 1880 and 1900. When the two data sets are correlated by measuring the number of sinkings against tonnage, however (figure 31), it appears that the effective loss rate of the industry peaked in the 1880s following the shift from the old North Channel route to the progressively improved (but increasingly

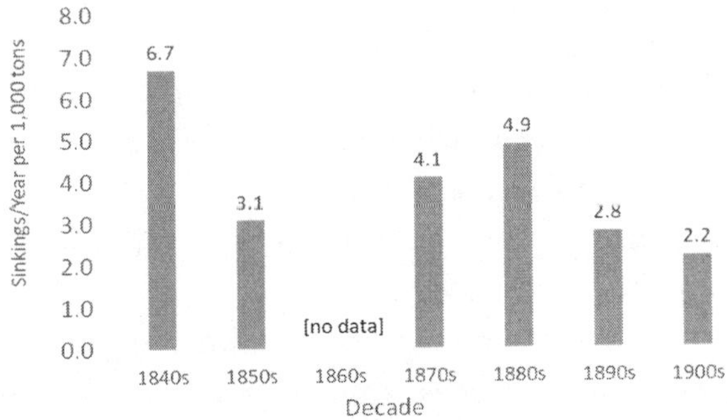

FIGURE 31. Rate of sinkings in St. Clair locale per 1,000 tons of shipping by decade, 1840s–1900s. Data for the 1860s are incomplete due to the disruption of the American Civil War.

crowded) South Channel between the 1840s and the 1850s. Thereafter it declined markedly as the waterway was improved and safe practices were implemented.

Class A Incidents: Patterns in Ship Sinkings

Of a total of 287 reported sinkings in the St. Clair locale, a selected sample of 252 incidents (87%) can be attributed to six principal causes, the remaining 35 incidents being poorly documented or outliers. Capsizes (n = 26) dominated the early results but by the 1860s were overtaken by fire, the scourge of wooden ships (n = 85), and collisions (n = 100)—mostly (n = 49) between steamboats but involving sailed, towed, and even docked vessels as well. Running aground was more common than the number of total losses would suggest (n = 10), as such vessels were almost invariably refloated or salvaged. Abandonments (n = 20) entered the picture in the 1860s; after peaking in the 1890s and again in the 1920s, they dwindled as wooden vessels aged out of the population.

Boiler explosions were among the most horrific and feared accidents. Anna Jameson's 1838 comment about bursting boilers was soon outdone by her countryman Charles Dickens. Aboard the steamer *Constellation* at Cleveland in 1842, he described it as "a large vessel of five hundred tons, and handsomely fitted up, though with high-pressure engines; which always conveyed that kind of feeling to me, which I should be likely to experience, I think, if I had lodgings on the first floor of a powder-mill" (Dickens 1868, 117). While common elsewhere on the Great Lakes, they were comparatively rare in the St. Clair system (n = 9). Their infrequency along the Strait was possibly owing to the slower speeds necessitated by piloting and towing through the restricted waterway. The exception is the Civil War period of the 1860s (n = 5), which likely reflects the exigencies of the war effort, as ships and their crews were driven to their limits and beyond (Thompson 2000, 331–32).

Viewed in terms of their mode of propulsion at the time of their sinking, sailing vessels with their initially greater numbers predictably dominate the mid-nineteenth century. After maintaining a relatively constant accident rate of 8.4 losses per decade between the 1850s and 1910s, sailing, while still commercially viable on the open waters of the Great Lakes, became rare in the Strait. There the towing of schooners had long since become the rule. The two accident types most characteristic of sailing vessels—capsizing (n = 12) and being driven ashore (n = 8)—collectively comprised 38% of all sinkings by ships under sail (n = 59). By comparison, those two causes account for only 7 of 119 sinkings (6%) by self-propelled vessels. By their very nature, sailing vessels proved to be more at the mercy of the elements than steamboats.

Vessels sinking while under power quickly equaled those under sail by the 1840s, and dominated the casualties thereafter, peaking in the 1900s. As the practice of towing caught on, towed schooners or barges soon became the victims of collisions, peaking in the 1890s. Problems of control, particularly when moving downstream, made the practice risky, especially when multiple towed ships were involved. These accidents declined as the practice of towing multiple aging wooden hulls astern decreased, replaced by dedicated barge and tug consorts with rigid connections. A handful (n = 7) of ships sank while at anchor out in the river, not surprisingly the victims of collisions with passing traffic. These sinkings cease after the 1890s, reflecting both improving ship handling and improved dockage inshore.

More remarkable is the number of ships that sank while docked (n = 40), even into the 1930s. Closer examination reveals that 31 of the docked ships (78%) perished by fire, typically caused by sparks from a boiler falling on flammable decks or cargo and often exacerbated by the absence of crew aboard. Fire was a deadly threat to wooden ships under power (n = 48), equal to that of collision (n = 49). Throughout the nineteenth century, advances in the technology of propulsion outpaced that of shipbuilding, with predictable results. The notion of placing a fire-breathing iron contraption inside a wooden container, seen in retrospect, was a recipe for inevitable disaster. As the cost of doing business, it speaks loudly to us of the magnitude of risk deemed acceptable in order to gain an economic or military advantage. The end of the era of wooden ships, whether sailed, powered, or towed, clearly occurred between the 1920s and 1930s. Burnings dropped from 12 to a single instance and abandonments from 5 to zero. Simply put, there were virtually no wooden hulls left either to burn or to abandon.

An overall decline in sinkings of all types, regardless of cause or mode of propulsion, occurred between the 1920s and 1930s, from 21 incidents to just two. Such a precipitous fall (90%) suggests a multitude of factors, ones that improvements in the waterway alone cannot account for. More tonnage was moving through the Strait, but it was in fewer and much larger ships, resulting in fewer encounters. Improvements in the clarity and enforcement of navigational "rules of the road," requirements for locally certified pilots in rivers and harbors, fire-fighting technology, the supplanting of external combustion (steam) by internal combustion (diesel) engines, wireless telegraphy followed by ship-to-shore and ship-to-ship radio, improved weather forecasting—all contributed to reducing the number and severity of maritime accidents throughout the Great Lakes, particularly in the confined waters of the Strait.

Class B Incidents: Vessels Reported as Total Losses

This reduction in collisions and other sinking incidents contributed to an even steeper decline in total losses, and thereby long-term wreck site formation. Unlike their wooden predecessors, the new iron- and steel-hulled ships were not prone to burning to the waterline. While still liable to sink in a collision, metal hulls had considerable value even as scrap and were seldom abandoned when accessible, particularly in shallow water and proximity to salvors and shipyards. As a result, there are no instances of long-term wreck sites of metal-hulled ships in the St. Clair locale.

The steel freighter *Joliet* nearly qualifies. Rammed and sunk at its Sarnia dock in 1911, it was dynamited, leaving a debris field that remains in situ. Its larger fragments, relocated a mile downriver, were finally removed as an obstruction in 1963. By that time, larger ore boats built to use the new St. Clair

Cutoff through the Flats required a wider and deeper waterway. As the built environment evolved, obstructions like the shattered *Joliet*, formerly allowed to reside at its margins, became "matter out of place"—anthropologist Mary Douglas's classic definition of dirt—and required purification: that is, removal from the reclaimed periphery (Douglas 1966). This scenario played out repeatedly throughout the twentieth century, as dredging operations in channels and harbors encountered obstructions both natural and man-made.

A comparison of 265 sinkings where the outcome and water body are known shows that the St. Clair River was the scene of the most incidents (n = 154, 58%), with the Flats and Lake St. Clair accounting for 61 (23%) and 19 (19%) sinkings, respectively. Throughout the corridor, however, recoveries where vessels were returned to service were comparable, averaging 57%. The slightly lower recovery rate for the St. Clair River (56%) versus the Flats (57%) and the lake (60%) may be attributed to its swifter current and greater depth. Both these factors complicate recovery from the river. Rather, wrecks in obstructing position are liable to be promptly demolished, as the *John N. Glidden* and the *Joliet*, or if outside the waterway's envelope in sufficiently deep water, allowed to remain in situ.

Such is the case with a half-dozen wrecks that litter the rapids at the head of the St. Clair River. Typical is the *M. E. Tremble*, a towed schooner sunk in a collision with the steamer *W. L. Wetmore* on the night of September 7, 1890. It is now accompanied by two barges capsized in the attempt to raise its cargo of coal (Kohl 1987). With its upper structure dynamited, its remains rest in seventy feet of swift water, a danger only to the sport divers who attempt this advanced dive. In most other cases, a ship written off as a total loss by its owners remained an accessible resource to the St. Clair maritime community, if not as a recovered vessel, then as salvage, fish habitat, a recreational dive site, or occasionally as shoreline infrastructure such as a seawall or breakwater.

Abandoned Vessels as a Subset of Class B: Total Losses

Unlike accidental collisions and fires, vessel abandonment was an intentional mode of deposition: of eighteen verifiable long-term abandonment sites in the greater St. Clair locale, fourteen are in the river, with the lake and delta dividing the remaining four equally at two apiece. Sarnia's harbor, in particular, developed a notorious "boneyard" of abandoned vessels awaiting a rebuilding that often never came, or cannibalization for parts akin to an automobile junkyard. At least three—the bulk freighter *Yakima* and the steambarges *Sachem* and *Aztec*—were raised in the 1930s, towed into Lake Huron, and scuttled. Known now as the "ghost fleet," they have effectively been repurposed as artificial reefs serving as an attraction to both fish and recreational divers. Even so, at least a half-dozen abandonments remain on charts of the Sarnia vicinity.

Unlike losses resulting from mishaps, abandoned vessels do not indicate the locations of risk and danger in the landscape. Rather, as in the case of the *Joliet* and the *John N. Glidden*, they spatially define the margins of the waterway at the moment of their intentional deposition. At the same time, they mark the processes of aging and obsolescence of specific vessels, vessel types, hull materials, and uses: "Discarded vessels are not shipwrecks," states Australian maritime archaeologist Nathan Richards. "They are non-catastrophically made a part of the archaeological record. The array of decision-making processes that defines this makes them a reflection of the changing technoeconomic circumstances associated with their abandonment" (Richards 2002, 379). Disasters or mishaps may prove problematic regarding the contributing role of human intentionality. Abandonment, by contrast, often permits inferences regarding the human purposes of the depositional event (Törnquist 2013, 26). This is particularly true in cases of their repurposing as infrastructure, or by salvors creating a boneyard of recyclable wreckage (Ford 2013).

Abandonments, particularly when clustered in well-defined spatial contexts, are significant and interpretable, even when they remain anonymous. Such ship graveyards become greater than the sum of their parts (Richards 2013, 12). In a comprehensive study of vessel abandonment and archaeological site formation, Nathan Richards outlines a half-dozen categories of abandonment, ranging from ritual discard (Viking burials, pharaonic grave goods) and naval tactics (harbor blockades using scuttled ships) to artificial reef construction for fish habitat and recreational diving (Richards 2008). Two of his categories cover the majority of documented or archaeological cases of abandonment in the St. Clair locale: first, the salvage or recycling of component materials, also known as "ship breaking" (e.g., the Sarnia boneyard); also, structural adaptation or repurposing (typically as a breakwater or dock).

Of all Class B vessels reported as abandoned (n = 21) or repurposed as such shoreline structures as breakwaters (n = 4) in the St. Clair locale between 1867 and 1925, all were wooden. Their average age at the time of deposition was 34.1 years—a ripe old age for a wooden hull, even in freshwater. The majority (n = 16; 67%) were towed barges at the time of abandonment, schooners and steamers converted when already well past their prime. The time period that saw the greatest number of abandonments was the two decades of the 1890s and 1900s, which, when age is factored in, is a reflection of the post–Civil War explosion in shipbuilding in the St. Clair locale (figure 19): the years from 1850 to 1865 saw an average of only 9 vessels built per year; the postwar boom decade between 1866 and 1875 saw an annual average of 23 new hulls laid. The frequency of shipowners abandoning their vessels in shallow waters, away from extant shipping channels but accessible for salvage, made them less likely to be promptly removed or destroyed compared to accidentally wrecked vessels, which immediately obstructed the transport zone and its infrastructure—those lost to collisions, fires, or boiler explosions in shipping lanes or at docks.

To summarize Class B as a whole: vessel losses by mishap in the St. Clair locale increased dramatically in number between the 1850s and 1900s, with their causes shifting from capsizes and groundings (characteristic of sailing ships) to collisions, fires, and boiler explosions (characteristic of powered and towed vessels). Beginning in the 1890s, abandonment featured as a major component of vessel losses, as wooden vessels aged out of the commercial fleet. The subsequent steep decrease in vessel losses of all types signals the transformation of the natural environment into a modern commercial maritime landscape as part of a holistic process. The built environment, propulsion and shipbuilding technology, and maritime practice all had caught up with the runaway demand for waterborne commerce that had begun over a half-century previous.

Class C Incidents: Wreck Sites in the Submerged Landscape

This category provides the targets for archaeological field investigations of both known and unidentified wreckage, as it comprises all officially charted sites (n = 74), plus uncharted site locations (n = 21) obtained from local informants and remote sensing.[2] Clustering is evident in the Flats, both at the outer edges of the delta and at the head of the delta in the vicinity of Algonac. Additional clusters formed in the vicinity of American/Canadian maritime communities along the St. Clair River: Marine City / Sombra, St. Clair / Courtright, Marysville/Corunna, and Port Huron / Sarnia. A number of these wreckage sites along the river are decayed and abandoned infrastructure, usually wooden docks associated with vanished wharves and shipyards.

Class D Incidents: Identified Vessels in the Archival and Archaeological Records

Even more satisfying than locating a wreck may be the reunion of a ship's biography with its final resting place (or places). While not essential to conducting meaningful archaeology, a "powerful moment from the past" is generated when detailed knowledge of a vessel's career sheds light on its deposition and condition, offering insights not obtainable otherwise (Rönnby 2013, 17). Through chart annotations, archival research, informant interviews, remote sensing, and field survey, a significant percentage of the wrecks in the archaeological record (Class C) may be linked with their identities as historical vessels (Class B). As the intersection of those two sets, Class D sites (n = 30) represent 23% of Class B's total losses (n = 129) and 32% of Class C wreckage sites (n = 95).

What becomes clear as the history of a vessel is reunited with its physical remains is that the postdepositional careers of sunken ships can be complex and ongoing, especially those of accessible shallow-water wrecks. More than quantitative analysis alone, the qualitative, anecdotal past makes maritime archaeology socially relevant, and accessible to other disciplines (Rönnby 2013, 21). Shipwreck stories are powerful narratives that illustrate ongoing relationships—resource exploitation and heritage identity among them—between the archaeological record and society. In his critique of the

---

2 Charted wreck sites were obtained from archival and current NOAA charts, both in paper and digital formats, using the symbol set published in *U.S. Chart No. 1: Symbols, Abbreviations and Terms used on Paper and Electronic Navigational Charts, 12th Edition* (2013). Examples of fully submerged wreck positions appear in map 19; partially submerged wrecks are shown in map 18.

popular "time capsule" metaphor, Jonathan Adams finds the view of a shipwreck as a "single-event phenomenon" not only unrealistic but undesirable. A synchronic "freeze-frame" analysis may needlessly blind the investigator to the nuances of a diachronic approach (Adams 2001, 297). This is certainly true in the St. Clair Flats. As the maritime landscape transforms, so too does a wreck site's social role evolve over the decades, from working ship to navigational obstruction, salvage resource, or tourist attraction.

Three Wreck Clusters: The Ship Trap, the Dumping Ground, and the Boneyard

The value of the diachronic approach is thus scalable: from the site level, where changes to an individual wreck are meaningful and interpretable, to the regional landscape level, where the accretion of individual sites over the long term reveals broad patterns of change in movement by water. Within the larger spatial and temporal frames of reference, incremental transformations are marked by the clustering of cases—and causes. I have identified three wreckage site clusters in the Flats comprised of individual sites with unique and meaningful stories to tell that collectively form patterns of repeated behavior (map 16). They are labeled Clusters A, B, and C and form the subject of field investigations I began pursuing in 2018 in collaboration with the research program of the Noble Odyssey Foundation and the US Naval Sea Cadet training program. They form the initial phase of an inventory of the submerged cultural resources of the St. Clair locale. Under the acronym "Project SCRIMSHAW" (St. Clair River Inventory of Maritime Submerged Heritage and Abandoned Watercraft), it combines archaeological, historical, and ethnographic evidence in assembling a picture of the relationship between present-day maritime communities, their heritage and identity, and submerged material culture.

Cluster B: The Southeast Bend Ship Trap

This notorious hazard is the "crooked route" decried by General Cram—the upper stretch of the natural South Channel that remained after the creation of

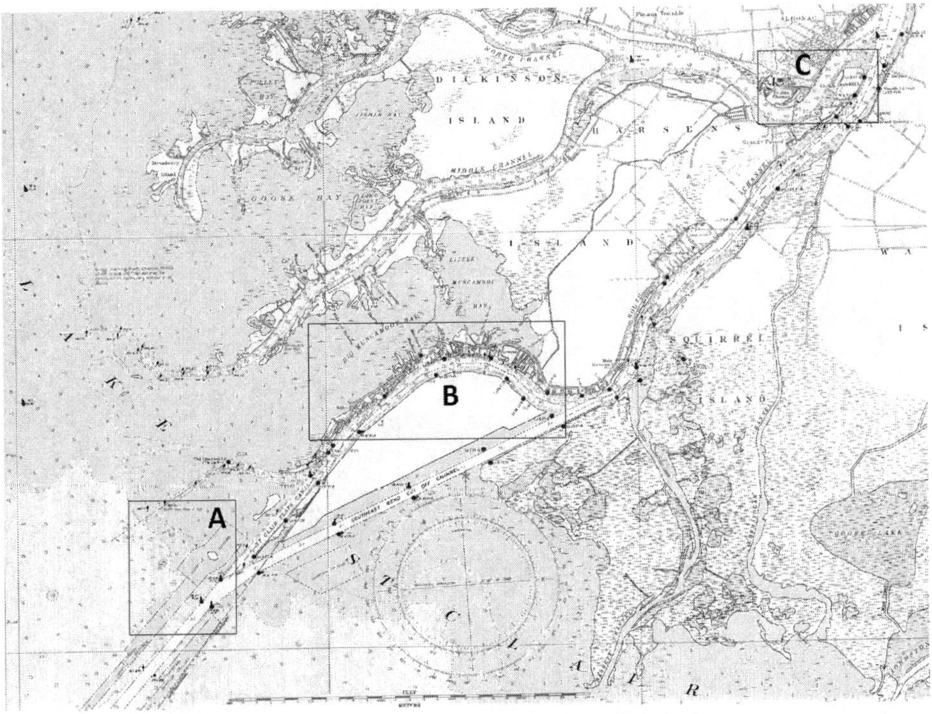

MAP 16. Wreck clustering in the St. Clair Flats: Cluster A, "Old South Channel Dumping Ground"; Cluster B, "Southeast Bend Ship Trap"; and Cluster C, "Russell Island Boneyard." (US Army Corps of Engineers)

the Flats Canal in 1871. The narrow, curving passage, poor sight lines, and lack of adequate ship-to-ship communications combined to provide the conditions for a classic "ship trap": a maritime hazard creating repeated wrecking incidents in a confined area (Conlin 1997, 377). In most ship traps, the enemy is a hidden shoal or reef or a treacherous tidal current; here, the enemy was other ships. Among innumerable accidents, at least eleven ships made the short trip to the bottom between 1870 and 1902. All were the result of collision, and all but two were either self-propelled or towed. Of these, at least four resulted in long-term site formation (map 17). The oldest is the schooner *N. C. West*, under sail when struck by the steamer *Sacramento* in 1898. It was moved out of the shipping channel a short distance to its present position in 1941.

The schooner *Gleniffer*, along with the schooner *Lothair*, was under tow by the steamer *Seaman* when the steamer *Admiral* struck and sank it in 1902. The Army Corps of Engineers dynamited its upper structure, leaving the lower hull

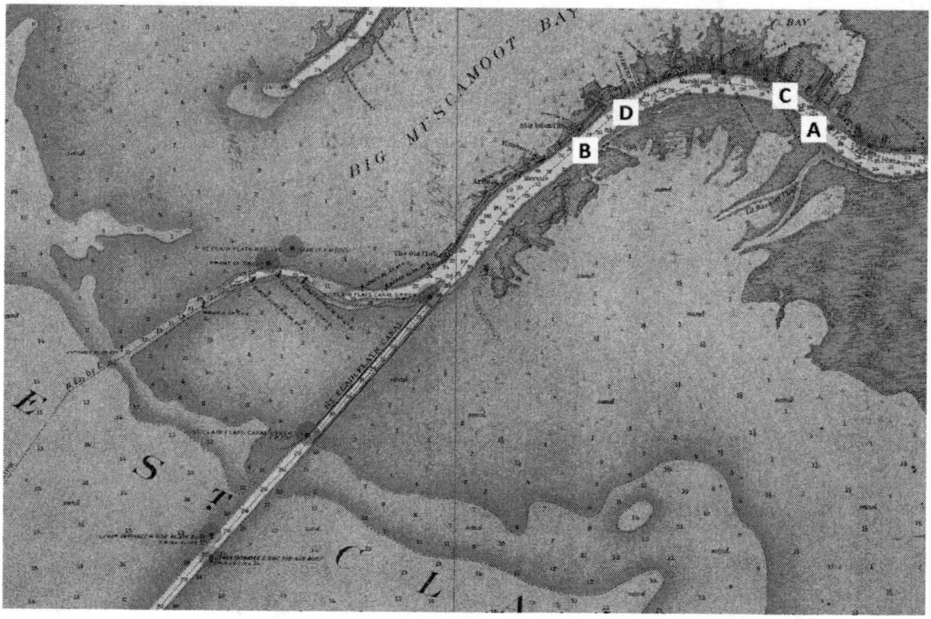

MAP 17. Wreck Cluster B, the "Southeast Bend Ship Trap." Superimposed on a 1903 chart are the present-day locations of (A) schooner *N. C. West* (1898); (B) schooner *Gleniffer* (1902); (C) steambarge *George T. Burroughs* (1905); (D) steambarge *Bothnia*, a.k.a. *Jack* (1912). All wrecks were the result of collisions. (US Army Corps of Engineers)

in situ. A similar fate befell the steambarge *George T. Burroughs* in 1905: sunk by the steamer *C. F. Bielman*, its engine and machinery were salvaged before its hull was dynamited. Finally, the steambarge *Bothnia* collided in 1912 with the steel steamer *S. S. Curry* and sank near the Star Island House resort, with one life lost. These four wreck sites were spared the fate of the *Joliet* and the *John N. Glidden*: the dredging of the St. Clair Cutoff in the mid-twentieth century allowed them to remain at the margins of the old channel.

The Southeast Bend ship trap illustrates the "law of unintended consequences," where addressing one issue creates others. Steam power solved the problem of being at Nature's mercy but worsened two man-made ones: first, fires (to say nothing of boiler explosions) were virtually unheard of before the arrival of steam. It also exacerbated an old one: collision. The ability to closely follow a marked and improved channel, even around a blind curve at full steam or at night, turned the Southeast Bend into a killing ground for three decades.

Cluster C: The Russell Island Boneyard

Opposite Algonac, on a broad, marshy shallows fringing little Russell Island, four wrecks lie in a row, their keels neatly arranged parallel to the shoreline (map 18). Their upper structures are gone, but their lower hulls are remarkably intact, considering they have been there well over a century. A fifth lies at the head of the island (map 18a). All are visible in remarkable detail, even measurable, using an inexpensive form of remote sensing—Google Earth.[3]

3 Google Earth's database of historical files varies widely with respect to image quality of submerged objects. As of this writing (2023), the historic files from 10/1/2013 show the greatest clarity and detail. The four clustered sites at Russell Island show such structural elements as keelsons, frames, and centerboard trunks. The image appearing as Figure 32 is from that date.

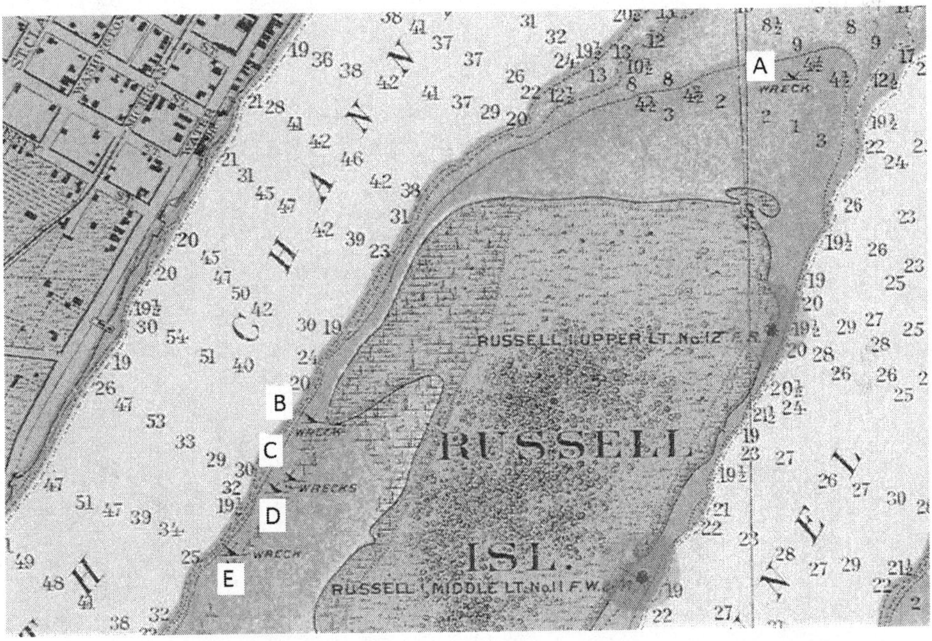

MAP 18. Wreck Cluster C, the "Russell Island Boneyard," as surveyed in 1903. Well-defined wreckage at each of the five marked sites is still extant. All identifications are provisional, requiring field survey: (a) unidentified; (b) barge *Champion* (collision, relocated 1903); (c) schooner *Ayr* (abandoned 1900); (d) unidentified; (e) steambarge *Virginius* a.k.a. *Thomas D. Stimson* (burned, beached 1903). The wreck symbol used indicates that the wrecks were partially above water at low water datum. All are now represented by the symbol for fully submerged wrecks. (US Army Corps of Engineers)

Their positions have not shifted since they first appeared on the Army Corps of Engineers' Lake Survey chart of 1903, although their condition has degraded. Pending field investigation, I have provisionally identified two sites by comparing observable features with archival records. One of the wrecks, code-named WR195SCR, has a length and beam measuring approximately 117′ and 24′, respectively, and a centerboard trunk is clearly visible. Allowing for measuring error and outward splaying of the hull, this fits easily within the dimensions (133′ × 23′) of the centerboard schooner *Ayr*, built in 1855 at Port Dalhousie, Ontario, and reported as abandoned in 1900 opposite Algonac.

Figure 32 shows WR190SCR lying just upstream (also map 18b). Its dimensions and hull structure suggest the *Champion*, built in 1863 in Cleveland as a barkentine, converted in 1868 to a 3-masted schooner, and finally to a towed barge in 1881.[4] It was carrying a load of coal behind the steamer *St. Louis* on July 13, 1903, when it was struck by the steamer *Robert W. E. Bunsen*, sinking in the channel between Algonac and Russell Island. Two weeks later, the press reported that both the owners and underwriters had abandoned the wreck: "The boat will be blown up by dynamite as it is directly in the channel and a dangerous obstruction to navigation. The steamer [Thomas D] *STIMSON*, also abandoned, will be blown up" (*Port Huron Daily Times* July 28, 1903). A photograph taken before the demolition (figure 33) shows only its two aft-raked masts, stripped of their spars as was customary. These were used, ironically enough, for hoisting running lights intended to prevent collisions. The river's current is clearly visible, indicating that its bow is pointed upstream. The mainland in the distance suggests that the wreck was already close to the Russell Island shore at the time of the accident.

The remotely measured dimensions of WR190SCR are 155′ × 28′, while those of the *Champion* were 182.5′ × 33.4′. Deprived of the graceful overhang at bow and stern typical of a barkentine hull, the dimensions of the *Champion* fit neatly into the footprint of the wreck site. Moreover, there is no obvious

4 Given that it was built during wartime, it may be significant that *Champion*'s original barkentine sail plan followed naval practice, employing square-rigged sails (figure 10.f), making her more suitable for operation in harm's way. Her conversion to the less labor-intensive schooner rig in peacetime suggests economic factors replacing military considerations.

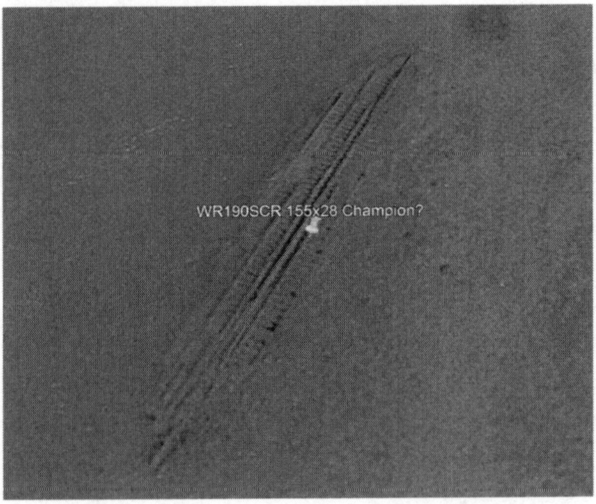

FIGURE 32. Aerial photograph of wreck site WR190SCR, tentatively identified as the barge *Champion*. (Google Earth)

FIGURE 33. The barge *Champion*, photographed shortly after its sinking by collision. The bow is pointed upstream, and it rests in water deep enough to submerge most of its deck structure. (C. Patrick Labadie Collection, Alpena County George N. Fletcher Public Library. Alpena, MI)

centerboard trunk, consistent with a hull originally laid as a barkentine. It cannot be determined from the aerial photo whether the bow is upstream—a diagnostic feature that would support, but not in itself confirm, its identification as *Champion*. Traces of coal, if found throughout the bilges, would likewise be supportive evidence: unlike a powered vessel, a towed barge carried coal in all its cargo holds, not just near its boilers as fuel. Planned field investigations will be required to answer these questions of identity.

Incidentally, the wrecked steamer *Thomas D. Stimson*, described in the newspaper report as slated for demolition at the same time as *Champion*, measured 160′ × 31′. The wreckage at WR205SCR measures 139′ × 24′ and is located only 300 meters away. Set afire by an exploded lamp, the *Stimson* was beached across from Algonac, where it burned to the waterline. Any evidence of charred timbers on WR205SCR would be a revealing but not conclusive diagnostic, given the substantial number of losses by fire in the locale, especially upstream.

Cluster C thus represents an opportunity to increase the number of known shipwreck sites in the Flats, and as part of Project SCRIMSHAW, to train young investigators in the basics of underwater survey and documentation. The Russell Island boneyard is less than 15 nautical miles from the home port of the Noble Odyssey's research fleet near Mount Clemens.

Cluster A: The Old South Channel Dumping Ground

Slightly more than one nautical mile (2 km) southwest of the Old South Channel Lights lies a cluster of charted wreckage sites. They appear on the 1962 Lake Survey, and all subsequent charts (map 19). None are present on the 1903 survey. By the time of the 1934 survey, a dumping ground had been designated in that area, evidently to receive dredge spoils and debris encountered in the ongoing maintenance of the St. Clair Ship Canal. Within this area appear two wreck symbols (map 19, A), which I code-named WR305LSC and WR310LSC. It appears that these two symbols mark wreckage deposited between 1903 and 1934, possibly relocated to the dumping area as part of nearby operations in dredging the second Flats Canal from 1906 to 1907, when a total of 2,044,801 cubic yards of material was excavated (Moulton and Thieme 2009, B.2.7). On the 1964 survey, a second pair of symbols appears (map 19, B), which may

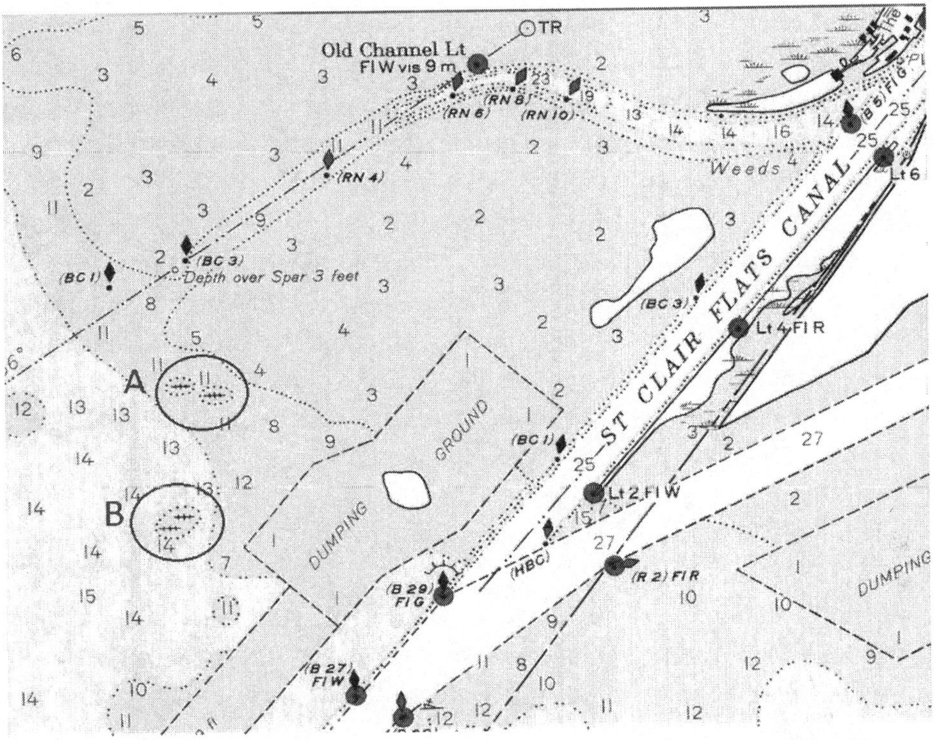

MAP 19. Wreck Cluster A, the "Old South Channel Dumping Ground," as surveyed in 1962. The pair of wreck symbols marked A first appeared on the 1934 survey, while the pair marked B appeared in 1962. Two designated dumping grounds appear here, their locations determined by the movement of dredging operations. (US Army Corps of Engineers)

mark further depositions of wreckage encountered by the Army Corps of Engineers between 1934 and 1962 in maintaining existing dredged channels and in constructing the new St. Clair Cutoff which opened in 1962 (Moulton and Thieme 2009, B.2.12–13).[5]

There appeared to be no contemporary documentation of the initial deposition or subsequent relocation of wreckage to the present positions. The two pairs of sites thus offered an opportunity to learn more about the scattering process of submerged material culture in creating large-scale maritime infrastructure. Sonar scans and reconnaissance dives in May 2018 aboard the Noble

5 Most of the dredge spoils resulting from the creation of the St. Clair Cutoff were deposited on the site which became Seaway Island, which lies almost entirely on the Canadian side.

Odyssey's research vessel, an 81′ decommissioned navy patrol boat renamed *Pride of Michigan*, failed to locate wreckage at any of the four chart positions. Three weeks later, however, we returned to the area for training dives to certify a group of new Sea Cadets as divers. Hoping that the wreckage might have shifted over time, I instructed the captain, Luke Clyburn, to anchor approximately 50 meters WNW from the charted position of WR300LSC. The position was an educated guess, based on the slope of the bottom and the direction of the current. As the divers hit the water, I told them to keep their eyes open—which they did, finding substantial wreckage only a few meters from the boat's anchor position. Since we only had basic survey gear aboard, I had to settle for a few quick measurements and photos, enough to tell me that we were looking at a substantial fragment of a large wooden ship. But which one? There had been literally dozens lost or abandoned in these waters.

In August 2020 we returned to the WR300LSC site with a new group of trainees and basic survey gear: stakes, measuring tapes, sketching slates, and video cameras. Our wreckage was 70′ in length, with a beam of 30′. It had been wider, indicated by its ribs being broken off short of the turn of the bilge, where the bottom meets the sides. Judging by the ratio of length to beam, it had also been considerably longer. There were four features that could serve as diagnostics in establishing its type, if not its identity: a stern post still standing erect at the aft end of its keel, a mast step along its keel, 50′ forward of the stern post, and a straight, clean break where the hull had been sheared, 70′ forward of the stern post. Moreover, there was no sign of a centerboard trunk. Those were enough clues to send me to the database I had compiled from shipwreck archives.

The "Pile of Planks" Speaks

In compiling three separate databases of ships built, sunk, and wrecked in the St. Clair locale, I could sort and filter by any number of parameters, including dimensions, vessel type, and location of loss. The results all pointed to one ship: the wooden freighter *John N. Glidden*, whose sad ending was described at the beginning of this chapter. Using a full-length photograph for scale (figure 34), I calculated that at 222′ overall, the distance between its stern post and the

FIGURE 34. Bulk freighter *John N. Glidden*. At 222′ in length, the distance between its mizzen mast step and stern post was calculated to measure 50′. (C. Patrick Labadie Collection, Alpena County George N. Fletcher Public Library. Alpena, MI)

step of its mizzen mast was 50′. Its beam of 35′ agreed with the width of our truncated fragment. Most striking of all, a remarkable photograph taken at the very moment it was dynamited amidships shows the demolition charges were placed 20′ before the mizzen mast—precisely the location of the clean break in WR300LSC's hull (figure 35). There were, in fact, so many photos taken while the freighter was blocking the channel that I was able to triangulate the location of the original collision. The distance from there to the wreckage deposition was 1.1 nautical miles (2 km), a journey aided by a downward slope and a following current. The wrecking crew had literally followed the line of least resistance.

While still in the area, we turned to WR295LSC, the other wreckage site of the southerly pair. I applied the same correction factors we had tried with WR300LSC, hoping that both had either been inaccurately charted or had shifted position in a similar fashion. We found a second large hull fragment almost directly beneath our boat. Time constraints prevented us from collecting the data needed to determine if it is also a part of the *Glidden*. A

FIGURE 35. Dynamiting the *John N. Glidden*, October 15, 1903. The center of the explosion was located 20′ forward of the mast. (C. Patrick Labadie Collection, Alpena County George N. Fletcher Public Library. Alpena, MI)

future comparison of fastening methods, timber dimensions, and frame spacing should tell the tale. I have also applied the same error correction factor to the charted positions of the other two wreckage sites, WR305LSC and WR310LSC, to be checked out in upcoming field seasons using side-scan sonar and remotely operated vehicles (ROVs). The Sea Cadets are literally diving into one of the most dynamic fields of Great Lakes research: the explosive growth in shipwreck studies made possible by the availability of remote sensing and imaging technology.

The Lessons of Failure

Collectively, the wrecks of the St. Clair Flats form a microcosm of the diverse site formation processes at work in the Great Lakes maritime landscape. More than that, they create Rönnby's "powerful moments from the past" that reunite a ship's mortal remains with its biography—what I earlier called "evidence-based storytelling" (Harrison 2017b; also Brink 2015, 103). They beckon us to reengage with them and their stories in a tactile and visceral as well as a narrative manner, examining their remains for signs of their lives and deaths: shattered timbers, twisted metal, scattered ballast piles. Because their stories are genuinely knowable if we make the connections, we indeed find ourselves posing socially relevant research questions to a pile of planks (Törnquist 2013, 26), which is to say, asking the fundamental question of the archaeologist: "What happened here, and what does it mean?"

By the mid-nineteenth century, the carrying capacity of the Great Lakes maritime system at last matched the demand—but at a price. Risk-taking behavior throughout the entire transport zone resulted in losses of ships, cargo, and crews. On the open waters of the big lakes, sudden storms, especially late in the shipping season, were a principal risk, as was the tendency to keep vessels in service well past their prime, while short-changing their maintenance. These two forms of pushing a vessel's limits have been termed "one more voyage syndrome" (Murphy 1983, 75). In the Strait, however, the risks that produced the greatest number of sinking incidents were those associated with haste and congestion: collisions, fires, and boiler explosions.

The transformation of the maritime landscape to its modern configuration was not complete until its ample, well-marked new channels were complemented by metal-hulled vessels propelled by internal combustion (diesel or diesel-electric) engines and guided by new communications technologies: radio, electronic navigation (radar and GPS); and weather forecasting. The emergent paradigm of *maritime landscape* and *material culture* was completed by *behavior*: nautical practices aimed at risk reduction, notably rules of piloting and vessel maintenance. Until that new triad of the modern era established a functional equilibrium, failure was a mode of disruption, and shipwrecks were a measure of failure.

12

Maritime Heritage in a Transformed Landscape

Even to a diver like the present author, it appeared that it was of more lasting interest to interview living people than to find shipwrecks.
—Christer Westerdahl, "The Maritime Cultural Landscape"

As the St. Clair landscape increasingly became a built environment, the constant revision of representations, notably nautical charts, and sailing directions, reflected critical knowledge of the evolving relations between the features of dwelling and movement coevolving in the maritime landscape and its transport zones. The operations of these long-term processes are inscribed everywhere: in the physical landscape itself; in the archaeological record; on charts, in voluminous accounts from newspapers to government inquests; and in the living memory of the maritime community. The outcome of these ongoing and incremental processes remains a constant transition and transformation. It is manifested in myriad ways, places, and times, creating a web of people, places, and things—or, as the anthropologist terms them, informants, sites, and artifacts.

Maritime Heritage: A Sense of Identity, a Sense of Place

The historical events marking transitions between dominant groups and their landscapes were often associated with territorial and ideological contestations in larger social and geographical contexts: the Beaver Wars, the French and Indian War, the American Revolution, the War of 1812, and the Civil War. During the relatively peaceful interim periods, other watershed events occurred. Disruptions and innovations were sparked by novel interactions between closely networked factors: technology and tradition, materials and environment, economy and ideology. Apart from the arrival of Europeans, the advent of steam technology for transportation, manufacturing, and landscape modification may have been the most disruptive of all in the St. Clair locale. The replacement of wood with iron and steel as a material for the fabrication of watercraft was a technological disruption shared by all modern maritime cultures but was particularly felt by the St. Clair locale's shipbuilding industry.

Disruptions and innovations are uniquely contingent phenomena, situated within a geographical, historical, and cultural context. Maritime identity, as reflected in the nautical practice of Great Lakes sailors, was conditioned by the landscape but also reflected the ideology of the greater society. Hence the evolving approaches to commercial shipping by three entrepreneurs reflected their respective eras. The French administrator Cadillac expediently turned to Indigenous and vernacular small craft, while his British counterpart Patrick Sinclair enlisted the naval might of the Empire to build and supply his eponymous fort—each seeking to carve out a colonial fiefdom on the frontier in the name of the mother country (Dunbar and May 1995, 47–48; Mitchell 1884, 405). By contrast, the anonymous captain of the steamer *Sheldon Thompson* opportunistically used Yankee ingenuity to coax a few extra dollars out of a routine trip upriver—a hallmark of American identity.

The subsequent development of the purpose-built steam-powered towboat, applied to the specific task of moving sailing ships through the Strait economically (if not always safely) was a truly revolutionary development, and one central to the positioning of the Strait as a hub of maritime industry. The scope and magnitude of the technological and social cascade precipitated by steam power cannot be overstated. Steam powered not only the ships but the sawmills that converted the forests into those ships; moreover, it powered the dredging of channels that allowed those ships to grow to enormous size. In the American mind, the balance of agency had tipped decisively from Nature to Culture—specifically, a shared American ideology of expansion and prosperity through innovation and exploitation.

As the transport zones of the Great Lakes became progressively interconnected with the Eastern Seaboard and transatlantic shipping, maritime practice and nautical technology were continually redefined in an increasingly anthropogenic and managed landscape. This process can be seen in the coevolving dimensions and capabilities of ships with their infrastructure—the canals, locks, and harbors they used—and in the standardization of aids to navigation to produce a seamless process of piloting throughout the entire system. Such expedient and informal landmarks as plum bushes and log cabins inevitably gave way to illuminated beacons and radio transmitters.

As the declining costs and risks of movement converged with rising demographic trends of an urban labor force with time and money for leisure, the "golden age" of the Flats literally emerged from the marshlands. In time, however, the palace steamers and grand resorts were obsolesced by a new proletarian elite that could afford its own cars, boats, and cottages. While transformations of all kinds have been the overarching and constant process at work during the *longue durée* of the historical period, their cumulative effect has been to shift the balance point of the forces defining the maritime landscape, from the transformation of Culture by Nature (behavioral adaptation) to that of Nature by Culture (anthropogenic modification), empowering an ever greater and more diverse population. Over time, layers of diverse representations, practices, ideologies, and identities become sedimented into the cultural landscape as heritage—connected to the outside world but uniquely localized—in short, a sense of place.

Conclusion: Maritime Heritage as a Community Resource

Ultimately, the social significance of the maritime landscape lies in its ability to transform and be transformed. In that sense, the St. Clair locale is unique but not anomalous. The social and cultural phenomena and trends that played out there are those that were driving the historical *durée* of the Great Lakes region and the North American continent from the seventeenth century to the present. The practices and technologies attempted, adapted, and adopted by Great Lakes mariners are comparable to those of their seagoing counterparts around the globe and to their North American contemporaries along the frontier. The complementary ideology and technology that transformed the Flats are the same as those that built the Union Pacific railroad and the Panama Canal: connectivity on a continental scale.

Across the span of nearly four centuries, the warp and weft of Nature and Culture have produced not a palimpsest, but a tapestry with a pattern: a motif of movement and dwelling with repetitions, variations, and innovations. Not every thread is visible at all times: they submerge and reemerge like the reed beds. Together, they tell a story. Better still, many stories—not just the triumphalist frontier narrative, but tales of separation and survival, endurance and identity. We want to know who these mariners and dwellers were.

The archival research and archaeological fieldwork described here show promise of strengthening the links between descendant maritime communities and their heritage, the family history that is embedded in the surrounding landscape (Leone 2010, 49; Clark, Wilson, and Binder 1979, 27). Blessed with such an opportunity, the maritime archaeologist begins and ends as an ethnographer, an observer whose interviews may lead not only to sites but to the recovery and sharing of community identity (Price 2013). In gathering and sharing their stories, we become the storytellers.

References

Abert, John J. 1847. *A Report from the Topographical Bureau, in Relation to the Commerce, Navigation and Means of Defence of the Western Lakes and Rivers* (Senate Exec. Doc. 4). Washington, DC: n.p.

———. 1853. "Report of the Colonel of Topographic Engineers." In *Message of the President of the United States* (House Exec. Doc. 1). Washington, DC: Robert Armstrong.

Adams, Jonathan. 2001. "Ships and Boats as Archaeological Source Material." *World Archaeology* 32 (3): 292–310.

Amherst, Jeffery. 1931. *The Journal of Jeffery Amherst*. Edited by J. Clarence Webster. Chicago: University of Chicago Press.

Andreas, Alfred T. 1883. *History of St. Clair County, Michigan*. Chicago: A. T. Andreas.

Andrews, Israel D. 1853. *Communication from the Secretary of the Treasury, Transmitting, in Compliance with a Resolution of the Senate of March 8, 1854, the Report of Israel D. Andrews, Consul of the United States for Canada and New Brunswick, on the Trade and Commerce of the British North American Colonies and upon the Great Lakes and Rivers*. Washington, DC: Robert Armstrong.

Anonymous. 1869. *Memorial of the Chippeway, Pottawatomy, and Ottawa Indians of Walpole Island! Touching Their Claim of the Huron Reserve, Fighting, Bois Blanc, Turkey and Point Au Pelee Islands*. Sarnia, ON: Canadian Book & Job Office.

———. 1888. "Return of all the Vessels upon Lake George, Champlain, Ontario, Erie, Huron & Michigan, &c. Quebec, 30th July 1778." In *Collections of the State Historical Society of Wisconsin*, edited by Reuben Gold Thwaites, 11:198–99. Madison, WI: Democrat Printing Company.

Arnshav, Mirja. 2013. "From Wreck to Heritage: A Matter of Time?" In *Interpreting Shipwrecks: Maritime Archaeological Approaches*, edited by Jonathan Adams and Johan Rönnby, 140–50. Southampton, UK: Highfield Press.

Aron, Stephen. 2005. "The Meetings of Peoples and Empires at the Confluence of the Missouri, Ohio and Mississippi Rivers." In *Untaming the Frontier in Anthropology, Archaeology, and History*, edited by Bradley J. Parker and Lars Rodseth, 174–202. Tucson: University of Arizona Press.

Atalay, Sonya. 2006. "Indigenous Archaeology as Decolonizing Practice." *American Indian Quarterly* 30 (3/4): 280–310.

Balée, William. 1998. "Historical Ecology: Premises and Postulates." In *Advances in Historical Ecology*, edited by William Balée, 13–29. New York: Columbia University Press.

———. 2006. "The Research Program of Historical Ecology." *Annual Review of Anthropology* 35:75–98.

Balée, William, and Clark L. Erikson. 2006. "Time, Complexity, and Historical Ecology." In *Time and Complexity in Historical Ecology*, edited by William Balée and Clark L. Erikson, 1–17. New York: Columbia University Press.

Barkhausen, Henry N. 1990. *Focusing on the Centerboard*. Manitowoc, WI: Manitowoc Maritime Museum.

Barnet, James. 1887. *Barnet's Coast Pilot for the Lakes, on Both Shores Michigan, Superior, Huron, St. Clair, Erie and Ontario; Green Bay, Georgian Bay, Grand and Little Traverse Bays; Straits of Mackinaw; the Rivers St. Mary, St. Clair, Detroit, Niagara and St. Laurence. Courses and Distances, Sailing Directions, etc. Rearranged, Rev. and Additions Made from the Latest United States Coast Survey Charts. Also, a Description of All the Lights and Lighthouses. With a Valuable Appendix, and an Alphabetically-Arranged Index of the Names of Places*. Chicago: James Barnet.

Barnett, Leroy. 2023. "Digging from Detroit to Windsor: The Michigan Central Railway Tunnel." *Chronicle: Official Magazine of the Historical Society of Michigan* 45 (4): 16–19.

Barry, James P. 1973. *Ships of the Great Lakes: 300 Years of Navigation*. Berkeley, CA: Howell-North.

———. 2002. *Hackercraft*. St. Paul, MN: MBI Publishing.

Barton, Barb. 2016. "Wild Rice: A Return to the Past." *Michigan History* 100 (5): 16–22.

Basso, Keith H. 1988. "'Speaking with Names': Language and Landscape among the Western Apache." *Cultural Anthropology* 3 (2): 99–130.

Beauharnois, François de La Boische, Sieur de. 1906. "1731: Post of Detroit." In *Collections of the State Historical Society of Wisconsin*, vol 13, edited by Reuben Gold Thwaites, 141–44. Madison: State Historical Society of Wisconsin.

Beckford, Clinton L., Clint Jacobs, Naomi Williams, and Russell Nahdee. 2010. "Aboriginal Environmental Wisdom, Stewardship, and Sustainability: Lessons from the Walpole Island First Nations, Ontario, Canada." *Journal of Environmental Education* 41 (4): 239–48.

Berg, Lawrence D., and Robin A. Kearns. 2009. "Naming as Norming: 'Race,' Gender and the Identity Politics of Naming Places in Aotearoa/New Zealand." In *Critical Toponymies: The Contested Politics of Place Naming*, edited by Lawrence D. Berg and Jani Vuolteenaho, 19–52. Burlington, VT: Ashgate.

Biersack, Aletta. 1999. "Introduction: From the 'New Ecology' to the New Ecologies." *American Anthropologist* 101 (1): 5–18.

Bigsby, John J. 1850. *The Shoe and Canoe; or, Pictures of Travel in the Canadas*. 2 vols. London: Chapman and Hall.

Bintliff, John. 1991. “The Contribution of an *Annaliste*/Structural History Approach to Archaeology.” In *The Annales School and Archaeology*, edited by John Bintliff, 1–33. London: Leicester University Press.

Blois, John T. 1838. *Gazetteer of Michigan*. Detroit, MI: Sidney L. Rood.

Bolsenga, Stanley J, and Charles E. Herdendorf, eds. 1993. *Lake Erie and Lake St Clair Handbook*. Detroit, MI: Wayne State University Press.

Bourdieu, Pierre. 1977. *Outline of a Theory of Practice*, translated by Richard Nice. New York: Cambridge University Press.

Bradford, John. 1957. *Ancient Landscapes: Studies in Field Archaeology*. London: Bell.

Brehm, Diederick. 1883. “Lieut. Brehm's Report to His Excellency General Amherst of a Scout Going from Montreal to La Galette [1761].” *New England Historical and Genealogical Register* 38:22–26.

Brehm, Victoria. 2018. *White Squall: Sailing the Great Lakes*. Tustin, MI: Ladyslipper Press.

Bright, William. 2004. *Native American Placenames of the United States*. Norman, OK: University of Oklahoma Press.

Brink, Yvonne. 2015. “Historical Archaeology, Language, and Storytelling at the Cape of Good Hope and Elsewhere.” In *Materializing Colonial Encounters*, edited by F. G. Richard, 97–127. New York: Springer.

Bryan, P. W. 1933. *Man's Adaptation of Nature: Studies of the Cultural Landscape*. New York: Henry Holt.

Bryant, William Cullen. 1851. *Letters of a Traveller; or, Notes of Things Seen in Europe and America*. New York: George P. Putnam.

Buchanan, James. 1860. *Message from the President of the United States Assigning His Reasons for Not Approving a Bill, Entitled “An Act Making an Appropriation for Deepening the Channel over the St. Clair Flats, in the State of Michigan,” Passed at the Last Session of Congress* (Senate Exec. Doc. 6). Washington, DC: n.p.

Butzer, Karl W. 1992. “The Americas before and after 1492: An Introduction to Current Geographical Research.” *Annals of the Association of American Geographers* 82 (3): 345–68.

Cadillac, Antoine Laumet de Lamothe. 1904. “Account of Detroit; Description of Detroit; Advantages Found There [n.t.].” In *Historical Collections: Collections and Researches Made by the Michigan Pioneer and Historical Society*, 33:131–51. Lansing, MI: Robert Smith.

Cain, P. J., and A. G. Hopkins. 1980. “The Political Economy of British Expansion Overseas, 1750–1914.” *The Economic History Review* 33 (4): 463–90.

Campbell, Donald. 1762. *A Court of Enquiry Held by Order of Major Gladwin*. Jeffery Amherst Papers 49:111. Clements Library, University of Michigan.

Cangany, Catherine. 2014. *Frontier Seaport: Detroit's Transformation into an Atlantic Entrepôt*. Chicago: University of Chicago Press.

Carroll, Francis M. 2001. *A Good and Wise Measure: The Search for the Canadian-American Boundary, 1783–1842*. Toronto, ON: University of Toronto Press.

———. 2004. "The Search for the Canadian-American Boundary along the Michigan Frontier, 1819–1827: The Boundary Commissions under Articles Six and Seven of the Treaty of Ghent." *Michigan Historical Review* 30 (2): 77–104.

Carver, Jonathan. 1781. *Travels through the Interior Parts of North America in the Years 1766, 1767, and 1768*. London: C. Dilly, H. Payne, J. Phillips.

———. 1976. *The Journals of Jonathan Carver and Related Documents, 1766–1770*, edited by John Parker. Saint Paul: Minnesota Historical Society.

Cass, Lewis. 1827. Review of *American State Papers: Indian Affairs*. *North American Review* n.s. 29:365–442.

Charlevoix, Pierre de. 1966. *Journal of a Voyage to North-America* [n.t.]. Facsimile of 1761 ed. Ann Arbor, MI: University Microfilms.

Chauvignerie, M. 1855. "Enumeration of the Indian Tribes Connected with the Government of Canada; the Warriors and Armorial Bearings of Each Nation, 1736 [n.t.]." In *Documents Relative to the Colonial History of New-York; Procured in Holland, England, and France*, edited by E. B. O'Callaghan, 9:1052–58. Albany, NY: Weed, Parsons.

Chiarappa, Michael J. 2005. "Great Lakes Commercial Fishing Architecture: The Endurance and Transformation of a Region's Landscape/Waterscape." *Perspectives in Vernacular Architecture* 10:217–32.

Clark, John, Claudia Wilson, and Gordon L. Binder. 1979. *Small Seaports: Revitalization through Conserving Heritage Resources*. Washington, DC: The Conservation Foundation.

Cleland, Charles E. 1992. *Rites of Conquest: The History and Culture of Michigan's Native Americans*. Ann Arbor: University of Michigan Press.

Cole, Leon J. 1903. *The Delta of the St. Clair River*. Lansing, MI: Robert Smith.

Colton, Calvin. 1833. *Tour of the American Lakes, and among the Indians of the North-West Territory in 1830: Disclosing the Character and Prospects of the Indian Race*. 2 vols. London: Frederick Westley and A. H. Davis.

Conlin, David L. 1997. "Ship Trap." In *Encyclopaedia of Underwater and Maritime Archaeology*, edited by James P. Delgado, 377. London: British Museum Press.

Considine, Glenn D., ed. 2008. *Van Nostrand's Scientific Encyclopedia*, 10th ed. Hoboken, NJ: Wiley-Interscience.

Cooney, Gabriel. 2003. "Introduction: Seeing Land from the Sea." *World Archaeology* 35 (3): 323–28.

Costa, Ricardo L. 2006. "The Logic of Practices in Pierre Bourdieu." *Current Sociology* 554 (6): 873–95.

Cram, Thomas J. 1867. "Revised report on the improvement of the St. Clair Flats, Michigan." In *River and Harbor Improvements: Report of the Chief of Engineers Respecting Certain Public Works*, Appendix N, 43–58 (House Exec. Doc. 56, pt. 2). Washington, DC: n.p.

Crumley, Carole L., ed. 1994. *Historical Ecology: Cultural Knowledge and Changing Landscapes*. Santa Fe, NM: School of American Research Press.

———. 1996. "Historical Ecology." In *Encyclopedia of Cultural Anthropology*, edited by David Levinson and Melvin Ember, 558–60. New York: Henry Holt.

———. 2021. "Historical Ecology: A Robust Bridge between Archaeology and Ecology." *Sustainability* 13 (8210): 1–12.

Crumley, Carole L., and William H. Marquardt. 1990. "Landscape: A Unifying Concept in Regional Analysis." In *Interpreting Space: GIS and Archaeology*, edited by Kathleen M. S. Allen, Stanton W. Green, and Ezra B. W. Zubrow, 73–79. New York: Taylor & Francis.

Cunliffe, Barry. 2008. *Europe between the Oceans*. New Haven, CT: Yale University Press.

Curwood, James Oliver. 1909. *The Great Lakes, the Vessels That Plough Them: Their Owners, Their Sailors, and Their Cargoes*. New York: G. P. Putnam's Sons.

Dappert, Claire P. 2006. *Oaken Whale with a Cast Iron Tail: The Single-Decked Wooden Bulk Carrier* Monohansett. Greenville, NC: East Carolina University.

Darby, William. 1819. *A Tour from the City of New-York to Detroit, in the Michigan Territory, Made between the 2nd of May and the 22nd of September, 1818*. New York: Kirk & Mercein.

Deetz, James. 1990. "Prologue: Landscapes as Cultural Statements." In *Earth Patterns: Essays in Landscape Archaeology*, edited by William M. Kelso and Rachel Most, 1–4. Charlottesville: University of Virginia Press.

Delafield, Joseph. 1943. *The Unfortified Boundary: A Diary of the First Survey of the Canadian Boundary Line from St. Regis to the Lake of the Woods*, edited by Robert McElroy and Thomas Riggs. New York: privately printed.

Delâge, Denys, Helen Hornbeck Tanner, and Pierre Chazelle. 1994. "The Ojibwa-Jesuit Debate at Walpole Island, 1844." *Ethnohistory* 41 (2): 295–321.

Delgado, James P., Tomás Mendizábal, Frederick H. Hanselmann, and Dominique Rissolo. 2016. *The Maritime Landscape of the Isthmus of Panamá*. Gainesville: University Press of Florida.

Dewdney, Selwyn. 1975. *The Sacred Scrolls of the Southern Ojibway*. Toronto, ON: University of Toronto Press.

Dickens, Charles. 1868. *American Notes and Reprinted Pieces*. London: Chapman & Hall.

Dickinson, Henry W., and Arthur Titley. 1934. *Richard Trevithick, the Engineer and the Man*. Cambridge: Cambridge University Press.

Dixon, Michael M. 2002. *Life at the Flats: The Golden Era of the St. Clair River Delta*. Mt. Clemens, MI: Mervue Publications.

Dodge, C. K. 1914. "The Flowering Plants, Ferns and Fern Allies Growing without Cultivation in Lambton County, Ontario." *Reports of the Michigan Academy of Science* 16:132–200.

Dolwick, Jim S. 2008. "In Search of the Social: Steamboats, Square Wheels, Reindeer and Other Things." *Journal of Maritime Archaeology* 3:15–41.

———. 2009. "'The Social' and Beyond: Introducing Actor-Network Theory." *Journal of Maritime Archaeology* 4:21–49.

Doolittle, William E. 1992. "Agriculture in North America on the Eve of Contact: A Reassessment." *Annals of the Association of American Geographers* 82 (3): 386–401.

Doty, James Duane. 1895. "Official Journal, 1820: Expedition with Cass and Schoolcraft." In *Collections of the State Historical Society of Wisconsin*, edited by Reuben Gold Thwaites, 13:163–67. Madison, WI: State Historical Society of Wisconsin.

Douglas, Mary. 1966. *Purity and Danger: An Analysis of the Concepts of Pollution and Taboo*. New York: Routledge.

Douglas, Stuart L. 1906. "Westward Ho!" *Outing Magazine* 48 (5): 614–18.

Douglass, David Bates. 1969. *American Voyageur: The Journal of David Bates Douglass*, edited by Sydney W. Jackman and John F. Freeman. Marquette: Northern Michigan University Press.

Duluth, Daniel Greysolon. 1902. "Account of Detroit Post." In *Collections of the State Historical Society of Wisconsin*, edited by Reuben Gold Thwaites, 16:127–30. Madison: State Historical Society of Wisconsin.

Dunbar, Willis F., and George S. May. 1995. *Michigan: A History of the Wolverine State*, 3rd ed. Grand Rapids, MI: William B. Eerdmans.

Dunnigan, Brian Leigh. 2001. *Frontier Metropolis: Picturing Early Detroit, 1701–1838*. Detroit, MI: Wayne State University Press.

Du Vernet, Henry. 1908. "Stores etc., Taken upon Lieut.-Gov. Hamilton's Expedition." In *Historical Collections: Collections and Researches Made by the Michigan Pioneer and Historical Society*, edited by Henry S. Bartholomew, 9:409. Lansing, MI: Wynkoop Hallenbeck Crawford.

Eid, Leroy V. 1979. "The Ojibwa-Iroquois War: The War the Five Nations Did Not Win." *Ethnohistory* 26 (4): 297–324.

Eldredge, Robert F. 1905. *Past and Present of Macomb County, Michigan*. Chicago: S. J. Clarke.

Erickson, Clark L. 2010. "The Transformation of Environment into Landscape: The Historical Ecology of Monumental Earthwork Construction in the Bolivian Amazon." *Diversity* 2:618–52.

Ericson, Bernard E. 1968. "The Evolution of Ships on the Great Lakes, Part II: Steam and Steel." Paper presented at the Annual Meeting of the Society of Naval Architects and Marine Engineers, Cleveland, OH.

———. 1969. "The Evolution of Great Lakes Ships, Part I: Sail." *Inland Seas; Quarterly Journal of the Great Lakes Historical Society* 25 (2): 91–104.

Evans, Amanda M. 2016. "Improvise, Adapt, Overcome: Vernacular Boats as Environmental Adaptations." In *The Archaeology of Vernacular Watercraft*, edited by Amanda M. Evans, 9–18. New York: Springer.

Evans, Amanda M., and Sheli O. Smith. 2016. "Vernacular Watercraft: In Concept and in Practice." In *The Archaeology of Vernacular Watercraft*, edited by Amanda M. Evans, 1–7. New York: Springer.

Ferretti, Christine. 2010. "10,000 Boaters Party at Jobbie Nooner: Police Report Few Problems at Annual Gull Island Event." *Detroit News*, June 26, A8.

Ferris, Neal. 2009. *The Archaeology of Native-Lived Colonialism: Challenging History in the Great Lakes*. Tucson: University of Arizona Press.

Firth, Anthony. 1995. *Three Facets of Maritime Archaeology: Society, Landscape and Critique*. www.wessexarch.co.uk/files/splash-import/wp-content/uploads/2010/04/Firth-1995-Three-Facets-of-Maritime-Archaeology-140410.pdf.

Fitting, James E. 1965. *Late Woodland Cultures of Southeast Michigan*. Ann Arbor: University of Michigan Press.

———. 1970. *The Archaeology of Michigan: A Guide to the Prehistory of the Great Lakes Region*. New York: Natural History Press.

Fitting, James E., and Charles E. Cleland. 1969. "Late Prehistoric Patterns in the Upper Great Lakes." *Ethnohistory* 16 (4): 289–302.

Fitzpatrick, Charles. 1917. *The Rush-Bagot Agreement*. New York: Lawyer's Club.

Fontenoy, Paul E. 1994. *The Sloops of the Hudson River*. Mystic, CT: Mystic Seaport Museum.

Ford, Ben. 2011. "The Shoreline as a Bridge, Not a Boundary: Cognitive Maritime Landscapes of Lake Ontario." In *The Archaeology of Maritime Landscapes*, edited by Ben Ford, 63–80. New York: Springer.

———. 2013. "The Reuse of Vessels as Harbor Structures: A Cross-Cultural Comparison." *Journal of Maritime Archaeology* 8:197–219.

Ford, Benjamin, and Kevin J. Crisman. 2018. *The Shore Is a Bridge: The Maritime Cultural Landscape of Lake Ontario*. College Station: Texas A&M University Press.

Fuller, George Newman. 1916. *Economic and Social Beginnings of Michigan*. Lansing, MI: Wynkoop Hallenbeck Crawford.

Galinée, René Brehan de. 1917. "The Voyage of Dollier and Galinée, 1669–1670," translated by James H. Coyne. In *Early Narratives of the Northwest*, edited by Louise P. Kellogg, 163–209. New York: Charles Scribner's Sons.

Gibbins, David, and Jonathan Adams. 2001. "Shipwrecks and Maritime Archaeology." *World Archaeology* 32 (3): 279–91.

Gibbs, Martin, and Brad Duncan. 2016. "Cultural Site Formation Processes Affecting Shipwrecks and Shipping Mishap Sites." In *Site Formation Processes of Submerged Shipwrecks*, edited by Matthew E. Keith, 179–207. Gainesville: University Press of Florida.

Gibson, James J. 1979. *The Ecological Approach to Visual Perception*. Boston, MA: Houghton Mifflin.

Gilman, Chandler. 1836. *Life on the Lakes: Being Tales and Sketches Collected during a Trip to the Pictured Rocks of Lake Superior*. New York: George Dearborn.

Glacken, Clarence J. 1967. *Traces on the Rhodian Shore: Nature and Culture in Western Thought from Ancient Times to the End of the Eighteenth Century*. Berkeley: University of California Press.

Goddard, Ives. 1978. "Mascouten." In *Handbook of North American Indians*, vol. 15: *Northeast*, edited by Bruce G. Trigger, 668–72. Washington, DC: Smithsonian Institution.

Goggin, John M. 1960. "Underwater Archaeology: Its Nature and Limitations." *American Antiquity* 25 (3): 348–54.

Gould, Richard. 2000. *Archaeology and the Social History of Ships*. New York: Cambridge University Press.

Graham, J. D. 1856. "St. Clair Flats Improvement, Michigan." In *Report of the Secretary of War, Communicating, in Compliance with a Resolution of the Senate of the 23rd Instant, a Copy of a Report from Lieutenant Colonel Graham of the Harbors, &c., in Wisconsin, Illinois, Indiana, and Michigan, under His Superintendence* (Senate Exec. Doc. 16). Washington, DC: n.p.

Griffin, Henry A. 1893. "Ship-Building on the Great Lakes." *Engineering Magazine* 4:815–35.

Haldimand Papers. 1892. "Memorial of the Merchants of Montreal." In *Historical Collections: Collections and Researches Made by the Michigan Pioneer and Historical Society*, 19:620–21. Lansing, MI: Robert Smith.

Halsey, John R., and Janet G. Brashler. 2013. "More Than Grave Lots? The Jack's Reef Horizon in Michigan." *Archaeology of Eastern North America* 41:145–92.

Hamil, Fred Coyne. 1951. *The Valley of the Lower Thames 1640 to 1850*. Toronto, ON: University of Toronto Press.

Hamilton, Henry. 1908. "Letter to the Earl of Dartmouth, 22 September 1776." In *Michigan Historical Collections*, edited by M. Agnes Burton, 10:264–69. Lansing, MI: Wyncoop Hallenbeck Crawford.

Harley, J. B. 1992. "Deconstructing the Map." In *Writing Worlds: Discourse, Text and Metaphor in the Representation of Landscape*, edited by Trevor J. Barnes and James S. Duncan, 231–47. New York: Routledge.

Harrison, Daniel F. 2014. "Frontier Arms Race: Historical and Archaeological Analysis of an Assemblage of Eighteenth-Century Cannon Recovered from the Detroit River and Lake Erie." *Historical Archaeology* 48 (4): 27–45.

———. 2017a. "Change amid Continuity, Innovation within Tradition: Wampum Diplomacy at the Treaty of Greenville, 1795." *Ethnohistory* 64 (2): 191–216.

———. 2017b. "Maritime Archaeology as 'Evidence-Based Storytelling.'" In *Interpreting Maritime History at Museums and Historic Sites*, edited by Joel Stone, 85–98. New York: Rowman & Littlefield.

Hay, Jehu. 1911. "Letter to Col. Henry Bouquet, 24 September, 1762." In *Michigan Historical Collections*, edited by M. Agnes Burton, 19:165. Lansing, MI: Wyncoop Hallenbeck Crawford.

Hayes, Bruce N. 1964. "An Ecological Study of a Wet Prairie on Harsens Island, Michigan." *The Michigan Botanist* 3:71–82.

Heckert, Paul A. 2016. "Little Ice Age (LIA)." In *Encyclopedia of Climate Change*, edited by Steven I. Dutch, 2:712–15. Ipswich, MA: Salem Press.

Hennepin, Louis. 1903. *A New Discovery of a Vast Country in America* 2 vols. [n.t.]. Facsimile of 1698 ed. Chicago: A. C. McClurg.

———. 1966. *A Description of Louisiana*, translated by John Gilmary Shea. Facsimile of 1880 ed. Ann Arbor, MI: University Microfilms.

Herman, Douglas. 2009. "The Aloha State: Place Names and the Anti-conquest of Hawai'i." In *Critical Toponymies: The Contested Politics of Place Naming*,

edited by Lawrence D. Berg and Jani Vuolteenaho, 101–36. Burlington, VT: Ashgate.
Himmler, Frank, and George C. De Long. 1963. "The Mesothermal Climates of Michigan." *Papers of the Michigan Academy of Science, Arts and Letters* 48:413–18.
Hinsdale, Wilbert B. 1931. *Archaeological Atlas of Michigan*. Ann Arbor: University of Michigan Press.
Hodder, Ian. 2012. *Entangled: An Archaeology of the Relationships between Humans and Things*. Malden, MA: Wiley-Blackwell.
Hoefnagels, Anna. 2002. "Powwow Songs: Traveling Songs and Changing Protocol." *The World of Music* 44 (1): 127–36.
Howland, Henry R. 1903. "Navy Island, and the First Successors to the Griffon." In *Publications of the Buffalo Historical Society*, edited by Frank H. Severance, 6:17–33. Buffalo, NY: Buffalo Historical Society.
Hoxie, Robert David. 1980. "A Formal Analysis of the Prehistoric Ceramics from Draper Park (20-SC-40): A Wayne Tradition Occupation on the St. Clair River in Southeastern Michigan." Master's thesis, Western Michigan University.
Hudgins, Bert. 1935. "Human Occupance of the St. Clair Delta." *Economic Geography* 11 (1): 53–61.
Hughes, Charles. 1895. "Proceedings of a Court of Inquiry Held on the 25th Day of November 1805." In *Historical Collections: Collections and Researches Made by the Michigan Pioneer and Historical Society*, 23:355–66. Lansing, MI: Robert Smith.
Ibrahim, Kamal A., and John A. McCorquodale. 1985. "Finite Element Circulation Model for Lake St. Clair." *Journal of Great Lakes Research* 11 (3): 206–22.
Ilves, Kristin. 2006. "Place Names about Life by the Sea: An Archaeological Perspective on the Estonian-Swedish Landscape." *Folklore: Electronic Journal of Folklore* 34:87–102.
———. 2009. "Discovering Harbours? Reflection on the State and Development of Landing Site Studies in the Baltic Sea Region." *Journal of Maritime Archaeology* 4:149–63.
Ingold, Tim. 1993. "The Temporality of the Landscape." *World Archaeology* 25 (2): 152–74.
Jameson, Anna. 1838. *Winter Studies and Summer Rambles in Canada*. London: Saunders and Otley.
Jenks, William Lee. 1912. *St. Clair County Michigan: Its History and Its People*. 2 vols. Chicago: Lewis.
Jensen, John Odin. 2019. *Stories from the Wreckage: A Great Lakes Maritime History Inspired by Wrecks*. Madison: Wisconsin Historical Society Press.
Johnston, Basil. 1976. *Ojibwe Heritage*. New York: Columbia University Press.
Karamanski, Theodore J. 2017. *Great Lakes Navigation and Navigational Aids: Historical Context Study*. Chicago: Loyola University Press.
Kaszicki, C. A. 1985. "History of the Glacial Lake Algonquin in the Haliburton Region, South-Central Ontario." In *Quaternary Evolution of the Great Lakes*, edited by P. F. Karros and P. E. Calkin, 109–23. Toronto, ON: Geological Association of Canada.
Keehnen, Floris W. M., Corinne L. Hofman, and Andrzej T. Antczak. 2019. "Material Encounters and Indigenous Transformations in the Early Colonial Americas:

Archaeological Case Studies." In *Material Encounters and Indigenous Transformations in the Early Colonial Americas*, edited by Corinne L. Hofman and Floris W. M. Keehnen, 1–31. Brill. www.jstor.org/stable/10.1163/j.ctvrxk2gr.7.

Kidder, Tristram R. 1998. "The Rat That Ate Louisiana: Aspects of Historical Ecology in the Louisiana River Delta." In *Advances in Historical Ecology*, edited by William Balée, 141–68. New York: Columbia University Press.

Klein, Kerwin Lee. 1996. "Reclaiming the 'F' Word, or Being and Becoming Postwestern." *Pacific Historical Review* 65 (2): 179–215.

Knapp, A. Bernard, ed. 1992. *Archaeology, Annales, and Ethnohistory*. New York: Cambridge University Press.

Knapp, A. Bernard, and Wendy Ashmore. 1999. "Archaeological Landscapes: Constructed, Conceptualized, Ideational." In *Archaeologies of Landscape: Contemporary Perspectives*, edited by Wendy Ashmore and A. Bernard Knapp, 1–30. New York: Blackwell.

Kohl, Cris. 1987. *Shipwreck Tales: The St Clair River (to 1900)*. Chatham, ON: Mercury Press.

Kost, Michael A., Dennis A. Albert, Joshua G. Cohen, Bradford S. Slaughter, Rebecca K. Schillo, Christopher R. Weber, and Kim A. Chapman. 2007. *Natural Communities of Michigan: Classification and Description*. Lansing: Michigan Natural Features Inventory. mnfi.anr.msu.edu/reports/MNFI-Report-2007-21.pdf.

Labadie, C. Patrick, and Larry Murphy. 1987. "Major Vessel Types on Lake Superior: Sail to Steam." In *Shipwrecks of Isle Royale National Park: The Archaeological Survey*, edited by Daniel Lenihan, 26–36. Duluth, MN: Lake Superior Port Cities.

Lafferty, William, and Valerie Van Heest. 2009. *Buckets and Belts: Evolution of the Great Lakes Self-Unloader*. Holland, MI: In-Depth Editions.

Lafitau, Joseph François. 1977. *Customs of the American Indians Compared with the Customs of Primitive Times*, edited and translated by William N. Fenton and Elizabeth L. Moore. 2 vols. Toronto, ON: Champlain Society.

Lahontan, Louis Armand de Lom d'Arce, Baron de. 1905. *New Voyages to North-America*. [n.t.]. Facsimile of 1703 ed. Chicago: A. C. McClurg.

Lajeunesse, Ernest J., ed. 1960. *The Windsor Border Region, Canada's Southernmost Frontier: A Collection of Documents*. Toronto, ON: University of Toronto Press.

Landes, Ruth. 1968. *Ojibwa Religion and the Midéwiwin*. Madison: University of Wisconsin Press.

Langouët, Loic, and Marie-Yvane Daire. 2009. "Ancient Maritime Fish-Traps of Brittany (France): A Reappraisal of the Relationship between Human and Coastal Environment during the Holocene." *Journal of Maritime Archaeology* 4:131–48.

Larson, John W. 1981. *Essayons: A History of the Detroit District U.S. Army Corps of Engineers*. Detroit, MI: US Army Corps of Engineers.

Latour, Bruno. 1999. *Pandora's Hope*. Cambridge, MA: Harvard University Press.

Lefebvre, Henri. 1991. *The Production of Space*, translated by Donald Nicholson-Smith. Cambridge, MA: Blackwell.

Leone, Mark P. 2010. *Critical Historical Archaeology*. Walnut Creek, CA: Left Coast Press.

Lewis, G. Malcolm. 1998. "Maps, Mapmaking and Map Use by Native Americans." In *Cartography in the Traditional African, American, Arctic, Australian and Pacific Societies*, edited by David Woodward and G. Malcolm Lewis, 51–182. Chicago: University of Chicago Press.

Lewis, Walter. 2015. "Transition from Sail to Steam on the Great Lakes in the Nineteenth Century." *Northern Mariner / Le Marin du Nord* 25 (4): 345–74.

Little, Barbara J., and Paul A. Shackel. 1989. "Scales of Historical Anthropology: An Archaeology of Colonial Anglo-America." *Antiquity* 63:495–509.

Livingston, Patrick. 2008. *Summer Dreams: The Story of Bob-Lo Island*. Detroit, MI: Wayne State University Press.

Logan, James. 1871. *Notes of a Journey through Canada, the United States of America, and the West Indies*. Edinburgh: Fraser.

Loomis, Elisha. 1953. "Diary of a Trip from Rochester to Mackinac Island." *Michigan History* 37:27–41.

Luce, Stephen Bleecker, William Shepherd Benson, and Samuel Seabury. 1898. *Text-Book of Seamanship: The Equipping and Handling of Vessels under Sail or Steam*. New York: Van Nostrand.

Lydecker, G. J. 1900. *Delays from Accidents, to Navigation in St. Marys River and St. Clair Flats Canal, Michigan* (Senate Doc. 80). Washington, DC: n.p.

Magee, Dorothy M., ed. 1980. *Centennial History of Mount Clemens, Michigan, 1879–1979*. Mount Clemens, MI: Mount Clemens Public Library.

Mann, Gother. 1888. "Report on the State of Forts Lernoult, Michilimackinac, &c." In *Michigan Pioneer & Historical Collections*, 12:30–37. Lansing, MI: Thorp & Godfrey.

Martin, Ron. 1971. "Walpole's Happy Hunting Ground." *Detroit Free Press*, November 19, B1.

Mauss, Marcel. 2011. *The Gift*, translated by Ian Cunnison. Mansfield Center, CT: Martino.

Mayhew, Eugene J. 2003. *Fort Sinclair: The British Roots of St. Clair, Michigan*. St. Clair, MI: St. Clair Historical Commission.

M'Call, James. 1892. "M'Call's Journal of a Visit to Wisconsin in 1830." In *Collections of the State Historical Society of Wisconsin*, edited by Reuben Gold Thwaites, 12:179–82. Madison, WI: Democrat Printing Company.

McKenney, Thomas L. 1959. *Sketches of a Tour to the Lakes, of the Character and Customs of the Chippeway Indians, and of Incidents Connected with the Treaty of Fond du Lac*. Minneapolis, MN: Ross & Haines.

Meide, Chuck, and Kathryn Sikes. 2014. "Manipulating the Maritime Cultural Landscape: Vernacular Boats and Economic Relations on Nineteenth-Century Achill Island, Ireland." *Journal of Maritime Archaeology* 9:115–41.

Meinig, D. W. 1979. "The Beholding Eye: Ten Versions of the Same Scene." In *The Interpretation of Ordinary Landscapes: Geographical Essays*, edited by D. W. Meinig, 33–48. New York: Oxford University Press.

Mills, James Cooke. 1910. *Our Inland Seas: Their Shipping & Commerce for Three Centuries*. Chicago: A. C. McClurg.

Mills, Rodney H. 2002. *Wooden Steamers on the Great Lakes*. Vermilion, OH: Great Lakes Historical Society.

Mitchell, William T. 1884. "History of St. Clair County." In *Michigan Pioneer & Historical Collections*, 6:403–16. Lansing, MI: W. S. George.

Mollica, Anthony S., Jr. 1999. *Gar Wood Boats: Classics of a Golden Era*. Osceola, WI: MBI Publishing.

Monk, Kimberly. 1999. "The Development of Aboriginal Watercraft in the Great Lakes Region." *Totem: The University of Western Ontario Journal of Anthropology* 7 (1): 71–77.

Moore, Charles. 1915. *History of Michigan*. 4 vols. Chicago: Lewis.

Morrissey, Robert Michael. 2013. "The Terms of Encounter: Language and Contested Visions of French Colonization in the Illinois Country, 1673–1702." In *French and Indians in the Heart of North America, 1630–1815*, edited by Robert Englebert and Guillaume Teasdale, 43–76. East Lansing: Michigan State University Press.

Moulton, Ralph, and Scott Thieme. 2009. *History of Dredging and Compensation: St. Clair and Detroit Rivers*. Ottawa, ON: International Upper Great Lakes Study.

Muckelroy, Keith. 1978. *Maritime Archaeology*. New York: Cambridge University Press.

Murphy, Larry. 1983. "Shipwrecks as Data Base for Human Behavioral Studies." In *Shipwreck Anthropology*, edited by Richard A. Gould, 65–90. Albuquerque: University of New Mexico Press.

Nash, Roderick. 1982. *Wilderness and the American Mind*. New Haven: Yale University Press.

Nassaney, Michael S. 2015. *The Archaeology of the North American Fur Trade*. Gainesville: University Press of Florida.

Neumann, Roderick. 2007. "Wilderness." In *Encyclopedia of Environment and Society*, 5th ed., edited by Paul Robbins, 1954–59. Detroit, MI: Gale.

Nin.Da.Waab.Jig. 1987. *Minishenhying anishnaabe-aki: Walpole Island, the Soul of Indian Territory*. Wallaceburg, ON: Nin.Da.Waab.Jig.

Nute, Grace Lee. 1944. *Lake Superior*. New York: Bobbs-Merrill.

Nutley, David. 2008. "Submerged Cultural Sites: Opening a Time Capsule." *Museum International* 60 (4): 7–17.

Odle, Thomas D. 1956. "The Commercial Interests of the Great Lakes and the Campaign of 1860." *Michigan History* 40 (1): 1–23.

Owen, Geraint. 2014. "Seiche." In *Encyclopedia of Environmental Change*, edited by John A. Matthews, 987. Thousand Oaks, CA: Sage.

Parkins, Almon Ernest. 1918. *The Historical Geography of Detroit*. Lansing: Michigan Historical Commission.

Paskoff, Paul F. 2007. *Troubled Waters: Steamboat Disasters, River Improvements, and American Public Policy, 1821–1860*. Baton Rouge: Louisiana State University.

Pasternak, Shiri. 2017. *Grounded Authority: The Algonquins of Barriere Lake against the State*. Minneapolis: University of Minnesota Press.

Peebles, Christopher S. 1991. "*Annalistes*, Hermeneutics and Positivists: Squaring Circles or Dissolving Problems." In *The Annales School and Archaeology*, edited by John Bintliff, 108–24. London: Leicester University Press.

Pickles, John. 1992. "Texts, Hermeneutics and Propaganda Maps." In *Writing Worlds: Discourse, Text and Metaphor in the Representation of Landscape*, edited by Trevor J. Barnes and James S. Duncan, 193–230. New York: Routledge.

Pierce, Franklin. 1856. *Message of the President of the United States, Returning to the Senate the Bill (S. 1) Entitled "An Act Making an Appropriation for Deepening the Channel over the St. Clair Flats, in the State of Michigan, with His Objections Thereto"* (Senate Exec. Doc. 71). Washington, DC: n.p.

Pieters, Adrian J. 1894. *The Plants of Lake St. Clair*. Lansing, MI: Robert Smith.

Podruchny, Carolyn, Frederic W. Gleach, and Roger Roulette. 2014. "Putting Up Poles: Power, Negotiation, and Cultural Mixing in the Fur Trade." In *Gathering Places: Aboriginal and Fur Trade Histories*, edited by Carolyn Podruchny and Laura Peers, 25–47. Vancouver, BC: UBC Press.

Polk, James K. 1848. *Veto of the River and Harbor Bill* (House Exec. Doc. 49). Washington, DC: n.p.

Porteous, John. 1767. "Letter to Porteous (MS)." *John Porteous Papers*. Burton Historical Collection, Detroit Public Library.

———. 1939. "Schenectady to Michilimackinac, 1765 & 1766: Journal of John Porteous." In *Papers and Records, Ontario Historical Society*, edited by Fred Coyne Hamil, 33:75–98. [n.p.]

Price, Franklin H. 2013. "Notes from Mount Desert Island: Interviewing Maine Fishermen to Find Archaeological Sites." *Journal of Maritime Archaeology* 8 (1): 59–76.

Price, Franklin H., and Nathan Richards. 2009. "Conflict and Commerce: Maritime Archaeological Site Distribution as Cultural Change on the Roanoke River, North Carolina." *Historical Archaeology* 43 (4): 75–96.

Raphael, C. Nicholas, and Eugene Jaworski. 1982. "The St Clair Delta: A Unique Lake Delta." *Geographical Bulletin* 21 (2): 7–28.

Rayburn, Alan. 1997. *Place Names of Ontario*. Toronto, ON: University of Toronto Press.

Reynolds, Geoffrey D. 2019. "Keep 'Em Fighting: Chris-Craft's Contribution to WWII." *Michigan History* 103 (4): 18–24.

Richards, Nathan. 2002. "Deep Structures: An Examination of Deliberate Watercraft Abandonment in Australia." Doctoral thesis, Flinders University of South Australia.

———. 2008. *Ships' Graveyards: Abandoned Watercraft and the Archaeological Site Formation Process*. Gainesville: University Press of Florida.

———. 2013. "Abandoned Ships and Ship Graveyards: Exploring Site Significance and Research Potential." In *The Archaeology of Watercraft Abandonment*, edited by Nathan Richards and Sami Kay Seeb, 1–16. New York: Springer.

Rodgers, Bradley A. 2016. "Vernacular Craft of the North American Great Lakes." In *The Archaeology of Vernacular Watercraft*, edited by Amanda M. Evans, 205–30. New York: Springer.

Rodley, Edward. 2012. "The Ethics of Exhibiting Salvaged Shipwrecks." *Curator* 55(4): 383–91.

Rodseth, Lars, and Bradley J. Parker. 2005. "Theoretical Considerations in the Study of Frontiers." In *Untaming the Frontier in Anthropology, Archaeology, and History*, edited by Bradley J. Parker and Lars Rodseth, 3–21. Tucson: University of Arizona Press.

Rogers, Edward S. 1978. "Southeastern Ojibwa." In *Handbook of North American Indians*, vol 15: *Northeast*, edited by Bruce G. Trigger, 760–71. Washington, DC: Smithsonian Institution.

Rogers, Joseph Henry. 1955. "A Land-Use Study of the St. Clair Flats." Master's thesis, Michigan State University.

Rogers, Robert. 1765. *A Concise Account of North America*. London: J. Millan.

Romig, Walter. 1973. *Michigan Place Names*. Grosse Pointe, MI: privately printed.

Rönnby, Johan. 2007. "Maritime *Dureés*: Long-Term Structures in a Coastal Landscape." *Journal of Maritime Archaeology* 2:65–82.

———. 2013. "The Archaeological Interpretation of Shipwrecks." In *Interpreting Shipwrecks: Maritime Archaeological Approaches*, edited by Jonathan Adams and Johan Rönnby, 9–24. Southampton, UK: Highfield Press.

Rutherford, John. 1958. "John Rutherford's Captivity Narrative." In *The Siege of Detroit in 1763*, edited by Milo Milton Quaife, 219–74. Chicago: R. R. Donnelley.

Sabick, Christopher. 2004. "His Majesty's Hired Transport Schooner *Nancy*." Master's thesis, Texas A&M University.

Sabrevois de Bleury, Clement. 1902. "Memoir on the Indians between Lake Erie and the Mississippi, 1718." In *Collections of the State Historical Society of Wisconsin*, edited by Reuben Gold Thwaites, 16:363–76. Madison: State Historical Society of Wisconsin.

Sauer, Carl O. 1956. "The Agency of Man on the Earth." In *Man's Role in Changing the Face of the Earth*, edited by William L. Thomas Jr., 49–69. Chicago: University of Chicago Press.

Schiffer, Michael Brian. 2010. *Behavioral Archaeology: Principles and Practice*. Oakville, CT: Equinox.

Schoolcraft, Henry Rowe. 1821. *Narrative Journal of Travels through the Northwestern Regions of the United States, Extending from Detroit through the Great Chain of American Lakes, to the Sources of the Mississippi River, Performed as a Member of the Expedition under Governor Cass in the Year 1820*. Albany, NY: E. & F. Hosford.

———. 1847. *Notes on the Iroquois*. Albany, NY: Erastus H. Pease.

Sibley, Solomon. 1917. "Extract from a Letter written at Detroit, Aug 7, 1798." In *History of Detroit 1780–1850: Financial and Commercial*, edited by Clarence M. Burton, 40–41. Detroit, MI: n.p.

Smith, Hal Horace. 1939. *The Story of Lac Ste. Claire: A Paper Read at the Prismatic Club, Detroit, May 8, 1938*. Detroit: Press of the Round Circle.

Snead, James E. 2009. "Trails of Tradition: Movement, Meaning, and Place." In *Landscapes of Movement: Trails, Paths, and Roads in Anthropological Perspective*, edited by James E. Snead, Clark L. Erikson, and J. Andrew Darling, 42–60. Philadelphia: University of Pennsylvania Press.

Spoehr, Alexander. 1956. "Cultural Differences in the Interpretation of Natural Resources." In *Man's Role in Changing the Face of the Earth*, edited by William L. Thomas Jr., 93–102. Chicago: University of Chicago Press.

Staniforth, Mark. 1997. "The Archaeology of the Event—the *Annales* School and Maritime Archaeology." In *Underwater Archaeology*, edited by Denise C. Lakey, 17–21. Corpus Christi, TX: Society for Historical Archaeology.

Steckley, John. 1990. "The Early Map 'Novvelle France': A Linguistic Analysis." *Ontario Archaeology* 51:17–29.

Steele, Eliza R. 1841. *A Summer Journey in the West*. New York: John S. Taylor.

Stevens, Kenneth R. 1989. *Border Diplomacy: The Caroline and McLeod Affairs in Anglo-American-Canadian Relations, 1837–1842*. Tuscaloosa: University of Alabama Press.

Stone, Joel. 2015. *Floating Palaces of the Great Lakes: A History of Passenger Steamships on the Inland Seas*. Ann Arbor: University of Michigan Press.

Storrow, Samuel A. 1872. "The North-West in 1817." In *Report and Collections of the State Historical Society of Wisconsin*, edited by Lyman Copeland Draper, 6:154–56. Madison: State Historical Society of Wisconsin.

Stothers, David M. 1999. "Late Woodland Models for Cultural Development in Southern Michigan." In *Retrieving Michigan's Buried Past: The Archaeology of the Great Lakes State*, edited by John R. Halsey, 194–211. Bloomfield Hills, MI: Cranbrook Institute of Science.

Strang, Veronica. 2008. "Uncommon Ground: Landscape as Social Geography." In *Handbook of Landscape Archaeology*, edited by Bruno David and Julian Thomas, 51–59. Walnut Creek, CA: Left Coast Press.

Tanner, Helen Hornbeck. 1987. *Atlas of Great Lakes Indian History*. Norman: University of Oklahoma Press.

Taylor, Alan. 2010. *The Civil War of 1812*. New York: Vintage Books.

Taylor, E. G. R. 1949. "Position Fixing in Relation to Early Maps and Charts." *Bulletin of the British Society for the History of Science* 1 (2): 25–27.

Thompson, Mark L. 2000. *Graveyard of the Lakes*. Detroit, MI: Wayne State University Press.

Thompson, Thomas S. 1859. *Coast Pilot for the Upper Lakes, on Both Shores: From Chicago to Buffalo, Green Bay, Georgian Bay, and Lake Superior, Including the Rivers Detroit, St. Clair and St. Mary's*. Chicago: James Barnet.

———. 1861. *Thompson's Coast Pilot for the Upper Lakes, on Both Shores: From Chicago to Buffalo, Green Bay, Georgian Bay, and Lake Superior, Including the Rivers Detroit, St. Clair and St. Mary's*. Chicago: James Barnet.

———. 1869. *Thompson's Coast Pilot for the Upper Lakes, on Both Shores: From Chicago to Buffalo, Green Bay, Georgian Bay, and Lake Superior, Including the Rivers Detroit, St. Clair and Ste. Marie*. Detroit, MI: Free Press Book and Job Printing House.

———. 1878. *Thompson's Coast Pilot and Sailing Directions for the North-Western Lakes from Ogdensburg to Buffalo, Chicago, Green Bay, Georgian Bay and Lake Superior, Including All the River Navigation*. Detroit, MI: W. A. Scripps.

Thornton, Thomas F. 1997. "Anthropological Studies of Native American Place Naming." *American Indian Quarterly*, 21 (2): 209–28.

Tilley, Christopher. 1994. *A Phenomenology of Landscape: Places, Paths and Monuments*. Providence, RI: Berg.

Tilley, Christopher, and Kate Cameron-Daum. 2017. *Anthropology of Landscape: The Extraordinary in the Ordinary*. London: UCL Press. www.jstor.org/stable/j.ctt1mtz542.7.

Tocqueville, Alexis de. 1959. *Journey to America*, edited by J. P. Mayer, translated by George Lawrence. London: Faber and Faber.

Törnquist, Oscar. 2013. "The Skeleton in the Dune: Unlocking the Explanatory Potential of Shipwrecks through Physical Landscape Studies." In *Interpreting Shipwrecks: Maritime Archaeological Approaches*, edited by Jonathan Adams and Johan Rönnby, 25–35. Southampton, UK: Highfield Press.

Trowbridge, Charles C. 1942. "With Cass in the Northwest in 1820," edited by Ralph H. Brown. *Minnesota History Magazine* 23 (2): 126–48.

Tuan, Yi-Fu. 1991. "Language and the Making of Place: A Narrative-Descriptive Approach." *Annals of the Association of American Geographers*, 81 (4): 684–96.

Tuddenham, David Berg. 2010. "Maritime Cultural Landscapes, Maritimity and Quasi Objects." *Journal of Maritime Archaeology* 5 (5): 5–16.

———. 2012. "Ship Finds and Their Management as Actor Network." *Journal of Maritime Archaeology* 7:231–43.

Tunell, George. 1896a. "The Growth and Character of the Commerce on the Great Lakes." *Journal of Political Economy* 4 (2): 243–45.

———. 1896b. "Transportation on the Great Lakes of North America." *Journal of Political Economy* 4 (3): 332–51.

Tyler, John. 1843. "Message of the President." Appendix to *The Congressional Globe*, December: 1–4.

US Bureau of the Census. 1975. *Historical Statistics of the United States, Colonial Times to 1970*. 2 vols. Washington, DC: Government Printing Office.

US Bureau of Topographic Engineers. 1857. *Chart of St. Clair Flats*. [n.p.]

US Light-House Board. 1860. *List of Buoys, etc. in the Eleventh Light-House District*. Washington, DC: Geo. W. Bowman.

Van Gijseghem, Hendrik, and Verity H. Whalen. 2017. "Mining, Ritual, and Social Memory: An Exploration of Toponymy in the Ica Valley, Peru." In *Rituals of the Past: Prehispanic and Colonial Case Studies in Andean Archaeology*, edited by Silvana A. Rosenfeld and Stefanie L. Bautista, 267–94. Boulder: University Press of Colorado.

Veregin, Howard, ed. 2010. *Goode's World Atlas*, 22nd ed. Skokie, IL: Rand McNally.

Vigne, Godfrey T. 1833. *Six Months in America*. Philadelphia, PA: Thomas T. Ash.

Voegelin, C. F., and F. M. Voegelin. 1964. "Languages of the World: Native American Fascicle One." *Anthropological Linguistics* 6 (6): 1–149.

Vuolteenaho, Jani, and Lawrence D. Berg. 2009. "Towards Critical Toponymies." In *Critical Toponymies: The Contested Politics of Place Naming*, edited by Lawrence D. Berg and Jani Vuolteenaho, 1–18. Burlington, VT: Ashgate.

Warner, Edward S. 1998. "Towing with Steam Tugs: An Aspect of the Great Lakes Commercial Trade under Sail." In *"A Fully Accredited Ocean": Essays on the Great Lakes*, edited by Victoria Brehm, 45–57. Ann Arbor: University of Michigan Press.

Warrick, Gary. 2013. "The Aboriginal Population of Ontario in Late Prehistory." In *Before Ontario: The Archaeology of a Province*, edited by Marit K. Munson and Susan M. Jamieson, 62–76. Montreal, QC: McGill-Queen's University Press.

Waterman, T. T. 1922. "The Geographical Names Used by the Indians of the Pacific Coast." *Geographical Review* 12 (2):175–94.

Welcome. 1779–1782. "Log Book of His Majesty's Arm'd Sloop *Welcome* (MS)." *Alexander Harrow Family Papers*. Burton Historical Collection, Detroit Public Library.

Westerdahl, Christer. 1992. "The Maritime Cultural Landscape." *International Journal of Nautical Archaeology* 21 (1): 5–14.

———. 1994. "Maritime Cultures and Ship Types: Brief Comments on the Significance of Maritime Archaeology." *International Journal of Nautical Archaeology* 23 (4): 265–70.

———. 1996. *Beowulf's Ship Type and the Pivot of Denmark: Traditional Zones of Transport Geography in Relation to Vessel Types*. www.abc.se/~m10354/publ/transport.htm.

———. 1998. *The Maritime Cultural Landscape: On the Concept of the Traditional Zones of Transport Geography*. Institute of Archaeology and Ethnology, University of Copenhagen. www.abc.se/~m10354/publ/cult-land.htm.

Wetzel, Christopher. 2006. "Neshnabemwen Renaissance: Local and National Potawatomi Language Revitalization Efforts." *American Indian Quarterly* 30 (1): 61–86.

White, Richard. 1991. *The Middle Ground: Indians, Empires and Republics in the Great Lakes Region, 1650—1815*. New York: Cambridge University Press.

Wien, Thomas. 2003. "Nicolet, Explorations of." In *Dictionary of American History*, 3rd ed., edited by Stanley I. Kutler, 6:106. New York: Charles Scribner's Sons.

Williams, W. G. 1842a. *Report on the Survey of the Northwestern Lakes* (Senate Doc. 256). Washington, DC: n.p.

———. 1842b. *Extract from the Report of Capt. W. G. Williams* (Senate Doc. 393). Washington, DC: Thomas Allen.

———. 1842c. *Report on the Lake Harbors* (Senate Doc. 416). Washington, DC: Thomas Allen.

Witgen, Michael. 2012. *An Infinity of Nations: How the Native New World Shaped Early North America*. Philadelphia: University of Pennsylvania Press.

Wolf, Eric R. 1982. *Europe and the People without History*. Berkeley: University of California Press.

Wolfart, H. Christopher. 1988. "The Beginnings of Algonquian Lexicography." *Proceedings of the American Philosophical Society* 132:119–27.

Woodford, Arthur M. 1994. *Charting the Inland Seas: A History of the U.S. Lake Survey*. Detroit, MI: Wayne State University Press.

———. 2012. *Tashmoo Park and the Steamer* Tashmoo. Charleston, SC: Arcadia.

Index

Note: Page numbers appearing in *italics* refer to figures.

About the Author

DANIEL F. HARRISON, PHD, is a maritime archaeologist, sailor, and diver specializing in the Great Lakes region. Recently retired from a forty-year career as an academic librarian, he has had his research in maritime archaeology published in peer-reviewed journals including *Historical Archaeology*, *Ethnohistory*, and *Michigan Historical Review*. Harrison's research and theoretical motivations are focused on community-centered preservation and interpretation of maritime heritage and submerged cultural resources.

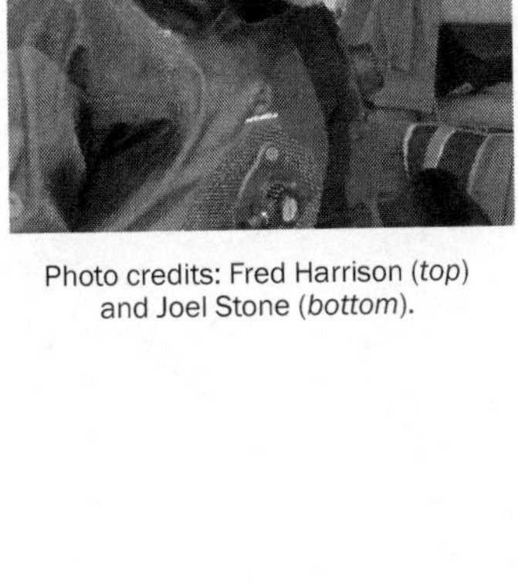

Photo credits: Fred Harrison (*top*) and Joel Stone (*bottom*).